HACHETTE MILITARY COLLECTION

REDBACK ONE

THE TRUE STORY OF AN AUSTRALIAN SAS HERO

ROBERT MACKLIN

All internal photographs are from Stuart Bonner's personal collection.

First published in Australia and New Zealand in 2014
by Hachette Australia
(an imprint of Hachette Australia Pty Limited)
Level 17, 207 Kent Street, Sydney NSW 2000
www.hachette.com.au

This edition published in 2016

10 9 8 7 6 5 4 3 2 1

Copyright © Robert Macklin and Emily Bonner 2014

This book is copyright. Apart from any fair dealing for the purposes of private study, research, criticism or review permitted under the *Copyright Act 1968*, no part may be stored or reproduced by any process without prior written permission. Enquiries should be made to the publisher.

National Library of Australia
Cataloguing-in-Publication data:

Macklin, Robert.

Redback one: the true history of an Australian SAS hero/Robert Macklin

ISBN 978 0 7336 3658 5 (paperback)

Bonner, Stuart.
Australia. Army. Special Air Service Regiment – Officers.
Australia. Army – Commando troops.
Combat patrols.

358.41310994

Cover design and illustration by Luke Causby, Blue Cork
Text design by Bookhouse, Sydney
Typeset in Garamond Premier Pro by Bookhouse, Sydney

For Kenzie and Jonathan

CONTENTS

Author's note vii

1. **They are out there** 1
2. **All too much** 13
3. **Growing up** 25
4. **Basic training** 38
5. **Selection begins** 52
6. **'Corporal punishment'** 65
7. **A massive challenge** 79
8. **'Most outstanding soldier'** 93
9. **'We had finally made it'** 105
10. **Meeting Emily** 118
11. **'Push ourselves to the limits'** 139
12. **Deployment** 151
13. **'Brave little people'** 164

14	To Afghanistan	175
15	Patrolling	185
16	Joint Task Force 106	197
17	Casualty	211
18	The hammer and the anvil	222
19	After Afghanistan	235
20	First into Iraq	248
21	'As close as possible'	262
22	Towards Baghdad	277
23	'Most difficult mission'	290
24	After Iraq	302
25	Providing security	314
26	After the SASR	327

List of abbreviations   339

AUTHOR'S NOTE

This is the second in my series of SAS biographies, and like *SAS Sniper* it is written in the first person, where in effect the author and the subject become one. It is, to put it mildly, an unusual experience for someone who has never fired a shot at anything more threatening than a retreating kangaroo, and that in my distant jackarooing days. But both occasions have been extraordinarily satisfying and even pleasurable despite the exhausting process and the demanding deadlines.

Rob Maylor, the subject of *SAS Sniper*, became and remains a close mate. We are developing a couple of TV and movie projects that flow from the experience, though Rob has moved his family headquarters back to New Zealand whence he came.

Stuart ('Nev') and Emily Bonner are very special, and I will always value the many hours we spent together digging into the past and unearthing the dramatic and powerful experiences that they both relished and endured. Stuart's were on the front lines of war while Emily's were in the exciting romance of their early days and the agonies of separation as she struggled to provide support for her man and their two great kids while battling her own demons. In situations like this the bonds between author and subject become indissoluble.

The drama is played out against the unique background of Australia's Special Air Service Regiment (SASR) during its most demanding operational activity since Vietnam – the first decade of the new century that began with East Timor then segued wildly to Afghanistan and Iraq. Stuart was among those who bore the brunt of it and, like many of his colleagues, he did not escape unharmed. The insidious effects disguised beneath the bland lettering PTSD are with him still. Post-traumatic stress disorder is a devil's brew and it is not confined to the front-line soldier. It spills over into the family and at times it must seem like a life sentence.

In my view Stuart would be justified in becoming very angry about the circumstances that permitted the condition to take root. It is not a new phenomenon. What was 'shell shock' in the First World War became 'combat fatigue' in the second great conflict, and a kaleidoscope of 'syndromes' in the Vietnam and Gulf wars. The army should have developed techniques to protect and prepare soldiers for its fierce onset. This is particularly true of the Special

Forces. But on the contrary, as our account demonstrates, the beginnings of the condition might well be traced back to an aspect of the actual selection process of the regiment itself. However, it is not in Stuart's nature to feed an anger or to hold a grudge.

I am less forgiving. I found the vicious interrogation techniques employed on raw recruits hard to take. As far as I know, there has been no previous public account of this aspect of selection, despite several SASR-endorsed documentaries on the subject. Readers will make their own judgement, but I would have thought the time to engage in interrogation resistance would be better scheduled when the SAS operator was more experienced and less vulnerable to its inevitable emotional backlash.

There are other elements in the book that will break new ground and might well cause official discomfort. For example it has never previously been acknowledged in Australia that we invaded Iraq through a US-negotiated corridor from the Kingdom of Jordan; and we actually led the Coalition forces streaming across the desert while the US Air Force delivered its 'shock and awe' bombardment of Baghdad. But we would not have included this unless it was easily obtainable in a five-minute trawl of the internet.

Similarly, we have been careful not to include any aspects of SAS operations that might break the rules of confidentiality or provide some future adversary with information that could put our soldiers in jeopardy. Nor have we touched upon those sensitive activities of the regiment that were outside Stuart's personal experience.

We have included the account – albeit in fairly brief form – of Emily's own struggles. The wives and loved ones of SAS operatives rarely get mentioned in the 'Boy's Own' approach of other books on the subject. I hope that this breakthrough will give other women the confidence to tell their stories, for it was never more true that, 'They also serve who only stand and wait.'

My gratitude to both Stuart and Emily for their trust and confidence is unbounded. I must thank my own wife, Wendy, for her warmth and endurance, since writers (and their partners) also have their moments of stress. And thanks again to my publisher, Matthew Kelly, a stalwart comrade-in-arms in the literary trenches.

Robert Macklin
www.robertmacklin.com

1

THEY ARE OUT THERE

In the darkness my hand closed over the grip of the hunting knife, the blade sharpened and honed to kill. They – the enemy – were out there in the night. They were silently closing in. But I had the knife and I had the training – 14 years in the SAS. I also had the experience – tours in Afghanistan, East Timor, Bougainville and Iraq. I was ready for them.

I moved silently through the darkness to a place where I could get eyes on. That was the first rule of surveillance: get yourself into a position of overwatch where you can see what the enemy is up to. That way you can make your counter-moves to take him out before he knows what's hit him.

I gripped the knife. I was sweating. Luckily I knew the terrain, so I could move quietly and confidently. No need to wake the sleepers; not yet anyway. It was my responsibility. I would protect them, come what may.

I reached the overwatch position. From here I would have an unobstructed view. The silence was deafening. Nothing moved. But they were there. I could feel them. Would they come in a rush, or one at a time? Either way, I was on to them, every sense on high alert. I checked the time – 0300 – just when an attack could come, when we were off guard in that dream time when all the senses closed down and we were at our most vulnerable.

Cautiously I reached out and gently lowered the blinds, making a kind of porthole in the window. Nothing moved. No lights showed. No sound reached me beyond the pounding inside my chest and the soft thudding in my ears. I looked again at where they might be lurking. The street lamp made shadows; they could be hiding in any one of them.

I made my way quietly to the door and inched it open. Still nothing. I stepped out into the cool night air. I moved the knife to the other hand and dried the palm on my t-shirt. I gripped the knife again. I turned left into the shadows. I made a tour of the perimeter. Still nothing. I checked the lock on the back door, checked the windows were firmly closed, then returned to the front and climbed the couple of steps to the door. I turned back for one last look along Meridian Street, Hocking, on Perth's northern suburban strip, so quiet you could hear a dog barking five clicks away.

Perth. Right, Perth; home; the other side of the bloody planet from that screwed up part of the world where I had spent much of the last few years, or East Timor, where the images drew me back to live again when I closed my eyes and tried to sleep. Perth, headquarters of the regiment, capital of the biggest richest state in Australia, a place of homecoming, of the family sleeping inside No. 22 Meridian Street – my lovely wife Emily, beautiful little baby Kenzie both sleeping inside. Safe.

Nev. Get your head together. Je-sus! There's nothing out there. It's all in your head, mate! I glanced across to the neighbour's place. Poor bugger. He was moving out and I don't blame him. Not after that 'incident' when smoke from his barbecue blew over the fence into our place and after a few beers I banged on his front door till he came out and I called him all sorts of things till he threw a punch and it was on. Blood everywhere. His. And next thing the cops arrived and told me I could be charged with serious assault, as he was in hospital with a head injury . . . Get your head together, mate!

I closed the door, crept through the quiet house and put the knife back under the mattress before climbing in. Emily was awake. She knew what I'd been doing. I did it nearly every night. 'You are a fruitcake,' she said.

I looked up to the ceiling. Maybe she's right, I thought. Maybe I am. Maybe after 20 years in the army, two-thirds of them in one of the front-line sabre squadrons of the SAS, maybe I've cracked, come to the end of my rope.

Nah, bullshit, I thought. Man up! Get your act together. You've never let anything get on top of you before this, never backed down before a challenge. Get over it. All you need is a good night's sleep . . .

Well, that was true, but it was also the problem. Because I knew, once I surrendered to sleep, just let myself drift off, the dreams were there waiting for me, terrible dreams, worse than you could imagine, so bad that I'd feel ashamed that I had them. I mean, what sort of person dreams of eating human flesh? Jesus, no . . .

So stay awake, think about the good times, the comradeship of the blokes in the regiment, the joy of meeting Emily in her native Kenya, the long-distance romance, the ups and downs . . . The ceiling is like a movie screen. Look at it long enough through the sleepless night and you don't need dreams – the images of the past come alive on the screen. And if you're lucky you can keep them under control, pick and choose the ones you want to see.

•

Strange how we all end up . . . the images blurring through time, random events, any one of which might have meant we never existed. Just like my great-great-great-grandmother on Mum's side of the family: little 'Dolly' Dalrymple. Her baby brother had been thrown onto the fire, but Dolly survived against the odds . . .

There she is, the daughter of George Briggs and her Aboriginal mother Woretemoeteyenner, who kept company with Briggs as he worked at sealing in the Furneaux Islands off north-eastern Tasmania around 1808. Woretemoeteyenner's life is one of hardship and cruelty from the Europeans who made their living from the seal colonies of the islands and of mainland Tasmania.

She is a daughter of Mannarlargenna, an influential native chief later convinced by George Augustus Robinson and his assistant/interpreter Truganini to leave their native homeland in mainland Tasmania and move to a settlement on Flinders Island, where they supposedly would not be subject to persecution by the white settlers. George Robinson at the time is employed by Governor Arthur of the colony to gather as many Aboriginal people as possible and resettle them in remote islands away from the wealthy white landowners. He promises them they can return to their tribal homelands once things settle down. It's a lie. Instead, the displaced people spend their remaining days in isolated colonies and disused penal settlements.

Truganini herself had also been brutally treated by the sealers. As a young woman she had travelled aboard a sealers' vessel as they made their way to Bruny Island. Her fiancé and several other native men had also come on board for the journey. En route, the native men were thrown overboard miles from land by the sealers while the women looked on in horror. The men would have attempted to swim back to shore but the sealers had severed their hands so they would drown or the sharks would smell their blood in the water ... here they come now, dorsal fins cutting through the water, turning on their backs for the lunge to kill . . . the screams . . .

It is not surprising that Aboriginal men, angry at some of the females in their tribal groups for associating with the white men, sometimes seized mixed-race children from their mothers to be killed, to be tossed on the fire. Luckily Dolly is saved from the awful fate of her brother and later fostered by a Doctor Jacob Mountgarrett and his wife, Bridget, and taken to mainland Tasmania. There she is brought up decently and provided with a basic education and safe accommodations.

Dolly later became a great success story in Tasmania. She was celebrated for her role as a protector during a siege on her farm house in 1831 when Aboriginals attacked. In recognition of her bravery she was given a government land grant. She and her husband went on to become wealthy land and business owners in Tasmania's Latrobe district. In later years Dolly petitioned the governor for her mother to be allowed to join her on the mainland. Woretemoeteyenner was now living at a mission called Wybalena on Flinders Island, where the conditions had led to the death of many of the people who had been sent there. The governor agreed, and mother and daughter were finally reunited.

•

The ceiling is wiped clean as the images of the Old People depart. Step forward now my grandfather, William George

Robert Keefe, born 1894 in Beaconsfield, Tasmania. He is a great-grandson of Dolly's and worked as a miner, labourer and timber cutter along the west coast, where he married and had several children. In the early part of the 20th century he abandoned his wife and four children and moved north to Queensland, where he met my grandmother, Muriel Amelia Ransley.

Just why he left his wife and children in Tasmania remains a mystery to me. Perhaps he became disillusioned with the routines and responsibility of fatherhood, or perhaps some trauma caused his actions. Whatever the case, William and Muriel spent time together in Mount Morgan and later Sydney. Muriel bore him a baby girl, my mother, Lila Del. Mum was always called Del, and I believe she was named after her famous great-great-grandmother – short for Dalrymple.

Muriel and William never married though, and this was shameful to Muriel, who always referred to him as her husband. She lived a very tough life as William was often away. She'd had another child some 20 years before my mother's birth. I knew her as my Aunty Bub or Prudence, and she was from a different father.

Muriel told us of her days as a child in Mount Morgan. Her mother ran a boarding house for the mine workers there, and Muriel, as a young girl and the oldest of her siblings, would cook and clean rooms to help make a living. On Sundays her mum would dress her in her Sunday best and 1920s knee-high leather lace-up boots. Off she'd go to Sunday school with firm instructions to keep her clothes clean but Muriel would find her mates and, instead of Sunday school, ride and race billy goats on the outskirts of town. On returning home she would get a hiding from her stern mother for the condition of her dirty torn clothes.

Muriel's parents were of English descent. Muriel's father and mother had a terrible and tumultuous marriage and her father George Ransley had big problems with alcohol. After discovering wife Ethel's extramarital affair with a local man, George went into a bout of depression and drinking, and in 1919 took his own life with a bottle of white arsenic he had told the shopkeeper he was using to cure goat skins. Muriel's brother Cecil found their unconscious father on the floor of a bedroom. He was rushed to hospital but there was nothing they could do to save him. His death certificate and coronial inquiry indicated suicide by poisoning.

Muriel was privy to all the sadness and turmoil in her parents' lives leading up to these events. In the inquiry it came out that, on the day prior to her father's death, he told her he intended to take his life and said goodbye to her and some of the other children.

In 1923, at only 18, Muriel married Henry Muller. She never spoke of this early marriage to anybody, and I suspect her daughter Prudence was conceived during this time. Court documents from 1926 indicate that Henry Muller applied to have the marriage dissolved in the magistrate's office in

Redfern, Sydney. He claimed at that time that Muriel was having an affair with another man, William George Robert Keefe, my grandfather.

Mount Morgan experienced a huge underground mine fire in 1927 followed by several mine closures. Muriel, with her mother and her other children, moved south to Sydney to try to find work and a permanent place to live. In Muriel's later life, when I was a boy, she would tell me how she could never stand the smell of boiled eggs, as she had cooked thousands of them looking after the working men of the mines at Mount Morgan, and later during the Depression of the 1930s in Sydney.

There she found a small house to rent and there she raised Prudence and Del. Life must have been a struggle but she educated her girls as best she could. Raising children in the Depression and then the war years in Sydney saw Muriel as a mostly single mum working in laborious government jobs to try to keep her family fed and housed. She told me that she was working near Circular Quay the day the Japanese mini-subs struck at Sydney and she saw the bodies of the men floating face down in the water in the aftermath. In the 1950s she worked in a government job at the Health Department for many years and processed human body parts for the department's medical laboratory.

William was an avid rock fisherman around the heads near Sydney and was often successful in catching big fish to bring home to the table. But on one such expedition he was washed into the sea by a big wave when trying to retrieve a fish close to the water's edge. He survived but the accident caused an infection in his legs that kept him wheelchair bound for the remainder of his short life.

William's accident meant Muriel was the sole provider for those tough years after the Second World War. She and my mother often told my three brothers and me stories of how grandfather Bill would sometimes get drunk and rowdy at the local pubs around Broadway and Del would be sent by Muriel to retrieve him, pushing him along in a wheelchair back to their rented home. I never met him, as he died in the early 1950s while my mum was just a young girl, but he must have been a real character.

At Muriel's funeral in 1999, after I had been in the army and SAS for some years, I saw how slight she had become with age but how immensely robust were her hands crossed over herself even in death. Those were working hands, and she toiled from the cradle to the grave till the age of 94 years.

Mum contracted Parkinson's disease in her forties and my dad Dennis cared for her full-time until the end. It was only in her late sixties that she discovered she had several step-brothers and sisters (William George Keefe's abandoned children) in Tasmania. William's grandchildren contacted us after some family tree searching by my dad and brother Mark, and let us know about the family William left behind all those years ago. Mum was disappointed to hear so late in her life that she had three half-sisters and a half-brother, some of whom lived and worked in Sydney, unknown to her while William was still alive. Did he visit them? Did he even know about them? It's one of those family mysteries that was still without an answer when Mum died at 69 in 2012.

My dad, Dennis Bonner, has been the rock in our family, looking after Mum 24/7 for over 20 years. He was born on 12 November 1941 in Sydney and went to primary school in Mascot, then high school at Botany Road, Rosebery. He became an apprentice plumber, worked in Banksmeadow for some years, then went to college and studied to become a health and building inspector. This scored him a job at Strathfield Council in 1966. He later moved to Sutherland council in 1970 as it was closer to his home at Heathcote. His dad, George, was a shoemaker and had lived his whole life in the Mascot area until his death at 95 in 2004.

•

Now I'm sitting at the airport in Sydney waiting to catch a flight home to see my own young children, Kenzie and Jonathan, and my beautiful wife, Emily. I have been visiting Mum in Kogarah hospital; Dad has been sleeping in a chair each night by her bedside in hospital and doting over her every moment. I knew he would be heartbroken when she passed on, as he shared his life with her since they first met at a Sydney matinee show when she was just 14 and Dennis was 17 years old . . . a young boy and girl post-war in Sydney whose love lasts from then to now, across a span of hardships and happiness and 56 long years. Mum did pass away a few weeks later, on Saturday 7 July 2012 at 1 p.m. And in my image of him I can see the tears rolling down his cheeks . . .

At Mum's funeral I spoke briefly with her lifelong friend Narelle after the service. Narelle had been at the pictures in Mascot when my dad Dennis had approached Lila Del and asked her if she would accompany him to a party. That is how they met. They were childhood sweethearts and then partners through life.

That is love. Dad consoled himself after her passing that he was lucky to have her all those years, but I believe they were lucky to have each other.

2

ALL TOO MUCH

I first noticed my strange behaviour on a combat operation – my first tour of Afghanistan in 2001–02. On patrol in the desert when we laid up for the night and I settled down next to my patrol vehicle, I couldn't sleep. I was attuned to every tiny sound; any noise would raise my heartbeat and produce both aggression and a sense of terrible foreboding. My stomach would knot up and I would bolt upright in my sleeping bag on the hard cold ground, searching for whatever was making the noise.

It got to the point where I would yell at our sentries to be quieter as they patrolled the perimeter. I felt angry that they were walking way too close; the sound of their quiet footsteps not only kept me awake but made me extremely anxious. I *knew* it was an enemy soldier sneaking up on me. The sentries would usually shout back, telling me to shut up.

I started to become a fearful soldier. In Iraq in 2003 on duty at a captured airbase called Al Asad I was startled by very close rifle fire. The other blokes near me heard it and casually looked to see what the commotion was. On the other hand I immediately thought that I was being fired at and began to duck for cover behind one of our patrol vehicles. It turned out to be our own lads firing at a feral dog that had entered the perimeter and threatened to bite someone and possibly spread rabies. For a few minutes my heart raced and I felt extreme anger that I had not been told of the likelihood of friendly weapons fire.

On my return to Australia I would find myself doing similarly odd things. For example when I went into a busy shop where people were crowding around I'd be on a hair trigger. I felt that at any moment I'd be attacked and would have to react immediately to defend myself. This paranoia meant that I was no longer happy to go out shopping. I would drive Emily crazy with my determination not to be in a crowded place and would always want to leave as soon as I got there.

Another time I was riding my motorbike home from the army barracks after work. A car with young men inside pushed past and yelled something like, 'Get out of the way.' I immediately felt a terrible rage towards them and began to chase their car on the busy highway. As I caught up with them, rationality began to kick in and I wondered what the hell I was doing.

My mind kept returning to incidents that had made a deep impact on me – the killing of a doctor in Iraq in a bombing mission, the strangling of a dog in the desert at night, seeing the bodies of dead soldiers in Afghanistan, watching young children screaming as their skin pulled free from sticky burn bandages in East Timor. These images still come back to me daily as I see mundane things that seem to remind me.

Dreams at night set the tone of my day. They can be grisly, bizarre or sometimes hardly remembered, but they'll mean I'm exhausted and depressed before I get out of bed in the morning. Some are too disturbing or embarrassing for me to recount and I keep them to myself for fear of being considered depraved and sick.

They are centred on military service, and being in the field while on operations. After one dream in particular I wake in a sweat with heart racing and the memory that I was in a hole in the ground surrounded by rotting dead corpses of soldiers. I look in my hands and find myself eating the severed hand of one rotting corpse. This is bizarre, as I've never been in any such circumstance, but the image and feelings are very real. I try to work out why I have them. Is it my mind trying to sort out some event, or is my imagination now twisted to a different level? I don't know and no one can tell me.

One day in Afghanistan while preparing to head out on patrol we got the word that a US special operations team and a group of anti-Taliban Mujahideen (Muj as we called them) had been calling in Coalition fighter aircraft to destroy a Taliban position when something had gone terribly wrong. The problem when using a ground-mounted laser to designate or light up a target is that either end of the laser beam could be interpreted by the laser-guided bomb as the target. When a Special Forces team on the ground shines a laser on the enemy to indicate its position to fighter crews flying above, the bombs can sometimes land on the friendlies' position instead. This had happened. Emergency medical teams were rushing about prepping the medical tent near our compound.

Suddenly vehicles from the medivac landing zone pulled up in the compound and stretchers were unloaded with badly injured soldiers who were carried quickly by the bearers to the medical tent. Minutes later more vehicles arrived and more marines this time ferried black plastic body bags heavy with limp dead men into the medical facility. I believe four members of the team lost their lives that day as well as the Muj. Seeing the body bags was a stark reminder of our vulnerability to human or technical error.

While at the Americans' Firebase Rhino in Afghanistan, we spent several days cleaning out the bomb-damaged buildings so they could be used as planning rooms and briefing areas for our 1 Squadron SAS blokes. The rooms were mostly empty except for the piles of discarded building materials lying about that the locals had been using to construct the place. We also went outside the compound to check out some other, older, mud-brick-style buildings that had also been badly damaged in the initial assault. Some of these still had unexploded ordnance (UXOs) lying about and had been taped off or marked with red paint on the brickwork warning all to stay away. There were some old water wells that had been blocked up with rubble and we suspected several bodies had been dropped down them. The smell was horrendous and I just can't forget it.

UXOs and mines were soon to be a constant companion and headache for all of us in the 'Ghan. When my SAS colleague Andy Russell was killed by a mine, my troop was about 20 kilometres away to the south. We got word on the radio that he had been mortally wounded. I went around to my soldiers and told them the bad news. Some didn't comprehend what 'mortally wounded' meant and I explained he was dead. It was a very sombre mood that day and I felt very detached from the whole scene, like I was watching from afar as the events occurred. We were down near the Iranian–Pakistani–Afghan border conducting reconnaissance, and the threat of mines was always there.

I was really angry at our OC at the time for venturing into the area where Andy had been killed. I felt the OC had been negligent, since he knew there were mines in the area and the one that blew up was in an obvious place for the Taliban to set it. When I got back to base, I didn't put my feet off the concrete for some time, and even then I stayed on the rocks and hard ground to avoid mines.

In the SAS you are conditioned to react to threats or danger with the 'fight' component of the 'fight or flight' reaction that is part of everyone's normal survival instincts. This reaction of aggression towards any threat is enforced through highly realistic training and then in operations. It becomes very normal to instantly prepare to fight whenever you sense any type of threat. This might come from mundane things like someone raising their voice, watching a threatening situation on TV, or having a dispute with a loved one.

You realise when it's happening and restrain yourself, but in my case the stomach cramps, raised pulse, increased breathing, anxiety and anger are still present. It cannot be switched off. It's just there and it never goes away.

While at Firebase Rhino I was shown a clip of a young Russian soldier having his head removed by Chechen soldiers with a blunt hunting knife. The image was haunting and set the mood for the remainder of the operation for me on what would be likely to happen to us if we were captured by the Taliban. Later, when searching Taliban training bunkers, we found photos of bearded Taliban men holding the severed heads of their captives.

Living like this continually for almost five months with little respite was a life-changing experience. It left me with great difficulty in planning ahead and a permanent sense of pessimism and gloom, a feeling I couldn't shake that the end is near. It's a frame of mind that affects all decision making and also life at home. And of course it affected my work and my ability to make vital operational decisions.

During our regular high-tempo training activities while I was a team leader on counterterrorist duties, I found myself treating the training exactly the same as if it were the real thing back in Iraq or Afghanistan. I felt real anxiety and fear even though I knew the bullets fired were just paintball or blank simulator cartridges. I became very angry when critiqued over any issues and responded verbally and aggressively to my peers.

I decided that I did not want to be promoted above the rank of sergeant and advised the unit commander of this decision. I then had to advise the regimental sergeant major (RSM), who was in charge of all promotional management within the regiment. I headed to his office.

When I got there, he told me he intended to send me on a range of courses leading to promotion. He expected me to be pleased. Instead I told him I'd rather not. That made him very angry. He told me – after I'd done almost 18 years of service and 12 years within Special Forces – that my decision meant I 'no longer had employability within the regiment'. He told me I should reconsider and let him know when I changed my mind.

I left his office with my mind made up, but not the way he wanted. I would seek discharge as soon as possible.

I considered myself a professional soldier and had dedicated myself to being a good soldier. I was only 37. I had excelled in the SASR selection, the patrol and regimental signaller's courses at the start of my SASR service, and I had done more combat operations than many of my colleagues. And I was proud of it. Now to be advised that my 'employability' was limited was a huge kick in the guts.

My sleep became severely affected, and it got to the stage where I would only sleep a couple of hours each night. Our first child, Kenzie, had only just been born in July 2004 and this added additional night-time duties, which contributed to sleep deprivation. As well as the inability to sleep and the anger and anxiety issues, my illness also manifested itself in other ways. I found my stomach was sensitive and painful, and I couldn't drink or eat things I usually enjoyed. A stomach specialist I consulted wondered if I was affected by some emotional disturbance. I decided to go to the army GP at the Swanbourne Barracks and tell him what was happening to try to get some help.

The doctor was very helpful and said he would try to be discreet. He knew it was not a good career move to admit to some psychological or emotional problem. So he gave me a referral to visit an outside psychiatrist, a Professor Robert Kosky, one of the leading specialists in Perth at the time. He got me to write down a list of my military operational experiences and asked me questions on each one, and I had to explain each experience in detail to him.

I became quite agitated in recounting some of the things I had been involved with. After one such session he said I should be careful on the drive home as these old memories can sometimes, once dredged up, cause difficulties coping shortly afterwards. I thought this was a bit of a laugh, as very few things worried me enough to affect my driving. But, sure enough, on the drive home the thoughts I had rediscovered and the feelings I had dug up did indeed come back at me with a vengeance and I had to stop and take time out from driving to regain my composure.

I had an overpowering feeling of guilt that I had done terrible things during my service and that I was no more entitled to be ill because of it than any of my work colleagues, as they had been through the same experiences as me and appeared perfectly normal. I was weak and not deserving of any special treatment due to some bullshit illness that no one else I worked with was suffering.

Eventually he came to the conclusion that I suffered from a condition known as post-traumatic stress disorder (PTSD). Professor Kosky described the symptoms in terms of a chemical imbalance in the brain. As I recall, the brain produces serotonin to help the body to relax and feel calm. My brain was no longer producing enough of the stuff and I was on high alert all the time.

I had to have some medication to try to regain this lost balance, and because of that I had to advise the regiment's psychologist of these developments and also my OC, so I could take some weeks off work to allow the medication time to take effect.

I fronted up to the OC, Paul, and our squadron sergeant major (SSM), Steve, who were extremely understanding. I indicated that I didn't want to lose my job over this 'lack of ability to sleep issue' (which was the way I understood it at the time). Steve said that it didn't even enter their minds that I should lose my job. I explained the 'imbalance' thing the same way Professor Kosky had explained it to me and they agreed that I should take a couple of weeks off to allow the medication to take effect.

I was now officially on extended sick leave for the first time in my almost 18-year army career. I was prescribed sleeping medication and also a strong antidepressant. This basically knocked me out for the first week or so until my body began to adjust to it, and then I was able to function almost normally again. For a time the bad dreams stopped and I stopped patrolling the house at night. I was more docile and less anxious. The downside was I put on weight and my short-term memory was shot.

After the sick leave I went back to work again. I felt much better and I was able to get some good sleep again for the first time in years. I continued to see the doctors regularly and I was eventually posted from my beloved 1 Squadron to the training squadron. There my new job was to be the lead instructor in the close-quarter battle (CQB) training cell. This posting was to be my last in SASR as an operator. It was the place from which I was to leave the regiment.

PTSD doesn't affect every soldier who is exposed to dangerous or traumatic circumstances. Most people are likely to have some kind of short-term stressful reaction to such circumstances but it will then subside, allowing them to live normally. Why I was not one of them, I don't know. Some of the incidents that I have been involved with continue to cause me distress. I find I recycle them over and over again in my mind. Some of the discomfort associated with those memories has subsided with time. The images are still distasteful to me and often shameful, but I can now usually think about them and not cringe and try to block them out as I once did.

Just what were the experiences that I believe contributed to the PTSD? Throughout these pages there are numerous such incidents where I still experience anxiety during recall. But I think it goes deeper than this. While many of my mates in the regiment are also suffering from it – and more are admitting to it all the time – there are others who have been through similar experiences who seem to handle it without any problem.

Maybe they are just better at covering it up, and I have no way of knowing if that's the case. But what I do know is that the life of an SAS operator puts you into the danger zone for PTSD. And unless the chain of command recognises this and finds a way to combat it, the casualty list will grow by the year. It really is that serious.

The story of female veterans is similar to those of some former SASR blokes I know who now live in their cars on the street. It's much more dangerous and traumatic for women, who are in constant danger from street predators. The post-deployment debriefings and questionnaires were just a 'tick the box' thing to cover arses so when things turned bad for veterans Defence could say they were given counselling.

3

GROWING UP

I had a pretty typical Aussie childhood. When I was born on 16 August 1967, I already had a two-year-old brother, Adam, and we lived for a while at Mum and Dad's original duplex in Mascot. But when we were followed by Mark two years later, we moved to Heathcote. Dad by then was a building and health inspector for the Sutherland Shire Council. They built their own place in Forest Road, land and house for a total £1325, and that's where we lived, surrounded by the Royal National Park, when our youngest brother, Glen, came along in 1977. I think Mum and Dad really wanted a girl but they got four boys instead.

It was a great life. We weren't rich but we didn't really want for anything. We sometimes had free takeaway Chinese food because the shop owners really wanted to impress the local inspector, who might come around to check on the hygiene at their premises. And the bushland of the National Park was our playground. We all grew up loving the outdoors. Adam, who became a lawyer, now spends much of his time on his cattle farm; Mark was a park ranger for a while before going into property development; and Glen lives on the New South Wales South Coast on a couple of acres with his wife, Kim, and their four children. They have built an eco-friendly home in a natural bushland area.

Mum was mostly one of the stay-at-home generation; it's lots of work looking after four boys. At times she did some household cleaning jobs. She also became involved with voluntary work assisting migrants in English language studies, which she really enjoyed. She loved language and was a fine poet, particularly about her struggle with Parkinson's. It's a terrible disease, and I think it helped that she was able to express herself in this way.

We saw quite a bit of our grandma Muriel, and as a small boy I often went with her to the Botany cemetery, where she would scrub her husband William's tile-topped grave with a bucket of water before placing fresh flowers by the headstone. This was a ritual for Muriel until the late 1970s. Although I was only six or seven, I always wanted to go along with her, as I worried she might stumble and hurt herself on the train journey to Rockdale, where her daughter Bub would pick us up and then deliver us to the cemetery. Afterwards we would go to Bub's for lunch.

My brothers and I walked the kilometre and a half to Heathcote Primary School from about the age of five or six. When we went to high school, we just had to jump over the back fence and walk across the footy oval and we were there.

Mum and Dad said I was a bright kid, but I didn't really like school and couldn't wait to finish each day. I remember that in Year 7 we had a French class and the poor French lady teaching us was hounded mercilessly by the rough-and-tumble 13-year-old kids from Heathcote, Engadine and Helensburgh to the point where she would often end up crying and fleeing the classroom. This of course was our goal, and after that a free-for-all reigned in the classroom until the bell rang for the next lesson.

During recess and lunch my friends and I would often take off in a mate's old Valiant Charger back to his place to get away from school. This was usually just before art class, as the teacher was easy to convince that I had some urgent medical appointment. Of course that wasn't the case, and maybe she was happy enough to get rid of me. I did get caught out a few times, however, and the principal would deliver a few strokes of the cane on the hand or backs of my legs. This was usually enough to keep me on the straight and narrow for a couple of days until the threat of punishment wore off.

Actually I liked art and English at high school. I enjoyed painting on canvas and got good marks for my work with the brush. In English we had a female teacher who was passionate about Australian literature, and she would often dissolve in tears when reciting an emotive story, a poem or a song like 'I Was Only 19', about Vietnam veterans.

We played rugby league in the last couple of years of high school. Ours was a fairly mediocre team, but we trained two afternoons a week and did okay against other local schools. I liked long-distance running and used to compete with some of the other reasonable runners in the school carnivals, where we'd race through the Royal National Park. I liked swimming, especially when my brothers and I swam in the creeks of the National Park or cycled to Cronulla for a surf. But what I really loved was cycling with my brothers, and we spent hours planning trips, building up to real expeditions from Sydney to Melbourne and north to Brisbane.

We did the Melbourne trip in the 1983 Christmas holidays when I was just 16. We left from Heathcote early one morning thinking that we'd take about ten days to reach our destination and then get a train back from Melbourne. We had to carry all our gear with us, so we rigged bike racks with pannier bags hanging on each side of the rear wheel. In these we carried the sandwiches Mum had made for us, a few spare clothes and a sleeping bag. The tent was a bit of a challenge. In the end Adam carried the tent and fly, and I had the poles and pegs. We also had a water bottle each.

Dad allowed us to withdraw $300 each from our pocket money savings accounts to buy food, pay for tent sites at van parks and also buy our tickets home. Mum no doubt was very worried about the safety of her boys, but being so young and carefree we were oblivious to the potential risks.

We took the coast road down the Princes Highway, and on day one we made it as far as Kiama, about 120 kilometres south of Sydney, without mishap. On the second day, just south of Nowra, a woman in a sedan failed to see Adam and turned left into a side street directly in front of him, knocking him off his bike. Luckily he only had a couple of bruises and scrapes and we were on our way again within a minute or two. Thankfully after this we didn't have any more accidents, but just about every day there would be a near miss when a large logging truck or a careless car driver would squeeze us onto the gravel shoulder. If we were belting down a hill at 50 km/h, running onto the gravel could be really dodgy. And as we had the bags on our backs, the bikes were already a little unstable, adding to the challenge.

Every couple of hours we would pull up near a small town and do minor repairs – fixing a flat tyre, tightening some loose nuts and bolts – or we'd just sit down in the shade of a tree and have something to eat. We usually bought a loaf of bread each day and we carried dried fruit and some honey; so this provided us with a high-sugar lunch. At night we heated up a tin of beef stew or beans on a small kerosene primus stove. We ate it on toast (basically burned bread) and finished off with a cup of tea.

On some occasions we could use a gas barbecue provided at the caravan parks where we spent the night. At one of these near the Victorian border we met an elderly couple named Harold and Esmay, who normally lived in Altona, a Melbourne suburb. They were surprised that I was 'so young and far from home' and invited us to stay in their granny flat when we reached our destination.

When we got to Melbourne, it took us hours of cycling around the suburbs to locate their address. No GPS in those days, and we didn't have a street directory. Eventually we came across their modest brick and fibro home on the main street of Altona. They were happy to see us and opened up the small granny flat in the backyard. They were a terrific couple and very generous. We ate most of our meals with them while we explored much of the Melbourne city by train each day. We also met their granddaughters, who were very pretty and about the same ages as Adam and me.

Years later, after I had joined the army, I had two opportunities to visit them again while passing through Melbourne. On the second occasion Harold had recently passed away and Esmay, now alone, was happy to see me again. I'm sure she now has a long list of grandchildren and maybe great-grandchildren to continue her family line.

It was a great experience for young teenagers, and at the end of the following year Adam and I did another trip to Brisbane with our younger brother Mark and his friend

Matthew. This time we stayed in a tent site near the high-rise palaces of the Gold Coast.

Back then there were no bike-helmet laws, and we certainly didn't wear them. Thinking back on these trips now, I wouldn't want my children to try such things when they get to that age. But I suppose I'm no different from all parents these days.

By the end of Year 11 in high school I'd had enough and, although I completed Year 12 in 1985, my heart just wasn't in it. Some of my other friends were already in the workforce and appeared to be making good money and I wanted to do the same. I was really keen on the outdoors and for a few weeks towards the end of that year I did a jackeroo's training course near Tamworth in northern New South Wales. I wanted to work on a sheep station. Dad had often told us stories about the farm near Grafton he visited as a boy. He made it sound like a great life. I loved watching TV shows by outback adventurers like Malcolm Douglas. I was also keen to see and experience the Aboriginal culture of the far north.

I liked horses. When we were all really young, Dad had taken us boys to the pictures to see a small production about some Aussie adventures by Alby Mangels and his mate, who had travelled the outback as stockmen, then around the world in their World Safari program. And there was a vacant paddock behind our place where we used to jump on the bare backs of the horses that roamed around there. Mark and I also went on a Blue Mountains horseback adventure for three days when we were about 12 and 14 and really enjoyed that as well. Mum loved horses and had a pony as a young girl. On weekends she would sometimes take us horseback riding south of Sydney.

I was quite excited as I rode my motorbike to Tamworth. I'd been mucking around with bikes and cars since I was 16 and bought an old, busted, two-stroke Yamaha road bike for $50. I fixed it up and sold it for $400. Later I bought a Mini for $700, which I tidied up and sold for $1500. I bought my first licensed bike, a 250 cc Honda motorbike, for $1400 with the money I'd saved from part-time jobs and the bike and car deals. It took me off to Tamworth as I made my way into the wide world.

It took me a full day to ride there, and when I arrived in the late afternoon there were around half a dozen other young people there just like me, eager to learn new skills that we could use in our future jobs.

The camp was really a beef and sheep farm about an hour's drive from Tamworth's town centre. It was quite old and was run by the son of the owner. His father was there as well, and they took us out each day to assist with the regular routine of the station. We travelled everywhere on horseback, and within a day we were mustering sheep and cattle, branding and gelding young cattle, and drenching or dipping the sheep. They showed us how to shear and slaughter a 'killer' – usually an old wether – for the dinner table. We also learned to shoe our horses and keep the saddles and reins soft and pliable with neatsfoot oil. It was a terrific experience and I often think it would be great for any young people today.

The one drawback was the food. They gave us such small helpings I was starving most of the time. At the end of a long dusty day branding cattle in the yards, I was ravenous and as a growing teenager I needed a big meal. The camp cook was a young woman who had the hots for the farmer's son, so always gave him triple rations, whereas we paying customers got the leftovers. We spent a lot of hungry nights until breakfast, and that was pretty meagre as well. They were obviously trying to save on their food bill.

Other than that it was a great experience and I learned a lot about the station and also about the types of people I would have to deal with. It was a real eye-opener for an impressionable youngster, especially seeing things like a sheep having its throat cut for the table or an injured cow slaughtered with a bullet to its head.

Also, I was at the stage where the country farm girls were starting to be quite interesting. They were good to look at but tough; at the dance at the end of the camp I was asked to dance by a local farmer's daughter, then thrown around like a rag doll. I reckoned she probably wrestled bulls before she could walk.

When I got home, I applied for a couple of jobs as a station hand in South Australia and other distant locations.

One was a massive property a few hundred kilometres north of Port Augusta. Another was a horse handler's position near Richmond not far from Sydney. Mum didn't really want me to go as far as South Australia, so I took the Richmond job.

The area at that time was semi-rural and the owner had a small acreage with about ten horses that he looked after for wealthy horse owners. I worked for the stable owner, and my job was to feed and exercise the horses every day but Sunday, for which I was paid the huge sum of $160 per week. I quite liked the work but it soon became apparent to me that my employer, who I stayed with in a spare room of his house, was gay. Normally I couldn't have cared less and I figured it wouldn't affect my work, but after a couple of weeks he started to make inappropriate remarks and gestures to me. One morning he came into my bedroom and jumped on top of me while I was still waking. I told him to get off, and when he didn't I picked him up and threw him back out the door.

Later, when we were in the kitchen getting breakfast, he came up behind me and pinned me to the bench with his body pressed up against my back and insinuated that he was stronger than me. I'm not tall but I'm pretty strong and I pushed him away. And after that I couldn't wait to get out of there. Luckily (or so I thought at the time) another horse hand arrived, a young woman, who was about 20, and my employer said she and I would be transferred for the next month to the polo ground south of Nowra, where we would care for the horses throughout the season.

She and my employer had known each other for a while, apparently, and he said she was to be my 'supervisor'. She was a bossy type and we didn't get along that well. We were accommodated in an old caravan near some horse yards. She slept up one end and I was down the other. The daily routine was to get up early, check and feed the horses we had there in the yards, and then come back and make breakfast. After that it was exercise time, and each horse had to be exercised for around two hours a day. I'd ride one and lead one or two others alongside. This was hard work for the uninitiated but I soon became used to all the horses and the routine.

The trouble was the young woman, who I'll call Sue, was a bit of a pain. She was dedicated to the horses but was lazy in other areas and liked to boss me around. And when my employer came to visit, she slept with him in the bed opposite mine. So he wasn't just gay, it seemed; he didn't care how he got his sex. They would carry on in the nearby bed and make crude jokes that I really didn't need to hear as a young employee just out of school. These days it would be called sexual harassment, but back then I didn't know better and just wanted to get on with earning some money.

Sue was also friends with an RAAF guy who worked at the nearby Nowra Airbase, and he came over to our van on a couple of occasions to hang out with us. He told me how great his work was and how much he enjoyed it. He also liked getting that regular pay cheque. He was really the only other person I got to know in the job. I didn't mingle with the owners, as we were definitely not considered in their class. As a horse groom I was flat out prepping ponies, saddling them up, plaiting their tails and generally running about.

One day I didn't fit a horse coat properly and Sue got really angry with me and told me the only job I was good for was picking up the horse shit. She forbade me to use a shovel to clean up the yards and made me pick it up with my hands instead. She said it would toughen up my work hands. I was very naive and thought she was a responsible person, but I soon realised she was just trying to belittle me. I did this for a couple of days until my anger welled up, and one morning when she criticised me again I turned and let her have both barrels. Then I told her I'd had enough of her crap and I was leaving first thing in the morning.

The following morning I jumped on my motorbike and headed back to Sydney. Along the way in Wollongong I saw the army recruitment office and thought back to what the RAAF guy had told me. I parked the bike and went in. I had an interview with a sergeant, who asked me a few questions, got me all sorts of forms to fill in and sent me on my way. He said I'd receive a letter in a few weeks to advise me of the next step in the process, so I jumped back on the bike and continued on up the Princes Highway towards Heathcote. As usual Mum and Dad were really happy to see me. When I told them about joining the army, Dad didn't seem too concerned but I could tell Mum was really worried about what I'd committed myself to.

Over the next few months I had lots of medical assessments and a couple of interviews with the army's recruitment office in Sydney. Finally they advised me that I had to turn up on 16 April 1986. So on the appointed day I caught the train to the city, carrying a few essentials and some lunch Mum had made in a paper bag. I was off to join the army.

When I arrived, I met a few other young men like myself who would be going through the same recruitment courses. Some of these guys would become good friends, and a few would go on to join the SAS and work with me on operations overseas. We were all loaded onto a couple of minibuses, which then headed south for the next five hours to Wagga Wagga.

Along the way we chatted about what was to come. I got increasingly nervous as we heard hair-raising stories about the treatment of soldiers during recruitment training (what the Americans call 'boot camp'). On arrival at the training school we were met by our platoon staff, which consisted of three corporals, a sergeant and the young captain. Those guys would babysit us over the next three months.

4
BASIC TRAINING

We would become 12 Platoon, a group of about 30 young men ranging between 18 and 30 years old. Our introduction to the army was definitely rough. During the first couple of weeks we spent many hours standing in our hallway just outside our rooms performing repetitive punishment exercises dictated by a small group of corporals who watched us like hawks and punished everybody for the minor errors of the individual. We soon learned that we had to make sure everybody performed to the same high standards expected by our staff. We were punished for the most minor infractions, like 'boots not clean enough' or 'beds not made properly'.

Some men even took matters into their own hands, and at night would gather and sneak into the room of one of the underperforming individuals who was making the group's life more difficult and deliver a severe beating. I knew this was going on because I could hear the commotion and cries of pain as the victims were struck over and over again by the hit squad. I never became involved in that sort of thing but I did see three of the other recruits in my room going AWOL as a result of not coping with the new lifestyle they'd signed up to. I never saw them again.

Some of these poor young fellows seemed really unstable to me and I wondered if they could not have been identified earlier as unsuitable for the army life. One of my roommates was so scared of the hit squad that he slept with his bayonet under his pillow. He was later removed from our platoon, I suspect on psychiatric grounds.

This routine of punishments and strenuous route marches and firearms training in the harsh Wagga Wagga winter went on for three months. I found I was good at shooting and most of the physical stuff, like the pack march. I was okay at the marching drill, which we practised a lot. At the end we had become a cohesive team and we competed with other platoons for the Vasey Trophy. It was awarded to the platoon that scored highest in marching drills, weapons handling tests, marksmanship, navigation, contact drills with a mock enemy, and route march times. It gave us a lot of satisfaction when we actually won it.

At the end of training I was given three options as to which corps I wanted to join: Infantry, Transport or Engineering. I had a corporal instructor who said Transport was great. It was just bullshit really as they always say their own corps' stream is the best. I imagined driving big trucks in remote parts of the world and decided that was for me. Shortly afterwards we had a big march-out parade, which was attended by my mum and dad and my two younger brothers. We were then loaded onto buses and shipped off to our various destinations. My bus trip wasn't far, as I was headed for the Army School of Transport located in Puckapunyal, Victoria.

Life in Pucka was much more relaxed and we got to see the less disciplined side of the army. The first night a young and really drunk lance corporal staggered into our dormitory, called us new recruits out into the hallway and complained that the toilets were not clean enough. Some of my colleagues slouched against the wall and just blatantly laughed at him, which enraged him. But he knew that he was in no state to follow through with his complaints and he staggered off to create more drunken mischief with easier targets elsewhere. This insubordination towards a lance corporal really shocked me, as until then anyone with rank had to be addressed appropriately or serious discipline would result. To me this was a rude awakening after a very disciplined and structured start at the recruit training school.

We spent the next three months at the 'School of Trucks' learning how to drive old Series 3 Land Rovers and relatively new army UNIMOG trucks, the six-tonne Mercedes used to transport goods and soldiers. This was all good fun but I struggled a bit as I had limited driver experience in anything bigger than a motorbike.

We also went to the boozer each night after training and drank as many beers as our measly pay cheques would stretch to. One night, while seated around the table at the army boozer with some mates in my troop, a really drunken army cook took a swing at me for no apparent reason. He was hastily ushered outside by the military police (MPs). I felt really pissed off at him for punching me, so I followed him over to his accommodation doorway from which he continued to yell abuse across the road at the other punters. He was so pissed he didn't remember me, and when I asked him the time he looked down at his watch and I smacked him a couple of good ones in the head and stomach. He went down and the MPs came running but I was young and quick and made a beeline out the back and up to my hut, where I hastily went to sleep. I think of it now as an act of cowardice, but at the time that's how we resolved things in the army, and anything less was considered gutless.

After passing through the Army Transport School I was posted to HQ Company at Lavarack Barracks in Townsville, Queensland. I was happy about this opportunity as I really wanted to go north to the tropics. I headed to Melbourne to buy a second-hand car that would get me there under my own steam. In a dealer's yard I found a small brown Mini with a sun roof and mag wheels. I used my saved pay cheques as well as some of the $900 the army gave me for travel and accommodation for the five-day journey. I still had a fair bit left over and I felt like a millionaire with a wallet stuffed with $50 notes and a 'new' car to go in.

It was really exciting and a friend from the unit, 'Sappy' Sapwell, joined me with his old Jeep as we headed, we reckoned, to tropical paradise. We had CB radios rigged up in our vehicles and we chatted as we drove. We'd only reached Albury-Wodonga when suddenly a young lady's voice came over the radio asking who we were and if we wanted to meet at the service station in Albury where we had to get petrol.

Of course I said, 'Yeah, you bet,' and Sappy and I pulled into the servo. I was filling the tank of the Mini when a big old Holden panel van pulled alongside with two young ladies in the front. One introduced herself to me as the girl on the radio. Her name, she said, was Lorraine. She was dark haired and attractive with the strong build of a farm girl. She asked where I was going and I told her Townsville.

I was a bit tongue-tied but when she said she had a friend there she wanted to visit I wasn't about to pass this up. I said, 'Sure, come along.' By then her friend in the Holden was ready to leave, heading south. Lorraine said she had no clothes with her except what she was wearing and a bag of women's stuff. With my small fortune burning a hole in my pocket, I offered to buy her a dress and she quickly agreed. Within minutes we were in the Mini and on our way to Townsville together.

Sappy was obviously jealous and he kept asking on the radio if she would join him in his Jeep; but for some reason she stayed with me in the tiny Mini. We travelled first to Sydney and arrived in the late afternoon at my parents' house. Mum and Dad were very happy to see me after three months away. They accepted Lorraine into their home with open arms. She even showed them her tattoos of birds on her shoulder blades, which Mum said she found 'quite interesting'. We slept upstairs on the lounge-room floor. I kept my distance as I'd only met her that day and anything else wouldn't have felt right. My parents were very accepting and genuine people.

I decided to stay an extra day there and get a new cassette player fitted to the car in the nearby suburb of Miranda. The salesman said it would take a couple of hours to be fitted, so Loraine and I walked to the nearby pub and proceeded to get a bit drunk. It only took me a couple of schooners as I was only 19 years old, weighed about 67 kilograms and before I joined up had hardly ever drunk much. We waltzed back to pick up the Mini and I let Lorraine drive the 20 kilometres back to the house.

Along the way an off-duty policeman pulled us over and was kind enough to advise us to walk to the nearest train station. This advice we promptly ignored and I took over from Lorraine and continued our journey. Around Engadine I didn't notice the car ahead pull up at the lights and I slammed into its rear. I pulled over to the side and when the police arrived they told me I'd be charged with driving under the influence (DUI).

My Mini sustained minor damage to the front end but was still driveable. I didn't let on to Mum and Dad, but I worried how I would explain it to my new unit when I arrived in Townsville – as a transport driver. A driver without a driver's licence would be no use to anyone. But there wasn't much I could do about it then, so I decided not to worry about it until we got there.

The next day we headed north again, this time to Ballina, where we stayed at the local hotel. We were getting along really well and having a great trip despite the minor legal hiccups. The following day we decided we would really push it and head to Airlie Beach halfway up the Queensland coast, where we could then stay two nights and enjoy the tropics before I would have to start work in Townsville. We struggled to make the long distance in the Mini but arrived around midnight at Proserpine.

The next day we made the short drive on to Airlie Beach where we rented a tinnie with an outboard motor and some dive masks and fins. The boat guy told us not to venture too far because we had to return the boat and gear by 4 p.m. or he'd call the local police and tell them we were missing. We took that with a grain of salt and headed off to a deserted island and parked the tinnie up on a white sandy beach. Then we went snorkelling for about three hours. Lorraine was a free spirit and walked around most of the day with her top off, which I couldn't complain about. Around 2 p.m. we decided to head back to the boat to start the long trip back to Airlie Harbour. But when we reached it, we got a nasty shock. The tide had dropped the water level a couple of metres and now our tinnie was on a sandbank about 200 metres from the water line. There was no way we were going to get the boat back to Airlie on time.

Lorraine reckoned we should try to drag it across the sand flats but we could hardly budge it. I decided to remove the engine, fuel tank and life preservers and leave them on the beach while we pulled and dragged the empty boat slowly, metre by metre, across the sand. This exhausted us both but after about an hour and a half we managed to get it to the shallows. We loaded the gear back on board, got the motor started and headed as quickly as we could back across the water.

We were about five kilometres from Airlie Harbour but the wind had come up and the boat was making slow progress and really bouncing across the white caps. As the spray hit our faces, we were bailing frantically to stay as high in the water as possible. The trip seemed endless but eventually we pulled into the harbour, really tired and thirsty. We were about half an hour late and the boat guy was not very impressed. But we survived and had a great day. That night was pretty good too.

After that it was on to Townsville, and I dropped Lorraine at her friend's house, hoping that I would see her again as I had become quite attached to her. I then went on to Lavarack Barracks and Headquarters Company 3 Brigade to report my arrival to the duty officer. It was a Sunday and he gave me a key to my new room. I told him about the DUI and said it looked like I'd lose my licence for three months. He said I needed to see the brigade officer first thing in the morning and tell him of my screw-up. He held little hope for me, I'm sure.

I headed over to the accommodation barracks, which was an old two-storey row of demountables with toilets at each end. Louvred windows and steel shutters lined the outside walls; they would be battened down when a cyclone hit. Inside was a large clothes cupboard that separated the room into two halves. I was on the left side and on the other was another young transport driver from Tasmania named Raynor. The rooms were stinking hot with no air-conditioning, just a ceiling fan directly above the clothes locker to circulate the tropical heat.

Next morning the brigade major gave me a stern word and said if he had his way I'd be working in the mess hall for the next three months washing dishes until I got my licence back. My sergeant was also not impressed but they needed a driver so they took me to a nearby police station and I applied for (and got) a full Queensland licence, no questions asked. I still had to face the court proceedings back in Sydney but a local military law officer advised I could plead guilty to the DUI charge to a legal representative in Sydney who would appear on my behalf. He also said I would probably have to pay a heavy fine and cover the cost of repairing the car I'd run into.

Since I had no savings left, I had to arrange a loan from the local bank in Townsville to pay the legal bills. It took me about a year to pay these back out of my meagre wage.

I saw Lorraine a few more times over the next week and we even took a weekend drive up to Cairns, but on the way back on Sunday she started up a conversation on the CB radio with a truck driver heading south to Melbourne. He said he had room for a passenger and she agreed to go with him. I was really sad to see her go, and that was the last time I ever saw her. I hope she stayed safe along the way, as she seemed to travel without fear of what could happen to a young lady a long way from home and relying on the charity of others.

My army company still remembered my DUI exploits, so when a three-month posting to the Tully Jungle Training School came up, I was the person earmarked to fill the spot. Within a week I was sent off to spend the last half of 1986 in the rainforest 300 kilometres north of Townsville. This new place was even more ramshackle than the Lavarack Barracks. The accommodation was really Vietnam-style jungle tin huts. The best that could be said of it was that it kept off the rain, and in Tully that was important as it has the highest rainfall in Australia.

I was issued a fold-up cot, which was just a sheet of canvas stretched out between three wooden supports and kept tight with some steel springs. This was what we slept on for the four months we were there.

The bunk houses were tin sheds, so during the heat of the day they were stifling hot, and when the tropical storms came the pounding of the rain on the roof meant you could not hear a single thing. At the time there were a few Vietnam veterans posted there, and some of them apparently suffered mental-health issues. They were probably there to keep them away from regular army postings. I recall a soldier telling me that one of the old vets would sometimes wander off away from the camp into the jungle and not be seen for days at a time. That was the first time I really got exposed to vets with battle fatigue, or PTSD as it is called these days.

Being a brand-new soldier, I was given every shitty driving job that came along. One was to drive the local wild pig catcher around in an old Land Rover and trailer to bait his many traps with bananas that we picked up from local growers. Peter the Pigman we called him; he was a local from the area but of European descent and hardly spoke a word of English. He stunk like an old camel and was really obnoxious, always yelling at me when I couldn't understand his lingo.

He was a cruel fellow, and when we caught a large bush pig in one of his steel traps he would pull out an old 22 rifle and try to kill it with a shot to its head. This rifle was underpowered and often the bullets bounced off or went through its ear and came out the other side. This enraged and petrified the wild animal and drove it insane, running headlong into the cage surrounding it and squealing like all hell. I could only stand back and watch as he fired again and again until one of the bullets eventually silenced it.

I complained to him about the cruelty, but this just angered him more and he would fly off his handle at me, swearing and bitching and then going back to the camp to complain to the commander that I wasn't doing my job driving him about. I got to hate taking him out into the forest to bait his traps and I sometimes felt I would like to hit him over the head with a shovel and leave him out there. Eventually the commander realised that the tension was too much for Peter or me to bear, so I was given a new job and no longer had to haul his smelly carcass around the jungle in my Land Rover.

The new job was as driver for the Jungle Training Centre commander, Major Donkin. This was much better. It got me out of the jungle to take him to various meetings all over North Queensland. I even stayed the night in hotels or army reserve bases in Cairns and other nearby towns. This was much more pleasant than the accommodation offered in the bunkhouses back at the jungle camp. I was surprised that no one else wanted the job as the commander's driver. I enjoyed it and started to like my place in the army.

After the four-month posting was up, I was posted back to Townsville's HQ Company 3 Brigade, where my old accommodation was waiting for me with the single fan circulating the heat and the dust in the room. Life as a truck driver in the army, I decided, was fairly easy, consisting of a series of three- to six-week training exercises throughout the year interspersed with local driver tasks and lots of mess duties – washing dishes or polishing the officers' silverware in their mess hall. Once a year we had an opportunity to go on a two-week adventure training camp up in the Far North at a place called Coen. This was a great adventure as it was a terrific opportunity to ride motorbikes, go fishing, shoot feral pigs and drink beer around the fire at night. That was where I got to meet a friend called Sean. He was a young bloke like me from Western Australia, and a real gun nut. He had a boot full of all types of rifles, shotguns and pistols, which he carried around in his old Valiant. After that trip Sean and I would often take a drive out west of Townsville and go shooting out in the dry bushland. One day Sean asked if I wanted to go shooting on Friday night, as we often did, but unfortunately I had been assigned a mess duty the following day and would have to get up really early to help prepare the meals for the barracks.

He went with one of the other lads. Along the way he was chased by a local farmer along the gravel highway, probably for shooting across his property. The farmer didn't catch Sean as they both sped along through the bush at night, but he did manage to call the Townsville police, who promptly set up a roadblock at the base of the escarpment and successfully collared the young army blokes. They were charged with several firearms offences and had to appear in court. Sean had to pay a fine and had his firearms seized. It was only dumb luck that I was on mess duty.

My two years in Townsville were soon up and I was then posted to 5 Transport Squadron in Brisbane. I enjoyed the position and got to make a few good mates, particularly Jeremy 'Scotty' Scott. I met Scotty in Rockhampton's Shoalwater Bay training area in 1989 in a foxhole we had spent the night digging. Sitting up for hours in a hole in the ground is not much fun, and to break the boredom we would crack jokes at each other's expense even though we had just met.

5

SELECTION BEGINS

In October 1989 I was offered the chance to deploy to Butterworth, Malaysia, for four months with an infantry company. There was a permanent RAAF unit stationed there and the army's responsibility was base security. There would also be opportunities to travel to Singapore and other training camps to take part in joint Australian–Malaysian training exercises.

That's for me, I thought.

I was quite excited as it was my first overseas trip. We travelled by RAAF C-130 from Brisbane via Darwin to Butterworth near Penang on the west coast of Malaysia. It was a hellishly long flight strapped in the narrow mesh seats of the cargo aircraft. On arrival we were ushered over to the accommodation area, which was only a kilometre from the airstrip.

SELECTION BEGINS

There we were given a briefing by the senior NCOs of the 6th Battalion RAR on the dos and don'ts of the barracks. The most serious don't was to try to get through the front guard post of the base without presenting your ID pass. A few years earlier someone (not an Aussie) had tried that and been shot dead by the sentry. Terrorism was a real threat, and it was taken deadly seriously by the Malaysian military.

The accommodations were ancient concrete single-level dorms with four to six beds in each small room. They had open ceilings with tin roofs. There was no cooling except the shuttered windows, which provided a passage for the tropical heat. Once or twice each day it rained heavily for about an hour and the shallow open-air concrete drains just outside the front door would fill to overflowing on the veranda.

Every day a local 'doby' or boot boy would come past and shine each soldier's boots for him. We would pay him a few ringgit a week for this extravagant novelty. He was not really a boy at all but a very old man who had followed his trade there since the Japanese occupation. He was bent over and burned black by the tropical sun but we would find him outside burnishing shoes each morning.

Scotty had not come along on this trip but I quickly made some new friends among the other support staff, as we stuck together as a unit. Rough treatment from the battalion boys could be expected if you got on their wrong side. On one occasion they took a dislike to one of the soldiers I worked with. They pinned him to a chair at the boozer after work and poured the cook's hot curry over him with their own captain watching on. There was hell to pay after that, as he rightly complained to the OC about the abuse.

On another occasion I was told to leave a regular drinking hole at the Georgetown area of Penang by an infantry corporal who accused me of misbehaving on the booze. Half an hour later the same fellow was completely naked and dancing on the barroom tables.

We didn't really mix with the air force blokes who were permanently stationed there. Their roles were mostly administrative or technical duties to do with the operational aircraft coming and going from Australia. They probably thought of us as a troublesome mob on a drunken holiday for three months, which to me it absolutely was.

My job was to drive the infantry and their equipment around in our Hino trucks. This was a dangerous exercise at times, as the roads were treacherous. There was lots of rain and the traffic congestion on the narrow highways meant you had to be on high alert behind the wheel at all times. On several occasions I came across serious and even fatal accidents when small motorbikes and other cars had collided with big trucks. Even one of our trucks was 't-boned' by a couple of locals on their mopeds when the riders failed to slow or give way entering an intersection and ran smack into the side of the truck.

SELECTION BEGINS

On one occasion while coming back from Singapore in convoy, there was a tropical downpour and two of our trucks were forced off the highway by oncoming traffic. One of the trucks put a wheel off the road and onto the grassy shoulder. Instantly the wheel sank into the mud and the entire truck and its load of army stores crashed over onto its side. A couple of kilometres up the highway another of our trucks faced the same problem and flipped on its side when it tried to avoid a collision in the slippery conditions. Chris, the driver, a friend from Townsville, was thrown through the windscreen and landed on his back on the highway. He suffered serious bruising but was not badly injured. When we got back to base, we tried to explain to the air force how the damage to two of their trucks came about. Our explanations didn't go down too well.

There was plenty of time off and we made the most of it. While I was out and about one evening, I met a young lady named Karen. She was one of the several local young women who served drinks at the bar, which was just a simple shop with a few seats along one wall. I was about 22 and she was around 18, and we became boyfriend and girlfriend. Karen was a Sikh – her parents were from the Punjab, the ancestral home of most Sikhs – and she didn't like being referred to as Indian or Malaysian.

She was always very worried that her parents would realise she was seeing a non-Sikh. They never found out, but her slightly older sister was aware of the situation and gave her grief for it. On one occasion we visited one of her friend's brothers and had a nice time in their small high-rise apartment. They were impressed that I was trying to learn their language, Bahasa Malaysia, and I'd already picked up many words at a colloquial level.

This was quite helpful when we were on training exercises. Local villagers would come around and I would talk with them and offer them money for their home-cooked fresh roti (flat bread) and delicious servings of curried chicken and other dishes as well as cold cans of Coke, which I loved. The infantry lads would look on in envy as my mates and I ate our fresh tucker while they were stuck with army ration packs. They could have done what I did had they wanted to but they didn't have the interest. In fact, while I didn't realise it then, the Bahasa I picked up on that first deployment would come in very handy later in my SAS career.

The posting passed very quickly. But when we were due to depart, orders came down that we would have to stay on a month longer owing to an aircraft shortage back in Australia. Most of the blokes were annoyed but I was happy to be able to see Karen a little longer. When I really had to leave the following month, that made it all the harder. I was very sad to go. I tried to stay in touch with her when I got back but I think it was too difficult for her and we soon lost contact.

After a year back in Brisbane at the Enoggera Army Camp doing the same old thing, I was beginning to get bored with the army routine. I had made a lot of good friends but I wanted to do something different and more challenging. I continued with my cycling and I even did a trip from Brisbane down to Sydney to raise money for charity with another keen cyclist. But that wasn't enough so I decided to apply for the SASR selection course.

I didn't really know anyone in the regiment except another truck driver called Craig, who Scotty introduced me to. But I'd read a lot of military history and had a basic idea of what it was all about. Most of my colleagues, however, were less than confident about my getting through the selection process, as they had heard how tough it was and obviously had little faith in my capabilities.

After training for several months and preparing myself for the 1991 selection, my Transport Squadron commander told me that I'd missed the boat with my paperwork and would have to wait another year. This was not such a big deal to me, as it meant I had more time to prepare myself. I was lucky actually because my squadron second-in-comand (2IC), a captain, had also attempted a previous course but was unsuccessful. He supported my goal and allowed me to do my own physical training (PT) during our regular sessions. This I did twice a day, starting around 8 a.m. for an hour or so and then again in the afternoon for about two hours after I finished work. And if I was on an army exercise out in the bush, I was allowed to go for PT runs along the bush tracks.

I occasionally saw some blokes from the infantry battalions doing similar training around the barracks and I'd sometimes ask to join them as they plodded along with their heavy packs. One time I joined a sergeant from 6th Battalion and I later came to know him well as he was in my section during the selection course. He was very fit and I struggled to keep up with the cracking pace he set as he marched along with his 40 kilograms of additional gear. I was a short bloke and my legs had to practically run just to stay alongside him.

On another occasion I met a bloke about my height who was also from the 6th Battalion. We arranged to do a pack-march session together on the weekend and set ourselves a difficult route through the hills at the back of the barracks. His pace was much slower and we stayed together for a few hours, but eventually he said he'd had enough and went back to camp. It shocked me that he would give up so soon. I knew if I was to be successful, I would always have to push on, even when I hit the wall. That fellow did start the selection course with me but pulled out after a few days; he just didn't have the drive to keep going at all cost.

During the pre-selection process I had to undergo a series of interviews and medical examinations. The interviews were mostly psychological evaluations by senior officers. They were long and tedious with lists of questions to answer. I guess they were trying to see if I was mentally stable. They also enquired if I was gay and other silly things like,

SELECTION BEGINS

'If you saw a cliff, would you have an overwhelming urge to jump off?' Fair dinkum.

There were several physical challenges I had to have supervised by my unit physical training instructor (PTI). One was a 3.2 kilometre run in belt order, boots and rifle. This sounds a lot easier than it really is. You had to carry around eight kilograms of equipment in your belt kit or webbing as well as your rifle, which was about eight kilograms, plus ammunition, plus your boots and army uniform. And you had to complete the course in just 16 minutes. The first time I tried this, I nearly threw up at the end, it was so arduous. It was pretty much a fast run for the entire distance and a sprint at the end just to try to make the time. I kept at it for many months to build up my stamina.

To add to the challenge, the base at Enoggera in Brisbane was quite hilly, so you had lots of gradients to take into account. To make it harder for myself, I would carry a length of solid copper pipe that weighed about ten kilograms. I figured that by training a bit harder than I really needed to, I would find it easier when I was tested.

About six months before the selection course in Perth I had to front a panel of SASR senior non-commissioned officers (NCOs) and officers and tell them why I wanted to get into the regiment. It was a hard-nosed bunch of characters I found facing me in the old timber office building just inside the front barracks gate at Enoggera. Straight away they wanted to know about the drink-driving incident some six years previously. I explained that I had learned a valuable lesson and was now on the straight and narrow. One of the sternest looking characters then asked me to tell him a joke, which I promptly did, and no one laughed at all. This bloke's name was Greg, and he was to become the senior instructor at the selection course. I would come to know and regard him very well over my years in the SASR.

After each of these critical assessments I had to wait several weeks to receive a letter advising me that I had moved on to the next stage prior to selection. I continued to train and never really doubted that I would get through it all. After nearly two years of daily training and building up my strength and stamina, I received a letter saying I would be on the May 1992 selection course that was to be conducted near Perth. I was really over the moon as I now had something more concrete to aim for rather than just another medical or psychological evaluation.

Just prior to my departure from Brisbane my good mate Scotty from our 5 Transport Squadron told me he was going to throw me a going-away party. He said he would come around to my barracks room with a few friends and have some beers; so I promptly bought a couple of cartons and some bags of ice and chucked it all in a clean garbage bin as a makeshift esky. I then waited in my room.

I was getting worried when no one turned up. I kept looking at my watch; maybe I'd mixed up the time. Next thing I heard a knock at the door and, when I was about

SELECTION BEGINS

to get up to open it, four or five blokes dressed in uniforms and black hoods or balaclavas burst into the room and bundled me downstairs. They pinched my Valiant's keys and pushed me into the boot with all my old spare parts, tyres and tools.

There I was, bouncing along the road in the darkness of the trunk for what seemed like an hour before the car stopped and I was hoisted out, blindfolded, hooded and led into a building and dumped on the floor. All I could tell was that I was surrounded by familiar voices laughing and I was getting the occasional kick in the bum or slap on the head but nothing hard. A beer was pushed in my hand and I tried to take a sip through the dark hood. Then they stood me up and removed the hood.

I looked around, a bit dazed by it all, but then it fell into place. We were at Scotty's house and all my friends from my army unit were there. 'Bastards!' I said but I really couldn't get the grin off my face. They'd brought my garbage-bin 'esky' along and with the beer they already had in Scotty's fridge there was enough to keep us going through a really great night – one of the best.

This was the last chance I would have to relax with a beer for many weeks. The rigours of the SAS selection course are legendary in the services. The regiment has even made a couple of television documentaries over the years that give a general outline of the course that candidates have to complete before they're considered to have the 'right stuff' for membership of a very exclusive club. But they don't convey just how gut-wrenching an ordeal it really is. That's something only the survivors know.

On the day before the course I boarded a C-130 cargo plane bound for Western Australia. It was crowded with many other lads like me headed for the selection course. The flight seemed to take forever, as those transports crawl through the air. I spent the time getting to know a few of the others around me. We were all nervous and knew that the ordeal we'd been training for would soon be upon us. After about 15 hours and a refuelling stopover in South Australia, the captain announced we were landing in Pearce Airbase, which is around two hours out of Perth.

Once on the ground, we unloaded ourselves and milled around. A cohort of tough-looking characters dressed in foreign camouflage uniforms were waiting on the tarmac. They told us to grab our gear and move over to another bunch of 'no-nonsense' soldiers, who turned out to be the cadre staff – the SASR personnel who would be running the selection on the ground. They were all unfriendly and demanding.

Within minutes another C-130 arrived and soon there were 160 of us all standing in ranks and waiting for orders. The cadres broke us up into several groups and told us to fill the two water canteens we carried on our webbing belts. Then they handed each of us an old self-loading-rifle (SLR) together with a few magazines.

SELECTION BEGINS

I couldn't help but wonder what would happen next. I didn't have to wait long. A soldier yelled, 'You are now going to undergo a 3.2 kilometre run around the airstrip.' It was just as I'd been practising back in Brisbane. As I lined up on the road ready for the start, I noticed that my kit definitely felt a lot lighter than it had been – the rifle was only half the weight of the heavy copper pipe I usually carried.

Someone then yelled, 'Go!' and we were off. Runners were almost tripping over each other trying to get a clear space. I knew I only had 16 minutes to complete the run, and after just a few minutes the pack really began to spread out along the airstrip boundary. I glanced at my watch and could see I was making reasonable time based on how far I estimated I'd already gone. After about 14 minutes I could look far enough ahead to see what I thought was the finish line – about 600 metres to go. As I got closer, people were already walking and some were bent over on the side of the road vomiting up their soggy aircraft lunch sandwiches. I figured I was still in the money, so I pushed as hard as I could until I crossed the line where the people stood; but then someone yelled, 'Keep going, you haven't finished yet!'

I looked across at my colleagues gasping as we continued to flog ourselves as hard as we could to get to the next finish line, which I could now see some 500 metres further up the road. I knew that someone was playing a nasty trick on us as we had already completed the 3.2 kilometres. Runners around me started to give up as we closed on the line. More were bent over vomiting and some threw up their lunch as they ran full tilt up the road. Finally I was within 50 metres of the finish and I made a last-ditch effort to increase my pace just a bit more. As I crossed the line, a soldier yelled my time and wrote down the number on the armband we had all been issued. I stood there, stooped and hyperventilating, and began to slow and control my breathing.

Soldiers who were staggering in after me were told to walk over to a different area and wait. Eventually we were all assembled again. Most had run, some had walked and others had arrived in an ambulance that was slowly trolling along behind us. I could see that those who had made it within the allotted time were in my group and the others who were unsuccessful – about half the total – had been separated from us. One of the cadres then fronted them and told them flatly they would be getting back on the plane and heading back to where they came from.

This was my introduction to the selection course. It was brutal but I had expected they would test all of us to the limit. Well, I was right about that. And there was much worse to come.

6
'CORPORAL PUNISHMENT'

After that exhausting test I'm sure a lot of the blokes reckoned that was it for the day. I wasn't so sure, and I was right. They marched us at a blistering pace about four kilometres to the base's Olympic swimming pool. I could see what was coming and I felt pretty confident about it because I've always liked swimming since our days in the creeks of the National Park and surfing at Cronulla. But now it was the middle of winter and we had to practically crack the ice on top before jumping in fully clothed in belt order and rifle to do a 200-metre surface swim.

The cold water took my breath away but I organised myself with my rifle across my back at the shallow end of the pool. They told us we had to swim eight laps of the 25-metre pool and gave us ten minutes to complete it. I was comfortable with this and when the starter called 'Go!'

I swam breaststroke up the pool and back. I found it fairly easy going but others tried to swim freestyle or some weird combination of styles they'd devised at the last moment.

Some guys were struggling and sinking, gulping water and disappearing under the surface trying to get to the end. I called to someone I had spoken with earlier, 'Swim breaststroke, mate, it's easier.' An instructor in the regiment's famous sandy beret said, 'Shut your mouth.' The cadre staff obviously had an agenda and they didn't need anybody helping those who were not up to speed. I continued to the finish and was then told to get out.

The next test was to swim under water. I actually enjoy this and had practised many times at the Olympic-sized Enoggera pool until I could do two laps without taking a breath. My body had adjusted to the water temperature by now and I completed the first lap under water then turned around and started to head back for another. I would have made it but for my camouflage uniform and boots, which were slowing us all down. However, I was sure I'd made a pretty good go of it.

There were plenty pulled aside and told to get their gear as they would not be continuing on the selection process. Luckily I was not among them, but by now the pace was frantic and, still soaking wet and cold, we were loaded into the back of UNIMOG trucks, which were tarped up tight so we couldn't see where we were going. As we headed down the road, we were all sitting quietly in the dark wondering what was coming next.

Night had fallen when we arrived at the front gate of the Bindoon army firing range. I had never been there but I expected there would be another quick march so I quickly got out of the back of the truck and set about getting my pack, webbing and echelon bag ready for a long walk. Others busily did the same. There were probably about 80 of us left and I could see that some blokes had brought far too much gear and were struggling to get it all up on their backs.

A staffer yelled, 'Start walking!' and we did. He set the pace at the front, and with all our kit it was literally blistering. Once again some started to lag behind. Whole bags of gear were abandoned unceremoniously on the roadside by their desperate owners. We marched at this pace for what seemed like kilometres, and eventually, almost exhausted, we came to a gravel area with a shed off in the distance.

It was now pitch black and we were told to go to sleep. So I set up a hoochie – a sheet of plastic to keep the rain off – and laid out my sleeping bag on the cold pea gravel. In about ten seconds I fell sound asleep. After what seemed like only an hour, I was jerked awake by loud music coming from the big shed around a hundred metres to our east. It was really blaring and obviously designed to shatter our slumber. This, I found, was the SASR trademark wake-up call – no bugle reveille for these guys. They were playing old songs from the sixties so loud that the sound was horribly distorted, but I think I recognised some theme songs from a popular Vietnam War TV show.

As I quickly jammed my sleeping bag back into my army pack, I could hear the crunch of boots in the gravel. It was the directing staff officers (DS) approaching. They yelled, 'Get up and be ready to move now!' They then marched us to the big shed, lined us up and ordered us to empty our packs and kit bags onto the freezing concrete floor. Thankfully by now they'd turned the music off. A major who was the senior instructor stood on a podium and gave a brief welcome speech. He said things like, 'Most of you won't make it, but give it your best.' It left me feeling like I was being welcomed to a concentration camp.

They then told us to strip naked. This was to ensure that no one was concealing anything and we were all on a level playing field. I guess it was also symbolic in a way that we were to be reborn, and this was my SAS birthday. Some birthday! All the great kit that I had brought over from the past two years of training, like my special 'bivy bag' that kept the water off my sleeping bag, was now chucked into a plastic garbage bag with my name on it. We were left with the most basic items of standard issue.

I could see that some blokes were really affected by this as they had banked on some of their gear getting them through. One guy had his feet all covered in Elastoplasts as protection against blisters. They ordered him to remove them and all his spare Elastoplasts were taken away. Once this process was complete, they told us to get our clothes and boots back on and move over to a chin-up beam inside the shed. This was to be another physical test – one that I had also been practising for. The requirement was to pump out 20 chin-ups. This I did and then followed it, as ordered, with 100 sit-ups.

Next was a five-kilometre run out on the bush tracks around the camp. I enjoyed running and kept up with the front runners until we finished in about 17 minutes. Once again the group was slowly being diminished by fatigue and lack of fitness.

We had barely recovered when they tossed us into a navigation exercise that was to last two days. This would test our navigation skills and our ability to operate effectively on our own both day and night. The rules were simple: don't walk on tracks; don't talk to other participants; and complete as many checkpoints as possible in the allotted time.

At the start I made an error that could have been costly. I calculated the navigation leg correctly on the map but then transferred the wrong bearing onto my magnetic compass. When I headed out, I saw I was going the opposite direction from everyone else. Something wrong here, I thought, and quickly realised the error, selected the correct bearing on the compass and set off in the right direction.

By now I was starving, so as soon as I got out of sight of the camp I sat down and had a big feed of army rations and hot tea. One other guy walked past and asked what

I was doing. He looked surprised when he saw I was just making morning tea. I soon continued on my nav leg feeling much rejuvenated by the meal. I really started to enjoy the navigation and loved going it alone in the bush. All those beaut times in the National Park with my brothers came back to me and I felt good as I went from one checkpoint to another.

Towards the end of the second day I had five completed and had covered over 20 kilometres through the scrub. I wanted to get at least one more under my belt by last light, so I pushed on to a checkpoint that the map indicated was in a creek bed. When I arrived at the dry watercourse, I didn't know whether the checkpoint would be to my left or right, so I ran left for about 500 metres. Of course it turned out to be in the other direction, so I backtracked until I eventually arrived panting at the checkpoint. A DS was located there and he quickly asked me how many others I'd completed, to which I answered five. He suddenly looked bitterly disappointed and said, 'If you don't get another two in by last light, you'll fail; you'll be on your way out of here.'

I looked at the sun, already low on the horizon, and knew the next checkpoint was five kilometres to the west. I had Buckley's of doing one let alone two. The DS, a short rugged fellow I later found out was named Kerry, said, 'You'll have to sprint the whole way if you want to make it, so get going.'

I checked my bearings on the map, then ran as fast as my legs would go. Barrelling headlong through the scrub in the low light was dangerous, and a couple of times I tripped and fell. After what seemed like ages, I knew I must be getting close and I pushed myself to the limit. Just as the last shaft of light was fading, I ran up a small hill and into the next checkpoint. There another DS asked me how many I'd completed. When I said, 'Six,' he seemed impressed and told me to go and sit down with some other guys resting nearby.

They all wanted to know how I went to compare their own performances. Most had completed three or four checkpoints and very few had five or six. I had actually done quite well and the DS who told me I needed to sprint to make it was just pulling my leg. This was to be a common theme throughout selection; the misinformation was designed to keep you constantly guessing and maybe even doubting your own ability. Such doubts could and often did cause some of the boys to give up. This was what the course was all about – to separate the self-doubters who would give up too quickly from the few who could push on regardless.

After the navigation exercise we were again bundled into trucks like cattle and sent off on another two-hour road trip. The conditions in the back of the trucks was terribly cramped and dark, so we continually jostled for leg room and tried to get a bit of rest, but it was really impossible. Eventually the trucks pulled into Northam Army Camp and we were again unloaded onto a dusty roadway. This camp was a former Second World War training and detention camp, so all the old wooden buildings were very basic: timber shutters for windows and a row of ancient steel-framed beds along each wall. In the winter night the buildings did nothing to keep out the cold and we nearly froze.

The best part of the camp was the mess and we were able to pile heaps of food onto our plates. Unfortunately we were only given the briefest time to eat and then had to race outside to begin the ordeal all over again. There we were introduced to a new group of DS personnel, one in particular who was known as 'Corporal Punishment'. This guy had a bad limp and I later found out his nickname was Stumpy and he had suffered serious injuries in an aircraft accident some years earlier. He was responsible for dealing out all sorts of punishments to our group when we made the slightest error or arrived late when called for a parade.

One of his favourites was to make the blokes stand for ages in the bitter cold night holding their rifles out at arm's length. Another was the eight-stage push-up, which was a combination of a push-up and a burpee, where you jump up during the push-up. One awful one was to run the blokes around the airstrip and run last man to the front continuously as the rest of his team sprinted along; and the worst was to continuously jump over and under the famous 1.5-metre-high and one-metre-diameter Golden Pipeline to

Kalgoorlie, which passed near the Northam Camp. It was not only taxing but your body was black and blue afterwards.

If he wanted to punish a group, there was always a handy pile of massive old truck tyres on the ground nearby. We'd be broken into teams of five and made to lift the tyres above our heads then hold them then raise, lower, raise, lower . . . great fun at 3 a.m.

The next few days consisted of continual periods of extreme physical exertion, new training methods, and late nights filling out questionnaires and stomping around the hills learning some essential navigation skills from our DS overseer Kerry. (Kerry was years later detained with his wife, Kay, in a prison in Laos for trumped-up charges of jewel theft, but that's another story.)

One of the most memorable and most testing sessions was called 'the airstrip run'. We were roused out of bed before sunrise and made to run hard together in a group up the hill from the camp to an old, disused, gravel airstrip. There we discovered two PTIs – 'The Two Robs' – who were both very fit. Over the next two hours they took turns at running our group around the gravel strip at full speed. When the instructor would begin to tire, the other would step in and take over again until he was tired and then they would change over again. The pace was insane and the group quickly spread out over a kilometre as the weaker runners lagged behind. Blokes were again throwing up and some even quit and were quickly picked up by a waiting Land

Rover, never to be seen again. At the end we were all given a dressing down for being such unfit candidates and then sent on another run back to the camp for more training.

During these strenuous sessions we were encouraged to sing old songs that we were told were the regiment's personal anthems, awful tuneless things like 'Happy Wanderer' and 'Lili Marlene'. This was just another tool in their arsenal to add to our misery. Often after an extremely long day we would stand on parade on the roadway near the mess hall with Corporal Punishment dealing out push-ups and burpees, or holding a half-push-up position with your nose just an inch from the ground. The trivial nature of our indiscretions was not the point. All the time the DS were searching for signs of weakness or a candidate who could be pushed to breaking point.

After about five days at Bindoon we were again loaded into the trucks and taken to the next phase of our selection course, which was codenamed Happy Wanderer. Normally this was conducted in the Stirling Ranges in the south of the state, but for this year's session we were heading to the sand dunes and coastal scrub of the navy bombing range at Lancelin, two and a half hours north of Perth.

On arrival we were issued with five ration packs and allocated our first checkpoints, to which we would have to navigate on our own. I liked this type of thing, so I was in my element. The area was essentially featureless, undulating scrub-covered terrain, and nearer the coast there were high sand dunes. Navigating was tricky, as there were very few features with which to orientate myself.

My first few checkpoints were close together, only five to ten kilometres apart, and I became overconfident. We had been told not to walk on any tracks, as there was a mock enemy force that would be on the lookout for us. I was walking parallel to a track and probably a bit close to it. I looked in the distance and saw a Land Rover approaching at high speed. I quickly took off my pack and lay down in the low prickly scrub. The DS in the vehicle must have seen me and assumed I was on a track. They stopped ten metres from me and looked out towards where they thought I should be. I could hear them saying things like, 'I know he's here somewhere.' I forced myself to relax and hug the ground. After a few minutes they moved on to search for other candidates. I got up and continued my journey, keeping well clear of the tracks.

The thick prickly scrub was almost impenetrable at times and I would have to lie on top of it and roll to get past the thickest sections. This was really soul-destroying when you knew you had many kilometres to the next checkpoint, but you were stuck doing only a kilometre an hour in this stuff. After a couple of days of this my trouser legs were almost worn through by the thorny scrub, and my knees and calves were full of centimetre-long thorns, which I was still pulling out weeks after the course was finished.

After two days of short navigation legs I got a shock when the next nav leg was 24 kilometres to the checkpoint. However, my experience of short trips taught me where most of the thickest scrub was, and I plotted my journey around it where I knew it would be clearer. This was a gamble, as it would mean adding kilometres to each leg, but it was worth a try. I started out and headed a good way south and eventually turned west towards the coast and my next checkpoint. At one point, after I had been travelling for the best part of a day, I heard a commotion away off to the north. I looked across and saw another candidate stuck in the thick scrub I'd come through earlier. He was really struggling and was using the butt of his rifle as a handle to try to club his way through the scrub. I could hear him swearing and yelling as he did this, and I wondered later whether he had actually made it through.

When I did arrive at a checkpoint, the DS there was standing next to a warm fire and would only offer me my next coordinate checkpoint and ask where I had just come from. It was almost dark, and instead of letting me put out my sleeping bag near their position, they insisted I must get at least two kilometres away before I could set up my night camp.

Travelling at night was not permitted, as a candidate had previously fallen off a cliff in the darkness. At night I always maintained a routine: put up a hoochie; cook a tin of army rations; and maybe have some dry biscuit and a cup of hot tea. Having a hot meal at the end of a long day when I'd probably walked 20 to 30 kilometres really lifted my spirits and gave me energy for the next day's walk.

After five days of this I estimated I had walked between 130 and 150 kilometres. When I arrived at the final checkpoint, I could see many blokes sitting around resting under their hoochies. After a brief rest a truck pulled up and we were called into the centre. A large plastic pallet with cooked chops and steak was dumped on the ground in front of us and the DS said to go for it. We were like a bunch of rabid dogs and everyone darted in to try to grab a morsel. I managed to grab a steak and like a dog scurried away to eat it without threat of it being grabbed by someone else. It was the best piece of meat I had ever tasted but there was not enough to fill my stomach.

Once again it was back onto the truck, and this time we all knew what was coming. It was the most difficult and strenuous part of the cadre course, known as the Lucky Dip. I don't know who came up with the name but there was nothing lucky about it. It turned out to be the most difficult physical torture I had ever faced in my life to that point.

It was conducted in the forests around Collie, a country town about three hours south of Perth. On arrival we were given one ration pack each, which we were told only to eat in an emergency. My team consisted of eight men including two officers. We would be thrown together over the coming week to complete impossible tasks in impossible times. This was where the final cut would be made, and those who didn't measure up would be pulled out or allowed to finish but then given the terrible news at the end that they had not passed, even if they had completed the course.

7

A MASSIVE CHALLENGE

On the first task our group of eight blokes was greeted by a DS who put on a strange and totally unconvincing accent. I thought, What is this bullshit? He was dressed in foreign camouflage gear and carried an AK-47 rifle. He told us we had to travel many kilometres on foot and cart the load of jerry cans of water sitting nearby to his soldiers, who needed them badly.

Together we figured out a system. To share the load, each of us would put one in our packs with our other gear. In addition we'd each carry one by hand and two teams of two would continually rotate carrying some jerrys hanging on a heavy, steel, three-metre pole as well as the ones inside their packs on their backs. All up, each of us would have to carry about 60 kilograms of water plus his own gear and rifle.

Initially this proved manageable. It was a very cold morning and the exercise warmed us up. But after a while the terrain got steep and the scrub became almost impenetrable. The crazy DS would direct our lumbering group down the roughest creek lines and through the thickest undergrowth. Blokes started to struggle and curse and, slowly but surely, one then another surrendered to temptation and just gave up. The DS would see their flagging willpower and approach them. He would offer them the comfort of a hot brew and a meal and a bus ride home. The temptation for those who'd had enough was too much to resist and they took the bait. Now our team was down to six, but these lads remained determined to stick with it.

One nasty trick that the DS used was to mark one of the jerry cans with a piece of string. This can was half full of water, so was only half the weight. They watched this jerry can like a hawk to see which soldier would realise it was a lighter burden and try to carry it more than his fair share of the time.

After the best part of a day, we had humped our load about nine kilometres. We came to another small group of DS at the bank of what seemed like a wide river. On the other side, about 400 metres away through the cold, evening, winter mist, I could just make out a big fire with some figures standing around it. The river was in fact a reservoir formed by the Wellington Dam. Dead tree trunks poked up through the murky frigid water. Our task was to swim to the other side with our load of jerry cans.

We decided that to get all our heavy packs and personal gear over without submerging it, we had to tie the lot in bundles inside our hoochies. That done, we stripped down to our undies, removed our boots and tied our rifles to our backs. We then bundled our gear up, secured it, and as a group we entered the water. This was a real shock. It was raining by now, and getting into that icy water was like submerging yourself in a bath full of ice cubes. It took my breath away and I had to fight to regain it as I began to swim breaststroke out into the dark water.

Once underway, my arms, legs and skin began to get numbed by the cold, which then turned to a burning sensation. The group stayed close together, with one crew of three a few metres out in front and the remainder clustered together. After what seemed like an hour, we all managed to get over, but we were in rough shape climbing the gravelly bank on the far side.

We undid the packs and laid out the jerry cans. Task completed. But then we realised we were starting to get hypothermia, so we madly unpacked all our gear from our bundles and hastily donned our smelly damp clothes again. This was not much better than being naked, but by running about we started to warm up a little.

I looked over my shoulder to where the DS group had deliberately stoked the big camp fire, and it was one of the most enticing things I could think of just to walk over and warm myself with a cup of hot tea in my hands. This was when a senior DS came over with his steaming mug of tea or coffee and said to me, 'What are you doing here?'

'I'm doing the selection, sir.'

'No, you're wasting your time; you won't be accepted even if you get through because you're too short. How fuckin' tall are you anyway?'

'I'm five foot six,' I said.

'Go over and get in the back of that truck right fuckin' now, you short-arse prick.'

I stood my ground. I guessed he was only bullshitting me to get me to pull the pin. I said, 'No way, sir. I'm gonna keep on going.'

He then walked away, shaking his head in dismay, and left me to get on with it. I remembered his face from my interview back in Brisbane. He was a senior officer in the regiment, a respected Vietnam vet who had worked his way up through the NCO level to become the RSM and then made the move to the officer ranks. And he nearly had me bluffed right there and then. But my small team and I resisted all their temptations and headed off into the rain-soaked scrub onto our next task.

After just a kilometre or two we saw a clearing in the distance, and when we reached it there was a huge pile of heavy wooden crates that I suspected needed to be shifted somewhere for no apparent purpose. And sure enough, out popped a soldier dressed in foreign camouflage gear with a phoney accent to describe the task. He gave us a time limit and a rough idea of the distance to be covered.

We began to design a system of poles to carry the crates; we could tell they were appallingly heavy. They were filled with gravel from the nearby tracks. Some were not overflowing, so the DS told us to use our steel cups to scrape up more gravel and jam it inside the already bursting boxes. This took what seemed like hours, as every time we thought they were full to the brim, the DS would come over and say, 'That's not good enough,' in his phoney accent and make us start over again. The idea of carrying huge boxes of useless gravel just added to the wonder of it all. I could see that it was really playing with some guys' heads because it was just so pointless. But I could appreciate the cruel humour and purpose in it. It was just another mental challenge that we had to confront and overcome.

By now we'd figured out a system. We had a team of three under the heavy boxes and a pair of blokes carrying a large single box, with one guy out front leading the way through the scrub. We would continually rotate the front man every five minutes so that everyone had a go. Being in front was much easier after moving through every position in the carriage team.

After several hours of this we realised there was no way we were going to make the distance in the required time, and that's when the DS really stepped up the pressure. He decided to target me again. He came up next to my ear while

I struggled under the terrible load and whispered, 'You're a weak link, Bonner. You're letting everyone on this team down. Pull the pin now because I'm gonna fail you as soon as you get to the next checkpoint anyway.'

I resisted. I said, 'No, sir,' and braced myself against the boxes even harder to show him I was pulling my weight. He kept on at me for another 20 minutes or so with similar taunts, trying to undermine my resolve. When I didn't crack, he gave up and moved on to the next bloke to try to wear him down. This was their routine now. They could see that most of us by now had great determination, and only overwhelming pressure or a serious injury might induce them to give up so close to the end of the course. We were completely dedicated to achieving our goal, which was just to get through to the next challenge.

Late one evening our small group was given yet another checkpoint to navigate to. But once there, we were told, we'd get a much needed feed. On arrival there was nothing there, so we sat and waited in the cold drizzling rain. We had now been without food for several days and I would literally eat anything if it came along on four legs. I sat back-to-back with my colleague Pete, both of us looking out to warn the other of anyone coming. The rain poured down continuously and it was very cold. I thought there was Buckley's of anyone bringing us food so I pulled out my hoochie and we shared it draped across our backs to get a little respite from the weather.

I said, 'Pete, do you have anything to eat? I'm starving.'

'Nothing,' he said.

Then I remembered I had a few sachets of coffee and sugar from an army ration pack ... but wait a minute, I'd already sucked those dry days ago. All I found was a small sachet of curry powder about the size of a sugar sachet. I pulled it out of my soaking web belt around my waist, tore the top open and emptied a small amount into my mouth. The powder was still dry and it felt good to have something with flavour in my mouth. I savoured the gritty powder for a minute or two before I swallowed it down. Poor Pete was almost drooling as he watched me eat. I passed the packet to him and he had the second half. He seemed to appreciate the dust as much as I did. I'll always remember that cold night; there was something about sharing what little I had with a friend who had suffered the same hardships as I had. It was typical of the kind of bond you made with workmates in the SASR selection. We might not meet again for another 25 years, but we would recognise each other immediately as brothers who had shared tortures and simple joys together. I still ask Pete whether he has any curry powder every time I see him.

The following evening, with the weather still miserable, they told us we'd get a really good feed the next day if we reached the designated checkpoint. In the morning at the start point we saw four three-metre-long and 75 mm diametre poles lying in the dirt. Beside them was a mannequin made out of old army uniforms with sand-filled hessian bags inside. It was sewn together in the shape of a man almost two metres long. The task was to construct a stretcher from the steel poles and then carry the sand man, who was supposedly an injured soldier, to a safe place to meet an ambulance. The cruel twist was that the steel poles were filled with cement. Each pole weighed about 30 kilograms. Multiply that by four and then add in the sand man, who had been out in the rain for a few hours and gained another 25 kilograms. Four men picking him up and heading off into the dripping scrub was another exercise in torture and determination. But we pushed on, with the thought of a meal to help us on our way.

At the end we finally found our checkpoint – another nondescript place in the scrub – where we waited for our food drop. The hours passed very slowly until, around 2 a.m., we heard the unmistakable rumble of the army UNIMOG truck approaching along the nearby track. We sent two of our team to the track's edge to shine a dull green torch as a signal to stop the truck.

Within a minute or so they had unloaded a big hot box food container from the rear of the truck and carefully carried it to our camp about a hundred metres from the track. I expected a rich stew to replenish some of the weight we'd lost, but when we opened it all we could see was a steaming brown liquid that appeared to have black feathers floating in it.

Reaching in, we soon discovered it was made from some kind of bird life that had been boiled – feathers, guts, beak and claws, every last part of it. But what the hell, we were *hungry*. Each bloke stuck his steel cup into the liquid and we drank it down. It was hot, chunky and very salty, but it tasted great no matter what it was. But then, as I drank, I found I was getting feathers stuck between my teeth as well as grains of seed that had floated in the hot water. I reckoned that was the stomach contents of the bird.

The feathers were very dark, so I thought it might have been a crow or, at best, a scrawny black chicken. It didn't matter though; we were all going to eat every last bit of it. Once all the liquid was gone, one bloke took the bird out by its wing and we plucked out the remaining feathers, pulled it into pieces and placed the meat on a hoochie we had spread on the ground. There were six of us to share the meal, so we methodically broke the bird up into equal portions. We then ate the thing and even crunched the bones up between our teeth. Nothing was left and, although we had each eaten only a small portion, we were full, as our stomachs had shrunk so much over the previous week. We kept it down too.

As soon as we had finished our food, the DS once again told us to move off through the scrub to complete the next task. It was still dark and bitter cold and, as we'd been stationary for some hours, our bodies had started to lock up through fatigue and exhaustion. It was a massive challenge to pull on our heavy packs once more and start moving again in the rain. Soon we came across a tent in the Jarrah Forest where a DS with an even more ludicrous accent ordered us to help him erect an old army VHF antenna mast.

I had seen these before when I was in Transport Corps and had put them up many times, so I started giving each guy a specific task. The other blokes in my team didn't seem too familiar with the kit, so I thought I should try to get the ball rolling. Within half an hour we had the ten-metre mast erected with the small antenna right at the top. There were six guide wires: three near the top section of the mast and another three about halfway up. These had to be pulled simultaneously to guide the mast from a prone position on the ground to a vertical position high up among the branches of nearby trees.

Once we got the mast upright, we called over the DS, who promptly told us that it was not straight enough and that we must pull it down and do it all again. After the meagre meal a few hours before, we were now all in an exhausted stupor, and even the most simple task seemed to take forever. Just thinking straight was a real challenge, but we all tried to help each other to get through as best we could. We pulled the mast down and then commenced putting it up again.

When we got it up the second time, the sun was starting to come up, and we could see that the middle section of the mast was slightly bent. This meant that the mast could never be straight, even if we put it up a hundred times. We promptly advised the DS and tried to explain that it would never be straight owing to the damage. The DS denied this and kept saying things like, 'You are letting my impoverished people starve and die because you cannot get the radio antenna to work.'

He knew full well that the mast was bent and that it would never be completely vertical. We must have put that antenna up another six or seven times before he finally got sick of the torment and sent us on to more miserable tasks. Our last job was to paddle an old engineer's barge up and down the Collie River system. This would have been a joy normally, but some cruel and twisted SASR operative had managed to find a way to turn a pleasant boat paddle into another exhausting and pointless torture.

Once we got the barge into the water and threw all our gear into the thing, the DS pointed to a 44-gallon drum about 50 metres away and a length of rope. He said, 'You must take the drum of water up the river for the thirsty soldiers.' Quickly we despatched three fellows to roll the drum over to the barge. It turned out it was empty, so it was easy to roll and even carry. The DS then said it must be filled with water, so we set about submerging the opening below the level of the river and slowly filled the drum to almost full. It was now very heavy, but we thought we could get it onto the aluminium boat and still manage it quite well. Of course this would have been the logical thing to do, but we were again thwarted by the strange softly spoken DS hovering nearby. He ordered us to tie one end of the rope to the drum and the other end to the rear of the barge. We then all began to paddle with small canoe oars out into the middle of the dam.

The drum was so full that it acted as a huge 200-kilogram boat anchor, and we made almost no progress as it lumbered along the floor of the dam at the end of the tether. The DS seated at the front of the boat sent us back to shore and explained in his limited English (with phoney accent) that we should empty 20 litres from the drum, which would lighten the load. This we did, and we were soon ready to go again. Now the drum was submerged but buoyantly hovering just below the surface and occasionally bobbing up, letting us know it wasn't sunk.

We began to paddle and tow the thing. The DS made us go from one end of the dam to the other, and then when we had exhausted all the tributaries we travelled along some of the small creeks leading off from the dam. This lasted all day, and as we paddled along at a blistering half a kilometre an hour or so, we were encouraged by the DS to sing songs that he appeared to be making up as we went along. They were more tuneless lunatic chants about his beleaguered people, and if we got them wrong, he would become belligerent and scream at us to paddle faster. Of course I knew it would all have to end eventually, as we all did, and we resigned ourselves to this miserable fate.

The end of the Lucky Dip phase came as something of an anticlimax. One minute our handful of remaining team members was completing a challenge and the next moment we were told to sit down in the rain and wait for a truck. They then gave us some tea bags and coffee, and we were able to make some hot drinks.

While it was a relief to have passed that phase, we all knew what was coming, and to me at least it would prove the most mentally challenging part of the selection course. It was called resistance to interrogation (RTI), and it was to last for another three days. It would be the final hurdle. And while I wasn't looking forward to it, I had no idea how tough it would turn out to be. In fact I sometimes think it might have been the first step into that dark place in the mind where PTSD planted its seed.

Sitting in the scrub in the dark with the remaining group of the selection course, I could see that there were only about half a dozen left in each of the combined teams. At least 80 per cent of the original candidates had fallen by the wayside. That's when one of the DS gave us a questionnaire to fill in. I looked it over. It asked each of us to rate the other team members on a scale of 1 to 10, 1 being 'useless' and 10 being 'a great team member'. It also asked for comments and observations on anything that I had seen that would be a positive or negative reflection on my colleagues' abilities and attitudes.

I felt quite attached to the few remaining members in my team, so I didn't fill it in. I didn't feel that it was appropriate for me to make negative comments about any of the blokes in my team. I tore it up into tiny pieces and disposed of it later. I didn't want to be caught with it in my possession when I was interrogated, as it might be used as some kind of ammunition against me. I did see that most of the others around me filled in their questionnaires, but that was their prerogative. Shortly afterwards the questionnaires were collected and no one queried where mine was.

We were all then loaded into a truck and again headed off into the dark on a long ride through the night. After a few hours I sensed signs that we were about to arrive at our destination. They had taken us to an old disused prison in the Perth Hills. The truck suddenly lurched to a stop and the back tarpaulins were thrown open and searchlights blazed into our bleary eyes. I could hear yelling and screaming and the barking of dogs. An arm reached into the back of the truck and gripped my shoulder, and I heard someone yell, 'Get out onto the ground!'

I stumbled out and lay down on the cold ground and immediately saw the snarling teeth of a dog only inches from my face. It was barking wildly and if not restrained by his handler would have taken my face in his slobbering teeth. Strangely enough I didn't feel so much threatened as amused that this part of the training was predictable and meeting my expectations . . . so far.

I would soon learn better.

Me after leaving the SAS.

My granddad – William George Robert Keefe.

Mountain warfare training in Kenya, 2001.

With a crowd of locals in East Timor.

Bogged in a creek.

One of our short-term medical clinics in the mountains of East Timor.

Struggling through a marshy area, East Timor.

At Al Asad Airbase, Iraq – Anzac Day 2003.

Above: Midway through our tour of duty in Iraq, April 2003.

Left: Our unofficial squadron badge – Redback One was our call sign between 2001 and 2003.

A local crossing the Helmand River in Afghanistan
– it is deceptively deep and strong in places.

My patrol in Iraq, 2003 – I'm on the far left.

The bridge over the Helmand River – the modern way of crossing.

One of the many local trucks that regularly travel between Iran, Pakistan and Afghanistan.

Patrolling through a desolate Afghan village.

An observation post on the border of Iran, Pakistan and Afghanistan.
The range of mountains is in Pakistan.

A US helicopter about to land supplies.

An old, old fort in the Helmand Valley.

8
'MOST OUTSTANDING SOLDIER'

Within a few seconds a white sack was pulled down over my head, I was stripped naked and someone secured my hands in front with plastic ties. Then, with one person on each side, they marched me into a building. Although I couldn't see through the bag, the sounds of footsteps and voices around me led me to believe that I was in some kind of shower cubicle or perhaps a small cell. There they roughly sat me down on a cold concrete floor and placed me in such a position that it was impossible to relax. I had to continually lean forwards to keep from toppling back onto the ground. Each time my body began to slump from the uncomfortable sitting position, a hand would slap me on the back of the head and a gruff voice would command me to sit up straight.

After about eight hours it was impossible to discern wakefulness from slumber, or to control either. At the end of this initial period, designed to isolate and induce severe sleep deprivation, a harsh voice ordered me to get up, and with someone on either side holding my arms I was taken to another room. They sat me down roughly on a cold concrete floor again, and what sounded like a tin plate was dropped onto the concrete in front of me. A voice behind me shouted, 'Eat.'

I was ravenous and grabbed with both hands at where I thought the plate was. I felt pasty-textured food and jammed it up under the sack to stuff some into my mouth. Most of it fell down around my face but I managed to get a mouthful before I heard the plate being quickly snatched away. The food seemed like cold tuna and rice mixed together and it tasted fantastic. They told me later that it was ground-up fish heads and boiled rice. That might explain the scales I felt sticking between my teeth for the next few days. Shortly afterwards I was led into a room where I could hear and sense lots of others like me also standing about or seated. This room was to be our place of confinement for however long they wanted to keep us there.

Each of us was given a timber platform about seven centimetres high, 35 centimetres wide and a metre long. We were commanded to remain on the platform at all times. Sometimes we would have to stand up and remain motionless, sometimes commanded to run on the spot. The rest of the time we sat on them with no part of our bodies touching the floor. The boards were too small to be even remotely comfortable. We were told to keep them clean, so I would brush off any sand or dirt whenever I thought it necessary.

I'm sure the interrogators walked around throwing sand onto our boards to have something to chastise us about. They were a constant presence, men and women, shouting at us, abusing us, or just moving around and coming close and threatening. There were times when I could feel myself getting angry and fed up with this treatment; but then I reminded myself it was just another test and forced myself to calm down.

The desire for sleep was soon overwhelming, and I could have collapsed anywhere and been asleep in seconds if the opportunity arose; but it never did. If I started to doze or slump forwards, another slap on the head would jerk me awake. The interrogators stood us up every few minutes and we had to repeat long-winded mystical chants, most of which made no sense to me, and I immediately forgot them. But they were insistent; we had to repeat them over and over until we had them down pat. The interrogators would also single individuals out and make them chant the phrases while the rest of us listened in a constant dazed stupor. One of my colleagues, Russell, who I came to know well, was formerly in the Intelligence Corps, and the interrogators seemed to know this and often singled him out to recite the endless verses. I was thankful that they chose him, as I would have forgotten most of them anyway.

After several hours thin cotton pyjamas were dumped in our laps. We had remained naked since being removed from the trucks and it was very cold. After a non-stop 24 hours of this treatment they took me out of the room to a separate building to be interrogated individually. I knew that I was only to provide my name, rank, serial number and date of birth. These, after all, were simulated enemy interrogators. Any additional information could be used against our own men.

When I entered the new location, the sounds suggested that I was in another bare room. They sat me down on a chair and lifted the hood. I was in front of a small table and on the other side was a bloke I recognised immediately as an instructor of a driver training course I had completed some years previously in Brisbane. My first instinct was to say, 'G'day, mate. How are you going?' But I could see he was playing his role seriously, so I went along. In fact it was a clever trick by the DS because each interrogation was to be different, and this was the 'friendly' approach.

He asked me some basic questions and appeared to write all the answers down. Then he interrupted the questioning and passed over a sheet of paper asking me to sign for the blue striped pyjamas I was wearing. I said, 'I won't sign for anything.' I shouldn't have answered his request at all and just quoted my name, rank and serial number, but in my semi-conscious state my thinking was blurry and I didn't really know where I was.

He then changed his manner and said if I didn't sign for my stuff I wouldn't be able to wear any clothing at all. He also added that I needed to sign for the clothes of all my colleagues; otherwise they would also have to go naked. And when I refused, he ordered me to undress. I had no choice and stripped off the PJs. They then marched me back to rejoin the main group on our wooden boards without a stitch on. As I sat there freezing, I began to hallucinate. Sleep deprivation was catching up with me and I was watching light shows with animals and dragons on the inside of my hood.

That was just the beginning. The interrogations continued one after the other, some friendly, others totally threatening. When I returned to my wooden board on one occasion, I could swear I heard the clapping of hands, but they weren't human hands; they were robots with rubber palms and fingers and thumbs and I was standing in the middle with them all around me. I was bewildered and stupid until suddenly, *smack!* One of the interrogators slapped me back into temporary reality – my colleagues had been ordered to run on the spot and clap in my absence.

On another occasion they told us we would be able to lie on our boards and sleep for two hours. Immediately I lay down and was fast asleep in seconds. Only 15 minutes later we were all wakened by the guards. When I woke, I had no idea where I was, so I immediately lifted off my hood and peered around in the dark room. The guards yelled at me to pull my hood back over my head.

The next interrogation was a repetitive series of questions asking for name, rank and serial number. This went on for an hour. The interrogator remained totally deadpan and monotone throughout the questioning. Towards the end he started to add in other questions, dropping them in casually, like, 'Oh, unit; what unit are you from?'

I gave no response. He tried again, then again. It was almost as though he was trying to put me into a hypnotic state and when my defences were down I'd drop the information automatically without realising what I was doing. Once I figured out what he was up to, I held the line and gave him nothing. Finally they dragged me out and returned me, still naked, to the main group.

The next interrogation was the nastiest, as the interrogator was openly hostile. He screamed his questions at me and threatened to injure or even kill me if I didn't cooperate. I was now so exhausted I was starting to believe that the situation was real and not a training and assessment scenario. He accused me of one certain thing to which I inappropriately responded by calling him a liar. He told me to lie naked and face down on the ground in a half-push-up position and continued to interrogate and scream at me. He then summoned two guards and they held me back in a chair and proceeded to pour cold water into my face while demanding responses to their questions. The water running into my mouth, nose, ears and eyes made it impossible to do anything except cough and splutter to try to get a breath. I fought for control. I was determined not to crack. And after a while they at last dragged me, still naked, back to the group area and sat me on my wooden board.

The last and worst was still to come. By now I wasn't sure how long I had been at the interrogation centre. I kept losing track of time and had to force myself to concentrate until reality re-emerged. I had to tell myself it was a test, that at some stage it would end and it was up to me to see it through. But then I was singled out with a handful of other blokes and marched outside into the cold winter daylight.

We were all still hooded, so couldn't see anything. They stood us up against a wall and without warning turned a fire hose on us. The water was powerful and freezing. It slammed me back against the wall; it thudded into my body and I had to turn aside to protect myself. God knows how long they kept it up for, but when they were done they commanded me to get on my hands and knees and crawl along the ground. And when they told me to stand up, two guards placed some kind of a lifting harness on me and tightly secured some buckles. I was then attached to a small crane or hoist and lifted off my feet.

I had no idea how high off the ground I was but while I was suspended in mid-air they fired questions at me and told me if I didn't respond I would be submerged into a tank of water. Immediately I felt the hoist drop and my entire body went under water into the iciest cold I had ever felt. After a second or two I was lifted up again and commanded to respond to the questioning; and when I refused they once again dropped me down into the icy tank.

This happened at least three times and after the last one I was unhooked from my harness and again taken back to the main group. I was now on my last legs and feeling really bad. My only consolation was I knew – because I had heard them say so – that the interrogation would only last three days, and I had been counting the periods of daylight I had discerned through my hood whenever I was taken outside into the sunlight. I knew that we must be in the last 12 hours, and so I slumped forwards on my wooden board pretending to be even sleepier than I really was... and that's saying something.

One of the guards even felt some empathy, and at one time I felt someone lift my hood and place a sweet into my mouth. This was very bizarre after being so badly mistreated for the best part of the last month.

The guards were a mixture of men and women and came from intelligence sections in the east. They used the SASR selection to hone and practise their interrogation skills and procedures. It must have been a great opportunity to do realistic interrogation techniques on Defence personnel, one that normally would arise only in times of war.

Of course they were not allowed to injure us, but they went about as far as they could without doing physical injury.

What mental trauma their actions may have caused, I cannot say, but I think there may be serious health ramifications from some of the techniques they used against us. Looking back now, I believe that experiences like these can leave a permanent mark and serve to shape the psyche of a person for the rest of his life.

On the final evening we were rescued from our prison by the SASR counterterrorist team, who used explosives to break into the facility and get us all out in the back of their old Ford Transit vans. We were then allowed to have our first real sleep in about three weeks. When we awoke, we were given hot dogs and soft drinks and advised by the squadron commander that we had now completed the selection course. We would be returned to Perth and advised if we were to be given a place in the SASR or not.

But first the interrogators who had dealt with us for the previous three days would take each of us aside for a debrief on our performance under interrogation. I sat across the table from a face I had seen 24 hours before. It was the nasty interrogator who had used water as a means to try to extract information from me. He told me that I had let slip some additional info like my old army unit (Transport) but had performed well overall. He also said that we were already too fatigued when we commenced interrogation, so it was very challenging for the interrogators to keep us awake or to get us to play along with the scenario, as most of us were incoherent much of the time.

One of the other blokes on selection, John, had actually told the interrogators a bullshit story that his mum had just died and was able to deceive them into allowing him some additional comforts. He had turned the game around and it gave me a lot of enjoyment to think that they could be manipulated the way they manipulated us.

Another great mate, Frosty, who would be killed four years later in the Townsville Black Hawk disaster, had played ill during the interrogation and been allowed a blanket and hot chocolate while the rest of us froze on our wooden boards. I think he was in fact suffering from low blood sugar and had actually been hypoglycaemic, but it worked to his advantage at that moment.

As we drove back to Campbell Barracks in Perth, we were alone with our thoughts, but my team of six blokes were all like brothers to me now. The following day we were advised who would stay in the SAS, and who would not be allowed to stay. This must have been awful for those who had got through everything successfully but for some reason or other would not be able to become a badged SASR operator – blokes like 'Donks', who I had seen as the strongest in our team, but maybe because of his seniority as a sergeant in the regular army the regiment felt he would be better off staying in his old unit back in Brisbane. Others were also disappointed, and of the 30 to 40 who had successfully finished the course with me in 1992, only about 25 would be chosen. From the original 160 people who got off the planes in Pearce Airbase some four weeks ago, that meant the success rate was around 16 per cent.

Those of us who were successful were told individually by a senior NCO of the regiment. We then made our way back to the barracks block, practically walking on air. We were all exuberant with the knowledge that we had made it. They told us we had the night off, so Dave, myself and a couple of others got together to decide what food we had been hungering for most. The consensus was pizza. We made plans to head into Perth and buy the biggest ones we could find.

The lads around me were gaunt, and some broken, but their eyes were full of excitement that we had made it this far. One of the blokes, Morrie, had a wife in Perth, who was coming to pick him up at the barracks gate. When she arrived, she didn't recognise him and drove straight past him. She soon realised when he called out, and she came back to meet her skinny husband. Morrie told us she began to cry when she saw him and asked what had happened to him as he was so emaciated.

We had a great night. We found the Pizza Hut in Murray Street near the cinema and we all ordered a large pizza; but when they arrived our ability didn't match our appetites. Because of our shrunken stomachs, no one got through even half their meals.

Later we had a small ceremony where the future governor general, Major General Michael Jeffery AC CVO MC, came and issued us each with a beret and wished us all well in our futures. I was lucky enough to be chosen as the Most Outstanding Soldier on the 1/92 SASR selection course – something that surprised me, but of which I am very proud.

9

'WE HAD FINALLY MADE IT'

For the next 12 months life was to be a series of training courses to prepare me to become a fully qualified operator in an SASR sabre squadron, the operational strike force of the regiment. I lived in the single men's quarters of Campbell Barracks in the Perth suburb of Swanbourne, with a frontage to the Indian Ocean. There were old oil heaters in each room but it was still cold in winter and had no air-con in summer. It was austere but reasonably comfortable after living on the ground for a month. We had our own mess, where the food was excellent and plentiful. The conditions were much better than I had been used to in the Big Army, and I was working with men I respected. It was all business, and the standards they set were at the top level.

During the initial few months in the regiment patrol members were sent away to complete a patrol signaller's course or alternatively a patrol medics course for around five weeks. I was lucky enough to be chosen for the signaller's course. In the early 1990s electronic secure data transfer technology was in its infancy. And because a clear signal was needed to transfer data, we very often had to revert to Morse code to get the messages to and from headquarters when we were in the field. So every sig (or 'chook' as we were known) had to become proficient in sending and receiving Morse.

Every day in the classroom we would listen for hours on end to random Morse code and write the letters or numbers on a piece of paper, which would then be reviewed by the instructor. After a couple of weeks you would almost dream in Morse code. On the weekends my mate Neil and I would practise it at the pub, asking each other to sound out the letters of the alphabet.

By the end of the course everyone had to be able to send and receive at least ten words per minute, and some were up to 20 if they had the ear for it. I was pretty good at sending and receiving, so when we had multiple patrols out in the field and we came together to plan an attack, the patrol commanders would get together and decide who of the three or four patrol sigs was going to be the primary source of communications. Sometimes I got chosen, which was flattering in one way but a real kick in the nuts as well, since instead of only having to send one patrol's worth of messages I would send and receive for all the patrols.

This was a difficult task. The poor sig would sit on the dusty ground for hours at a time encrypting and decrypting messages going out to HQ and coming back to the patrols. The rest of the patrol members, meanwhile, would be doing the fun stuff like reconnaissance, resting and battle preparation for the upcoming job. The sig's job would run all day and then all night and sometimes into the next day. If you had a good patrol commander, he would rotate you with another chook to give you a break from the tedious routine. The longest stint I did on the radio was over 18 hours, and by the end of it I could hardly move as I had been hunched over in the same spot the whole time tapping away on the Morse key.

There was one saving grace – you always knew what was going on before anyone else in the patrol, and that included the commander. He had to come and ask 'What's happening?' and 'What's the plan?'. That knowledge gave you a strong sense of value within the patrol and I really thought it was the best job despite the fact that I always had the heavy radio to lug around all day.

Then we moved on to the patrol course, which also ran for six weeks and was in some ways just as demanding as the selection course. It was designed to teach us the skills required for our special role in surveillance and combat. It was strenuous, but there was much more to it than simply staying the course. It was essential to see if the soldier had the awareness and weapon skills to move and fire when under stress. This was always done with live ammunition. To simulate incoming rounds striking near the individual, well-aimed bursts of machine-gun fire were laced across the ground near your feet by a highly experienced senior instructor.

I recall Gary, a young corporal, who would later become the RSM, firing a Mag 58 machine gun at a spot just metres from my boots as I conducted the patrol contact drills. This would have been frowned upon as an unsafe practice elsewhere, but in this regiment it was a great way to challenge a soldier's ability to be calm under fire in a combat situation.

On one occasion our small patrol had been sitting having a cup of coffee while waiting to be contacted to test our drills. Suddenly live ammunition started striking the white trunks of the Wandoo trees some six metres away. Immediately we sprang into action, one or two men returning fire towards some nearby automated targets, while others quickly dragged their heavy packs on. Half the patrol got their packs onto their backs and the remainder switched firing positions and also loaded their packs. There was no time to pack up coffee cups or things left out for lunch. We were up and moving away from the target area and trying to fade back into the scrub, all the while returning fire accurately at the pop-up targets.

At the end of the drill, when we were about 200 metres back from the starting point, everyone was gasping for air and sucking down water from their canteens as the instructors gave a debrief on our performance. They then told us to go and do it again, but this time better. I walked back to the spot where we had been sitting about five minutes before to recover my steel brew cup and saw that it had been shot to pieces. There were at least two holes in it where the bullets had gone through, and the exit holes had literally torn the bottom right out of the cup so it was completely useless. One of the instructors came up behind me and sniggered, 'How's your brew cup?' and then smiled dryly as he walked off. I tried not to leave any gear behind after that.

I found that being only 168 centimetres meant I had to work hard to keep up with the taller and longer-legged fellows in my patrol. Sometimes being short was a distinct advantage, for example when working in confined spaces like a hide. Also in hot tropical conditions I seemed to perspire less than some of my colleagues and could dissipate heat quicker. But at other times it was harder, like when I was carrying a stretcher with a heavy load and I had to try to match the others, who might have a 15 centimetre height advantage on me. Also when out in a Zodiac inflatable boat 20 kilometres off the Western Australian coast in midwinter, I struggled with the cold conditions as I lost body heat faster.

Carrying a heavy pack could be a challenge. The average patrol load for an operator was between 45 and 55 kilograms for a seven-day patrol. This was okay for someone who weighed 90 to 100 kilograms, but for me weighing only 75 kilograms the equipment was equal to 70 per cent of my body weight, and we had to carry these things for many kilometres over hills and across rocky creek beds day after day. To counter this I became very adept at weight minimisation. I would carry the very barest essentials to reduce the burden in my pack.

Being a patrol signalman in my early years in the regiment didn't help, as our antiquated radios weighed between ten and 20 kilograms and were around the size of a thick briefcase. This had to be jammed into our packs with all the other equipment: food rations, water, ammunition, explosives and sleeping bag. This meant any comfort items went first. Some blokes carried a thin foam sleeping mat to keep off the cold ground at night. I cut mine down to a size just large enough to support my head down to my backside. It could be folded to act as a seat when sitting for hours on the ground sending messages on the radio.

Other things like water could be minimised to reduce weight, but this was always risky, as it was easy to be caught short if the patrol got extended or we missed a resupply. I could manage on around two litres of water a day even in the hot desert environments but I would be constantly thirsty.

I always cut my rations to the bare minimum – a hot coffee or tea and biscuits for breakfast and cold tinned cheese and crackers with maybe a muesli bar for lunch.

Dinner was a hot brew of tea or coffee and a dehydrated meal, to which we'd just add hot water and stir. This was pretty typical for the patrol members and you would always lose lots of weight on a strenuous patrol.

I could also do small things to keep weight and bulk down, like not carrying toothpaste and even cutting the handle off my toothbrush. I would allocate just one-quarter of a hexamine tablet (our personal stove fuel) to heat the water just enough to warm my coffee and only carry socks for spare clothing, even on the longest patrol. Apparently you could get at least four days out of one pair of socks. Wear them normally on day one, flip them inside out on day two, swap feet on day three and then flip them inside out again for the fourth day. By the fifth day, they smell so bad they'd almost crawl away and die.

We flew over to the Army Parachute School in Nowra for the next course. We went through lots of drills on the ground but then my first jump was from a static line – which automatically opens the chute at 1500 feet (457 metres). We wore the old round parachutes and they were not very manoeuvrable; all you could do was rotate so that when you were landing you could orientate your body towards the wind to slow you down a bit.

As we gained height before the jump, I wasn't nervous. Some blokes talked about it and were a bit nervy, but when I focused on what I was supposed to do, fear didn't come into it. I was accustomed to just ticking all the boxes. But that first one, when I left the aircraft with only a parachute between me and certain death, was exhilarating . . . especially when I felt the chute open. There's not much time to enjoy it, but when I hit the ground and realised nothing was broken, I felt happy. I wiped the dust off and thought, I'm glad I did that.

The first six or seven jumps you do 'cleanskin' so you get used to flying under the canopy, but then towards the end of the course they load you up with combat equipment. We also jumped at night, and when you can't see the ground coming you can hit pretty hard. But I got through it in one piece.

Then came my favourite course: vehicle-mounted operations training. This became my passion and still is. We spent about six weeks up the Pilbara region of northern Western Australia. It's a spectacular area, and the best time to see it is in the late afternoon just before last light, when the spinifex grass has a blue tinge and contrasts with the red–brown soil of the hills and rocks. Otherwise it is very hot and the flies plague you mercilessly.

We spent a week or so patrolling in the Land Rovers in the bush and rarely saw a road. The local landowners who allowed us to use their properties were great and we visited them afterwards to thank them and let them fire the weapon systems on our cars as a bit of a thank you. Their eyes lit up as they arced up the Mag 58 into a termite mound or fired a 40-millimetre grenade into a paddock.

We then spent a week at Learmonth, an old airbase south of Onslow, doing a great range practice with live explosives and 50-calibre ammunition to develop our mobility skills. Unfortunately, while placing plastic explosives as simulation for battle effects, one of the charges exploded with Gary and me close by. Gary got the worst of it as he was closer, and I feared his head might have been blown off as he was leaning over the charges a moment before. I felt a sand blast on the back of my legs and body, and the pain in my ears was like the smack of a sledgehammer.

I turned around and saw Gary staggering in the dust. 'Are you all right?' I shouted and he stoically said, 'Yeah,' but he had been lucky to avoid severe injury. In fact it damaged our hearing permanently but at the time we saw the course as great fun. We wore our shorts and foreign 'cams' out on training patrols. Things are much more serious now.

Then there was the SAS Tactical Photographic course. We spent many cold hours in the middle of the night out in Coburn Sound off Fremantle navigating in Zodiacs and getting smashed by the Indian Ocean's winter swells. They gave us missions to get to a beach in the darkness, cache the boats and take imagery of the nearby facilities; then we'd withdraw tactically back into the ocean and return to Swanbourne or Fremantle. This was hard work, as caching the boats meant pulling them apart and burying them. Sometimes we'd do this twice in one night, then head back to the barracks and use wet photography skills to develop the images and compile a report. We'd have to hand it in at 0800 the next morning. Sleep optional.

This course spilled over into small craft handling and we spent more long winter night transits up the west side of Garden and Rottnest islands. The scariest part was coming alongside a navy frigate or patrol vessel at 3 a.m. in rough seas to be craned up on board. This was the tactical method of transferring an SASR Zodiac patrol without stopping dead in the water. As the navy frigate knifed through the waves at about ten knots (18 km/h), we would bring two Zodiacs alongside so close that we banged against the hull. The heavy sea meant the front keel of the ship was heaving and diving in and out of the water. One error and your boat would be sliced clean down the middle as the bow came crashing down beside us just a metre away. Cables were lowered to the water and the whole SASR patrol raced to hook the Zodiacs up to a pre-positioned harness so they could be hoisted aboard. It put me off boats for life. Even today I'd go for a ride in the *QEII* in open water but anything smaller and you can forget it.

Specialist weapons training went for just a week as we familiarised ourselves with all sorts of foreign weapons, mostly from the Soviet bloc. This ensured that we could pick up any weapon when overseas and still be functional should our own weapon be lost or broken.

Demolition explosives training was run at Bindoon over two or three weeks. It was great fun blowing stuff up under the instruction of Vietnam vets who could make explosives and booby traps out of just about anything.

Counterterrorist (CT) driving meant long hours of belting around Wanneroo race track and Bindoon range training facility. We slowly built up skills from gravel road manoeuvres to high-speed bitumen driving. The final test was to be able to deliver a team of assaulters to a stronghold at high speed in the dead of night with no lights and only night-vision goggles (NVGs). Later I became an advanced instructor in these skills.

The CT assaulter course was one of the most technically punishing and strenuous in the reinforcement regime. The hardest part was becoming a cohesive team member able to engage targets in short order out to about 20 metres with a Heckler & Koch submachine-gun variant. The failure rate was around 25 per cent. You had to know where your other team members were at all times, especially if you were pulling a trigger with live ammunition and explosives at night in a close-quarter battle scenario.

The last stage was a climbing course run on the coast west of Bunbury on 60-metre sea cliffs. Each day we had to achieve a set number of points with each climb. Every ascent had its own difficulty rating and they were mostly multi-pitched climbs so we had to complete each one with a partner in several stages. One fellow would lead climb and the other would belay as safety. Then on a perch partway up, we would swap roles and continue to the summit. Some guys bit off more than they could chew and ended up in very precarious spots. Exposure to the elements was a big factor and fear was ever-present. We used to call the bad climbs 'a real leg trembler'. Your whole body might lock up with fear and you'd wonder how you were ever going to make it any further. Fortunately when this happened, the belay partner could usually see a better option and would climb up and take over the lead.

Many blokes were injured during these courses – damaged eardrums, severe lacerations, broken bones and other injuries from fragmentation. Towards the end of the close-quarter battle course I was hit in the back of my leg by minor fragmentation from a metal-cutting explosive charge. Luckily I got something to take my mind off my leg when the razor wire on top of a security fence collapsed onto me and got hooked in the skin on my arm. A medic stitched me up, but when I got home to 'Swanny' I spent an hour pulling tiny lead pellets out of my skin with tweezers. The lead lining around the explosive core had liquefied on ignition and sprayed out in the form of molten lead. No one else was injured, as our team was hiding behind a large portable Kevlar shield. I must have had my leg hanging out at the side. At least it wasn't life-threatening. The rate of mortality in the regiment was one or two per 100 operators.

There was also some wastage from those who were sent back to the Big Army within a year or two after selection. This was mostly due to incompetence or silly misadventure.

'WE HAD FINALLY MADE IT'

The commanding officer (CO) used to remind us that 'each day is a renewable contract' to ensure that everyone always put in 100 per cent.

After completing all the courses, I was posted to 3 Squadron, where I was to be a patrol signaller in an operational squadron on war roles. Even though the old hands still called us 'reos' (reinforcements), we had finally made it into the ranks of Australia's most elite fighting force.

The pace was still hectic and we continually bounced between training exercises all over northern Australia for the first few years. In late 1993 I was advised I was to be part of a patrol deployment to the original British 22 SAS in Hereford, UK. And even better, we'd be going on a joint training deployment to Botswana. This was a real privilege as I was so new to the mobility troop. I couldn't wait to see some more of the world.

10

MEETING EMILY

We travelled by commercial flight to Hereford, capital of a typical English farming county on the Welsh border. It's a nice little town on the River Wye with a big cathedral and a pub on every corner. After we met the 22 SAS guys, we spent a week or so doing weapons training and patrol preparation. In the evenings we sampled most of those pubs.

The base was a two-kilometre walk out of town but it was quite difficult to find because it was surrounded on all sides by the urban area of Hereford. It was a bit like Swanbourne – headquarters buildings, individual squadron quarters, accommodation for the soldiers, messes and footy ovals. They had a lot of training areas outside the base because it was so urbanised and they weren't able to do much explosives work there.

On the way to town we passed their traditional cemetery for the operators killed in action. In fact tradition was big with them and they looked fondly back to the creation of the original SAS by David Stirling in North Africa during the Second World War. I knew the story quite well from my reading. While it started out disastrously when two-thirds of the force was lost in their first operational parachute jump, they regrouped and created a very proud record.

The base had great security: double layers of fencing and civilian police on the entrance with automatic weapons. This came as a surprise to us till we realised they were concerned about the threat from the IRA at the time. But after the week's preparation they said, 'Right, we're heading down to Botswana for four or five weeks; and we'll do a trip through the Okavango Delta.' As well, each of the three troops on the exercise – Mountain Troop, Vehicle-mounted Troop and Water Troop – would split off and do their own thing.

We were joining the vehicle-mounted guys, which suited me perfectly, as that was my specialty. We would do a trip through the delta, some intense training on a week's patrol, and would then marry up with the others for some range activity firing missiles and camp attacks using live ammunition and explosives. So that was the plan. I couldn't wait.

We jumped on a plane at Brize Norton, the RAF base in Oxfordshire. The aircraft was a British Tri-Star, which resembled a 707, and we were really comfortable on the first hop to Crete, where we landed at an airbase at Heraclion. It was quite late but the Poms said, 'Let's go and have a beer; take-off is not till 6 a.m.' I got absolutely stonkered on five or six large bottles of VB that I'd found somewhere, so I can't remember getting back to the base, but I managed to get on the plane and we flew to Nairobi to refuel at Kenyatta International Airport. That's when the Tri-Star broke down.

I had a shocking hangover; and there I was, sitting out on the tarmac for hours in 35-degree heat, waiting to hear what was happening next. Not my happiest memory. Eventually they said the RAF had decided they were going to put us up at the Intercontinental Hotel until they got the parts for the plane. We didn't mind. We assumed it would be an overnighter. Well, we got that wrong. We were to be stranded there for nearly two weeks. But it turned out to be the luckiest break that ever came my way.

On the second night the blokes said, 'Let's go out for a meal and a few beers.' We'd spent the day sitting around the pool and by then I'd recovered from my hangover, so I said, 'Yeah, let's go.' We went to a restaurant called Carnivore where they served roasted impala, ostrich, crocodile and other sorts of wild game. The waiters came to our table with a big skewer and sliced it onto our plates. After 15 minutes we'd probably tried ten or 15 different species. It was great.

At the back of the restaurant was a club where you could drink and dance in the open air. We all went out there and

I was talking to Mal, one of the characters in the ill-fated Bravo Two Zero patrol who was captured in the first Gulf War. He was interrogated and beaten up, and the survivors of that patrol were not released until the end of the war. He was a big tanned Aussie, about 185 centimetres, and I'd noticed a couple of really nice-looking local girls sitting together, so I said, 'Mal, why don't you go over and talk to them?' He said, 'No, I'm a bit shy; you go and I'll join you when you've broken the ice.'

That was *my* idea, but anyway I said okay and made my way through the tables and said, 'Hello, can I buy you a drink?' The one I really liked said, 'No, not really. I've got one thanks.' But I stayed anyway and we got talking.

I introduced myself as 'Nev' Bonner, because I'd been given the nickname practically the day I joined the army. It was after Senator Neville Bonner, the first Aboriginal person elected to the Federal Parliament, so I didn't mind a bit. Since then, nobody in the military has ever called me Stuart (and Emily only does these days when I'm in trouble). Anyway, she said, 'Hello, I'm Emily.'

Then Mal came over and we talked a bit more and had a few dances. The rest of the blokes said, 'We're going somewhere else now.' I didn't; I stayed there with Emily and we got on really well.

She spoke excellent English because, although she had been born to her Kenyan parents, James and Catherine Kipruto, in Tanzania, she grew up and was educated in

Canada, where her dad was a driver for the Kenyan Embassy. Later that night she and her girlfriend gave me a lift back to my hotel and we made a plan to meet up the following day.

We had dinner that night and over the next week or so we went out and she showed me the sights: Nairobi National Park, about 20 kilometres out of town, with its lions and elephants and other game; souvenir shops; downtown; and we had lots of meals together. It was really good. And at the end I really didn't want to leave. But I had to go to Botswana so I set off. I started writing her letters because there were no mobile phones.

EMILY'S STORY I

Emily is a beautiful woman. She is quick to smile, and when she does her face lights up with easy humour and quick intelligence. She glows. But very quickly it becomes clear that beneath the surface there is a delicacy in her emotional make-up that is easily disturbed. She has endured difficult times, not least as the loving wife and partner of a Special Forces soldier.

It is not an enviable role in life. And Emily brings to it her own challenging history. We speak quietly together in the covered outside entertaining area of the family home in a pleasant Perth suburb. She is hesitant at first but increasingly confident and articulate.

She was born to a large family in Arusha, Tanzania, in 1970, she says. Her father, James Kipruto, worked for the East African Community (EAC) of Kenya, Uganda and Tanzania. He was Kenyan but lived in Tanzania as a driver for the Kenyan minister.

It was a good life. She remembers playing with her brothers and walking to the shops with her mother, who, on the way home, would buy her a special strawberry ice-cream. 'Even now when I buy cupcakes for the children,' she says, 'I can smell the strawberry and it reminds me of when I was little.'

However, in 1975 the EAC, which had been formed in 1967, hit troubled political waters and the Kenyan representatives left the organisation, which would be dissolved two years later. It would not reform for another 16 years. Meantime Emily and her family spent two years back in Nairobi before her father was posted to the Kenyan Embassy in Canada.

'We lived in Ottawa until 1987 and I loved it there,' she says.

She was a star athlete with excellent school grades and a wide circle of good friends. 'I still stay in touch with some of them,' she says. 'It was a really good time in my life.'

She was just starting Grade 11 when, without warning, her life turned upside down. Her father, who had been driving for the ambassador, was posted back to Kenya and the family had no choice but to accompany him.

Emily enrolled in one of the top Kenyan schools for girls, and she was looking forward to the new challenge. However, she quickly discovered that the curriculum was totally different from Ottawa's, where she'd been an AB student specialising in the humanities. Her plan was to matriculate and study psychology at university. But while instruction at the school was in English, subjects like physics and chemistry were compulsory.

Her grades suffered. And so did her morale, particularly when it became clear that the headmistress had taken a set against her. If schoolmates were noisy in assembly, she was unfairly blamed. She was put back two full years and found herself taking classes with younger and less mature girls.

'I was finding it quite difficult to cope,' she says. 'I felt I couldn't trust the people around me at school.' And there was always the chance that her father's work would take her away, so she was reluctant to make firm friends.

The situation came to a head when she was approaching her final exams. The headmistress was very defensive about the school's academic reputation and she told Emily she would not be allowed to take the exams because she would bring the school average down.

'That was devastating,' she says. 'I became very depressed. It damaged my confidence and self-esteem. It comes back. It always comes back.'

We flew into a place called Francistown, in north-east Botswana – formerly the British protectorate of Bechuanaland – and then to Maun at the edge of the Okavango Delta. Unlike most river deltas the Okavango doesn't flow into the sea, since Botswana is landlocked. The water eventually just evaporates. The 22 SAS lads had leased an entire bush camp resort for the duration. It had little bungalows – thatched huts with ceiling fans and beds – and a few staff to look after us. The Brits obviously had a strong relationship with the Botswana Government and we were training with the local military as well.

In the patrols we had one or two Botswana soldiers in the Land Rovers with us. And when we had the big final camp attacks, we combined with a whole bunch of them. We built the target areas together and shared the firing of the weapons. They did most of the same things as us and the Brits provided the ammunition. So it was a really good couple of weeks.

The journey through the Okavango Delta was an amazing experience. We travelled in specially modified Land Rover V8s with the roofs removed and 50-calibre machine guns mounted in the rear. These were the standard mobility vehicles used at the time in the Gulf by British SAS. They were called Pinkys owing to their unusual light red–brown colour, which apparently made reasonable camouflage in the Middle Eastern deserts. Although quite powerful, they were a bit unstable at speed with a full load, and two were rolled en route to Francistown later in the trip.

The guys wanted to get photographs of everything. They'd see an elephant and want to get out and walk up to stand beside it for a photo. Not surprisingly the wild elephants would get really narky at them. This is the Brits – just crazy. One time I thought I'd have to shoot one (an elephant not a Brit). The 22 SAS guy was hiding on one side of a bush and the elephant was running into it to chase him away. A few more steps and I would have had to fire my assault rifle at the elephant. But thankfully common sense prevailed and the soldier retired slowly back to the vehicle.

On another occasion we came across an elephant's carcass decomposing in the baking heat. It stank to high heaven but our patrol, curious to get a closer look, dismounted from the Pinkys and wandered around the massive rotting thing, poking it with sticks. We figured it had been killed by poachers. There was a gaping hole in its stomach where wild animals had got into it. One of the Brit lads bent down to take a look up inside its chest cavity when there was an almighty ruckus and a vulture sprang out from inside. We got quite a surprise, as we were only feet away and this vulture was the size of a wallaby. When it tried to fly away, its leg was entangled in a piece of elephant's tissue and it was stuck fast – a prisoner entombed to have as much to eat as it wanted but probably never to leave. No one was game to help it, as its beak was massive and sharp. The temperature outside would have been 35°C, but locked inside the carcass it would have been more like 50. What a way to go . . .

Towards the end of the tour we were camped out in a thicket near a narrow lake that was home to an extended family of hippos – as well as a few crocs – so we didn't go swimming. At that time we called for an aerial resupply from 22 SAS's own dedicated C-130 aircraft. They flew over at midnight about 100 feet (30 metres) above the ground and we had set out some lights to guide them into the drop zone. They dropped some beers as well.

After a good feed and a few coldies I stretched out my hammock between two trees, but I noticed the Botswana guys slept on the ground and put glow sticks all around their beds. When I asked them why, they said, 'That's so when the elephants come down to drink at the waterhole they won't step on us.' Fair enough.

We did some parachute jumps. I was still on a static line from 1500 feet (457 metres). They just picked a big open area and out you go, provided the wind is not above 15 knots (28 km/h). On the way down you can see lots of acacia bushes, the big ones with lots of thorns. If you land in them, they hurt and you're picking thorns out for a week. We did six or seven jumps there and my mate Mal, the Bravo Two Zero bloke, who was freefall qualified, jumped out at about 12,000 feet (3657 metres) with his team. Afterwards, over a cold beer back at the camp, he said, 'I looked down and could see all these ants rushing in to where I thought I was going to land. But as I got closer, I realised they were kids, and even closer I could see I was going to hit an acacia bush.'

He managed to miss it but his parachute got tangled up in the bush. He tried to get it off but as he pulled it out the thorns ripped it to pieces. By now he had about a hundred kids all around him wanting to talk to him and touch his parachute. It was amazing for them. 'I got my knife out and cut the parachute up into squares and gave them all a piece each, They were all happy with that because they all had a piece of silk, something they'd never seen before.'

The big camp attack at the finale was really good. We went to a different area a few hundred kilometres away where it was much drier, practically arid. The Brits had all sorts of heavy weapons – 50-calibre machine guns, sniper rifles and surface-to-air and shoulder-fired anti-tank ground-to-ground missiles; a whole bunch of fancy stuff. However, as we were preparing for the attack, something pretty amazing happened that really gave me an insight into what the SAS is all about.

We had a big set of orders; that's when the commanders sit you around a map that they've constructed on the ground out of sand so you can get the full picture. The mobility troop included 30 blokes plus us Aussies, and a young British troop commander – an officer – who began giving his orders for the attack. It was a basic attack – you had your fire support group positioned up on the high ground and a mortar team back in the distance providing additional indirect fire support and the assault force coming in on vehicles. They'd dismount and then punch through on foot.

This troop commander looked like a British public-school boy – the aristocratic accent, the white scarf round the neck – and had a bit of an educated irony in his presentation. Anyway 'Dinga', another Bravo Two Zero vet, suddenly stood up and said, 'That's bullshit. Sit down.' This was a sergeant telling a captain in front of his entire troop to shut up and sit down. And he did! Dinga took over and gave the rest of the orders. I thought it was fantastic. But the poor old officer must have felt that big. I don't know what happened behind the scenes but we all thought it was very entertaining.

Everyone was allocated a task. The day before the attack the support guys set up a little mock village with the buildings made from hessian and with sandbags around so it looked like a defensive position. My job with some of the other Aussies was in the fire support group. We had to cart heavy weapons, ammunition and sandbags a couple of kilometres up the hill, where we would set up a fire position. The mortar team would be on the other side of the hill behind us lobbing mortars onto the position as well. The target was going to get absolutely pounded with live ammunition.

We were humping 50-calibre machine guns and Milan missiles, so we were pretty loaded up. That's when a bit of friction developed between the Brits and the Botswana Defence Force guys. I had to carry part of a machine-gun tripod as well as some ammo. You'd think it would be logical to fill the sandbags up at the top of the hill, but unfortunately it was all rocky up there, so we had to fill them in the creek bed down the bottom and hump them up the hill. That was all right as long as you didn't have to carry more than one. I did notice that the local officer from the Botswana Army was a bit upset because most of his men were not given weapons to carry; instead, they were allocated two sandbags apiece. I saw this guy struggling so I took one off him and gave him a bit of my kit. I carried the sandbag with my other gear. But then the officer had words with one of the British NCOs and halfway up they swapped the loads around.

Anyway, we got up there, and what followed was a fantastic camp attack. It went on for at least half an hour and then the mortars lobbed in and the ground force charged through and did their job. The mortars continued so that if the enemy was withdrawing, they could follow and smash them as they retreated.

I'd never seen a Milan wire-guided missile fired before. The operator holds the launcher on his shoulder or a ground mount and a wire is attached from the launching module to the back of the missile. When you fire it, the missile might

MEETING EMILY

go for a kilometre with this skinny little wire tracing behind it and you can actually guide it onto the target. When you look through the aiming device, you can see a little dot on the target. The missile will go to the point where the dot is indicated. They only have a limited range – about 1500 metres – and the wire can run out, but it's so thin it just snaps. (These days missiles like the Javelin are heat seekers, so they lock on to a heat signature and as soon as you fire you forget about it and load up the next one.)

After the battle we went back to the camp at Maun and spent a couple of days there just relaxing and cleaning the weapons. They then gave us a week off and said we could go anywhere we liked in the area. Most of the guys decided to go to the Victoria Falls but I said, 'Can I go back to Nairobi?'

They said, 'You can go wherever you want but you have to pay for your ticket,' so I went to the local Maun terminal, looked up the schedule and booked myself back to Nairobi. The idea was that I'd meet the SAS team back in Nairobi once our leave was over. I'd sent a letter to Emily from Botswana and I called her and let her know I was coming up and wanted to see her again.

She was there to meet me, and I got to meet her mum and dad. They were living in a little apartment with John, one of Emily's younger brothers, and younger sister Betty as well. I stayed in a spare room at Emily's older brother

Peter's house, where she was also living. We went out for dinner every night, and we even went to Mombasa for a couple of days and stayed in a hotel on the beach. It was a real adventure. By the end of that week I was really committed to Emily. I felt we were getting on really well and we wanted to see more of each other. I asked her if she wanted to come over to Australia for a holiday. Obviously, this was going to be a long-distance relationship.

Until then the longest relationship I'd had was probably three months, and that was with Karen in Malaysia. And I think Emily was really in two minds. Maybe she thought when I left Nairobi she'd never see me again.

EMILY'S STORY II

Emily was working as a marketing assistant for Sedgewood Ltd, owned by the famous Leakey family, when she met Stuart, and had had only one serious relationship – an American named Robert, who was a teacher at the International School. But when he was robbed during a break-in at his home, he decided to return to the States, quickly packed and departed. And when sometime later Emily applied for a visa to visit him in America, it was denied, as they had no serious marriage plans. 'I think they thought I'd go to America and not come back to Kenya,' she says. 'There were a lot of people doing that. But that was not what we planned. Things just didn't work out. And even when

I met Stuart, I remember saying that I wasn't playing hard to get, I just wasn't ready for another relationship.'

But Stuart was persistent and they were both aware of that special chemistry. 'When he went to Botswana, he wrote and he just kept on calling me and calling me,' she says. 'He never gave up.' However, that American visa refusal would bring extraordinary complications to their plans.

•

After Nairobi I went back to the UK with the lads for another few days, and before heading home we took leave and saw a bit of London and Scotland. By the time I arrived back at Swanbourne, I had been away about eight weeks, and if this was life in the regiment I thought it was fantastic.

I kept in touch with Emily and a couple of months later she came to Australia for that holiday. I didn't have a place for her to stay at the time as I was still in the single men's quarters. So I was relying on the good graces of some of my friends with houses in Perth to put her up. Pete was one mate who allowed me to stay with him at his rented three-bedroom villa in Scarborough. Frosty loaned me his sports car to meet Emily at the airport and Skip, a mate who came to the UK with me, said I could borrow his old Ford Falcon for a week to get around. I still only had an old Moto Morini 500 cc motorbike, which was not really practical for two. I also had an old Valiant sedan that was unregistered, and I eventually sold it to my mate 'Action Jackson' for a couple of hundred bucks.

Jacko was a mad bugger; he'd sabotaged my date with a girl in Cottesloe before I met Emily by eating her lipstick out of her handbag. Jacko used to do a back flip in the nightclubs of Perth while standing in front of you just talking. This was his undoing when he did the same off the second-storey balcony at Defence Language School Point Cook and broke his collar bone. He was sent off posthaste for a psych assessment and hospitalisation. He was more stable than most people I know; just a party guy.

Emily and I had a two-day trip to Bunbury on the coast in a beautiful part of Western Australia. We stayed at the Rose Hotel. It was a classic Victorian two-storey pub and it was there I asked her to marry me. She said, 'Yes,' and I thought all my birthdays had come at once.

Unfortunately, she only had a holiday visa and had to go home. I said, 'We'll get all this visa stuff sorted out and take it from there.' I had no idea how complicated that would become. Actually, in a portent of things to come, before she went back I got sent away on a military training exercise in the north and I couldn't tell her anything about it because I didn't see her off at the airport.

EMILY'S STORY III

'I don't know where he went but I knew that he worked in the army,' Emily says. 'I didn't know what SAS was. He never really said "Special Forces". But after I returned, he wrote every single day – from February to July. I still have the letters.

'I was shocked that he proposed so early, but I had a lovely time when I was with him on that holiday. I didn't know much about Australia but there was an atlas in my dad's house and as a child I would turn to Australia because I always wanted to live where the ocean is. I said yes.'

That was February 1994. On her return she began the process of organising a permanent visa to Australia and that's when the American refusal complicated the issue. Every time she went to an embassy, they'd ask, 'Why were you refused a visa by the Americans?'

Weeks went by without a response and the questions kept coming. Stuart was writing every day, as he had almost from the time they met. Finally he took leave and flew to Kenya. 'The Australian Embassy asked me to bring all the documents,' Emily says, 'even the certificate for the engagement ring. I gave them three shoeboxes full. I think they were shocked because I included all Stuart's letters.'

•

It took eight months to get all the paperwork in order – letters of reference and all sorts of stuff. It was harder for Emily because she was born in Tanzania, so there were problems of citizenship. Finally I had some holidays, so I flew over there and every day we went to the embassy to check to see if her visa had come through, until I had to return. On the final day, on the way to the airport, as a last hope we called by the embassy, and there it was. Emily didn't even have time to say goodbye to her mum. Her dad dropped us at the airport in one mad scramble for the plane.

I had thought we'd be back long before this, and had organised the wedding at the Perth registry office on 4 July 1994.

When we got to Australia, we stayed with my patrol commander, Gary, and his wife, Peta, for a night and the next day went down to the registrar's office and got married. Then we had some drinks with friends at the Burswood casino and stayed there overnight.

I couldn't get married quarters at Swanbourne because there were none available, but I was lucky enough to find a small two-bedroom apartment at Scarborough not far from the beach. I had no furniture – just a stereo and a small television and a bag full of clothes. So we madly ran about for the first week buying furniture – Ikea was our one-stop shop for everything. But then I was gone on an eight-week trip up through northern Australia to North Queensland to do two months' training. So Emily was left alone after just one week in Australia.

I tried to warn her about life as the wife of an SAS operator, but you can never properly warn someone about the full story because when you fall in love reality doesn't play a big role. When I left, she didn't even have a driver's licence. We had bought her a little car and she had to do her training with a driving instructor while I was away. Luckily she was within walking distance of the shopping centre at Scarborough. I'd send her a letter or give her a call every now and again, but I couldn't say where I was or what I was doing. I couldn't even say when I'd be back because we didn't know ourselves. It must have been pretty hard on her.

Welcome to Australia, babe . . .

EMILY'S STORY IV

'By the time of our wedding I knew he was Special Forces,' Emily says, 'but I didn't really understand what that was. After that first week together he went away for seven weeks and I was left in this villa in Scarborough. I didn't know anybody, except Nicole, who was married to Michael in the SAS. She introduced me to the other wives, but I was confused and missed my family, and really the SAS women don't talk about what the boys do. I think they just assumed that I knew.'

It was a steep learning process. 'It's a big hush-hush,' Emily says, 'but I eventually learned that you had to be careful what you speak about. When we moved into the village – the married quarters at Swanbourne – that was a big wake-up call. That's when I started knowing a lot of people but I'm very outspoken and I soon realised I was not supposed to say certain things.

'There's no introduction course for wives. All we had was the Ladies' Auxiliary. I just went to a few get-togethers. But they just didn't fit into the way I operate.'

11

'PUSH OURSELVES TO THE LIMITS'

In the early to mid-1990s training was a big part of the regiment's activities, as there were very few combat operations in that period. The SASR had deployed a small team on operations in Somalia but there were limited opportunities to rotate through that operation. The first Gulf War had finished before I joined, so I missed that one. In any case most of the Australians involved in that conflict were in a liaison role.

But that didn't mean we slackened off. Training meant many exercises in Australia with the regular army, usually on pathfinder or surveillance jobs. Occasionally there would be trips overseas to train with our Special Force equivalents in Indonesia, Malaysia, Thailand and Brunei, and 22 SAS in Hereford. But whatever exercise we were engaged in, we always operated to the limit of our capacity, always testing the boundaries. Even on leave, we tended to push ourselves to the limits.

Each year we had to complete a parachute training series to maintain competency even though it is rare these days to parachute into combat. The freefall guys who specialise in those skills have tried going in that way, but it's basically just to say they've done an operational jump. The highest I've jumped was about 13,000 feet (3962 metres) around Swanbourne, where the drop zone is the footy oval, but it's near the beach so is one of the windiest drop zones you could think of. On the other hand it's great as you come down to see your house, the barracks and the Cottesloe pub in the distance.

A friend of mine and I did some jumps there one year when the wind came up. The distance from the drop zone to the married quarters is only about a kilometre. He ended up landing on my roof. First he hit the neighbour's roof, landed on mine and then fell down between the two houses. The Land Rover came and picked him up. He was okay, with just a few bruises. If you got it right, it was fine but you could easily land in a nearby paddock, and some guys have landed in the water.

I've done lots of drops into deep water. Most years we trained up around Ocean Reef, about 20 kilometres north of the Swan River. The reason for doing it in the water is that there's such a high level of injuries when they drop blokes on the land, especially on static-line parachutes. When you drop eight blokes, there's a good chance one of them will do a knee or an ankle. But in water there's less chance of an injury, even though it's a bit more of a challenge because under canopy you've got to do a few more procedures. Just before you hit the water, you pop one of the capewells, which releases one side of the parachute; otherwise you could be pulled along like a jet ski and you could drown. They have some Zodiacs waiting in the water, and usually within two minutes blokes would be pulling the parachute in and helping you into the boat.

For water jumps you have your combat gear in a rubber bag; and when you're about 60 feet (18 metres) from the water you pull a cord and it drops the combat equipment down and it hangs about five metres below your feet.

When you hit the water, you drag the combat gear to you. You wear an inflatable vest, which you can inflate in an emergency but you float fairly well anyway. When you hit the water, you pop straight back up again.

Sometimes they drop you a couple of kilometres off the beach. It's always at night in an operational training exercise. You take off your parachute and let it sink – in fact you usually put a weight on it to make sure it sinks and is not visible – then you get your pack still in its waterproof bag; you'll have fins strapped to your legs and you put them on and swim to the beach.

The other way it's done is just before the stick of blokes leaves the aircraft, they push their boat out. It's on a parachute as well, and once they hit the water the guys swim to the boat. This can be a bit of a challenge because it could end up a kilometre or two away. And it could be dangerous because with currents and wind you might never get to your boat. The chances of doing it successfully and having your team and the boat in the one place are pretty slim. The boat would have one of those glow sticks attached so you could actually see it but it might be heading over the horizon. In perfect conditions where the water is really nice and flat you might manage it, but otherwise it can be very difficult indeed.

There is another technique: with steerable parachutes you can actually sail to the boat under canopy and land within 20 to 40 metres of it. But doing that at night from 1200 feet (366 metres) using static-line parachutes can be really difficult. Mostly we just hit the water and swim to the beach.

When you leave a plane, the first thing that hits you is the wind, and it's like falling onto a wall of fast flowing air. When you jump from a helicopter, the sensation is totally different: you basically drop like a stone until you get stable and then do your normal drills. For the first few seconds it's just like falling off a 20-storey building.

When freefalling, you try to jump out as close together as possible – sometimes as we jump we actually hang on to each other. You get stable hopefully within a few seconds and you stay in a fairly tight formation within 100 metres of each other until you get down to around 4000 feet (1219 metres). At that point you track away to get some space between you, then pull your ripcord; and once you're under canopy you can steer your rigs back on line and track to a target area.

I did about 150 jumps and I've seen some funny situations. I remember on our freefall course at Nowra back in 1997 one of the guys – his name's Bill and he was a signals bloke – just could not get stable; he was totally uncoordinated and looked hilarious. If they dropped him out at 10,000 feet (3048 metres), for the first 7000 feet he was just like a jellyfish falling. You couldn't help laughing. When he pulled his chute at 3000 or 4000 feet (914 or 1219 metres), he'd be okay, but until then he was all arms and legs, just like a rag doll. We took a video of him and we'd all sit around having a beer and have a good laugh at his misfortune. It was a classic. He'd get tired trying to get stable – because it's quite demanding on your belly facing down – and he'd end up giving up through exhaustion and basically just lie with his hands and feet up to the sky and his bum facing towards the ground, and he'd be falling like that . . . and then he'd be quite stable.

It was scary for him because everyone knows that you've got to get stable under your canopy so when you deploy your parachute it is facing the sky and your body's facing the ground; because if your body's facing the wrong way, your parachute can get tangled around you and you could die.

We had one guy who did die back in the 1990s when a pay and conditions review tribunal came around to look at how we did our work and our training. They were deciding whether they were going to give us a pay rise based on this and other special training. So we set up these different activities so they could see what we normally do. One of the activities was freefall parachute jumping out at Bindoon, which was surrounded by bush. The five or six boffins from Canberra were flown up there in the C-130 with the guys who were going to jump, so they probably got to meet them all.

After they landed the tribunal members at the drop zone, the SASR guys went back up and jumped, and as they came out one of the guys got his chute tangled around his arm and neck and he couldn't steer. So he went into a spin and apparently on the way down or when he hit the ground the chute was rotating at high speed and snapped his neck. I was a kilometre away and I could see them from a distance. We were setting up another scenario based on our vehicles and our mobility training. We got a pay rise, but it was a tragic way for that to happen.

There have been quite a few serious injuries. One guy, John, jumped out and he got a rotation going under canopy and he actually landed in the water. But he hit the water so hard that, even though he landed on his side, it was like hitting concrete, and that put him in hospital.

I've had situations where a bloke's feet are touching the top of my parachute or he's come so close I could practically reach across and touch him. I usually warn them to move away, which they can do in most cases, but when you first pop your parachute, that's the most dangerous time until everybody gets their bearings and you can steer away from each other. Most of my experiences have not been terrifying exactly, but a bit scary. It's that nerve-wracking few seconds when you deploy your canopy and you look up to see it's there. If it's not there or there's something wrong with it, that's when you go into the drills you've been taught to rectify it. That's probably the worst time.

Once we were jumping freefall at Swanbourne and it was cleanskin – just our parachutes and no equipment. It was a beaut sunny day – more of a fun jump opportunity – and they dropped us over the water and we were supposed to come in and land on the footy oval. I hadn't jumped for a while, so I thought I'd track like a missile through the air, arms at my side, so it felt a bit like flying. The idea was to get into a group and hang on to each other for 20 seconds or so. As I tracked down, I could see the group below me but I didn't put the brakes on soon enough and so I hit one guy's feet quite hard as I went past. I then had to turn around and come back in again.

But that's a dangerous mistake to make. I've heard of guys tracking towards each other and not blowing off enough speed and they hit like a car accident and knock each other unconscious. To put the brakes on, you use your hands and basically just grab the air. As well, you reshape your body so instead of being a bit like a torpedo your arms go out and it slows you down. When you've had a bit of experience and know what you're doing, it feels like flying – terrific fun.

Freefall parachutes are very controllable. If you're well enough practiced, you can land on a car roof. But the static-line square parachutes don't have much drive. They still use the round ones to get a large number of men on the ground. In a battle scenario under fire you would have to have a fairly pessimistic outlook on how many would reach the ground and still be able to fight. In the Second World War they had hundreds jumping, but the enemy were shooting them as they came down under canopy, and when they landed they broke legs or landed in creeks or whatever. If you dropped down 30 guys in a team in that scenario, you might end up with 15 or 20 of them left able to do the job.

One of my best mates, David ('Frosty') Frost, after our selection course and reinforcement cycle was posted to 1 Squadron. He was a big fellow with a gentle calm about him that some regimental seniors mistook for a lackadaisical attitude. That wasn't the case at all; it was just Dave's way. We became good friends on the patrol course and our friendship grew from there. At the end of 1993, with six weeks' leave coming up, Dave and I decided to drive his Honda CR-X sports car to the east coast. Along the way we stopped in South Australia and dived with the sea-lion colonies on the islands off the coast. When we got to Sydney, he went to visit his family and I mine. We then linked up after a week and went up the central coast to dive at a popular spot called Fish Rock Cave. It was a great trip and we always hung out together back in Western Australia. After Emily came to Australia, Dave would visit us in our married quarters at Swanny and liked to take our pet Staffordshire terrier Grungle for a walk along the beachfront at Cottesloe. He reckoned Grungle was a real chick magnet and got the girls talking with him.

From 1994 through to 1996 I had a couple of opportunities to travel overseas on exchanges, including one to Indonesia to train with Kopassus, the Indonesian Special Forces. At that time General Prabowo was the commander of Grup Tiga (Group 3) in Bandung, and we were given the royal treatment by the military there. Prabowo owned a five-star hotel in Jakarta, and we spent a night or two there on his credit card with the entire troop paid for. I also went to Thailand on a survival training exercise with the local Special Forces around the northern border region centred near Chiangmai.

Then in 1996, while Dave was on CT roles with 1 Squadron in Townsville, two Black Hawk helicopters collided and crashed to the ground in the High Range Training Area, killing 18 men: 15 from SASR and three from 5 Aviation Regiment. We knew Dave was with the boys and soon found out he was one of the dead. Emily was smashed and I felt numb, as I always would when a mate died. The reality of losing Dave and so many others took a while to sink in.

We went to Dave's funeral in Sydney, where we met his family, and I was a coffin bearer. We also went to the funerals of other lads who were buried near Perth. It was a very tough time for everyone. But soon after the funerals, blokes from my 3 Squadron were told to be ready to move to 1 Squadron to fill in the blank spaces and resurrect the CT capability. I was one of the blokes nominated to transfer.

I was okay with this, but I knew it would mean establishing myself in a different squadron with lots of unknown blokes. I was a lance corporal at the time, and it was difficult moving across and trying to fit in with other team members both above and below me in rank. The pace was hectic, as we were under the pump to achieve the same level of readiness that had been achieved before the accident, but we managed to do it.

At the end of about six months on team duties with 1 Squadron, we handed over the role to a different squadron and I was selected to attend the Defence Language School at Point Cook near Melbourne, as I'd done okay in a language aptitude test. And since I'd be learning Bahasa Indonesia I had a head start from my time in Malaysia and training with the Kopassus guys.

While it was a useful skill, it meant ten months away from the regiment from January to November 1997. So I was still a newbie in 1 Squadron when I returned. However, on the bright side, Emily had been allowed to accompany me and we had some good breaks in Melbourne.

Soon after our return Bougainville became a political issue, as the civil war there was coming to an end and New Zealand was attempting to broker a peace deal. This would be my first overseas operational deployment, and we were based on a navy vessel, a Landing Ship Heavy (LSH), HMAS *Tobruk*. A huge old craft with a drop-down ramp at the front, it could be run onto a beach to deliver men, vehicles and armour. It had been refitted several times over the years.

We were stationed just over the horizon off the coast of Bougainville, as our presence there was sensitive. Our job was to be ready to respond if there were any threats to Australians or Australian interests, since there were some Department of Foreign Affairs and Trade diplomats and other personnel involved in negotiations. There were also plans for peace talks to be conducted at Townsville, so a big part of our tour there was to facilitate those talks. At one time the village heads were invited onto the boat and we were dressed as navy personnel to remain clandestine. Of course the navy personnel knew who we were because we were all like peas in a pod. Suddenly there was a big influx of 40 people onto their ship, so of course they had to be advised who we were.

On the ship there was not a great deal to do. Most of our time was spent training using the helicopters on board. We practised fast roping and rappelling onto the deck as well as contingency planning in case some crisis occurred on the island. Occasionally we would fly to a spot on the island, pick up an official and move him back to the vessel.

We returned to Bougainville some time later and moved the negotiators to a northerly airstrip and then flew them to Townsville for the talks. By now I was really comfortable in 1 Squadron. I'd got to know the blokes well and they were a great team. But you don't really know how a bloke is going to perform in a combat situation until you're in it.

The situation in Kuwait at that time started to look bad, and soon enough part of 1 Squadron left Australia (while we were sitting in the boat off Bougainville) bound for the Middle East. The Kuwait thing turned out benign, and soon the entire squadron was back and readying up for the next challenge. I didn't know it then, but I'd soon discover all I needed to know about how the lads – and I – would perform in the real thing.

12
DEPLOYMENT

In the second half of 1999, 2 Squadron deployed to East Timor to assist in quelling the violence created by Indonesian soldiers and pro-Indonesian militia. Their operation was fairly brief, but in that time they were involved in numerous skirmishes with the militia and, on one or two occasions, the Indonesian military. By now the International Forces East Timor (INTERFET) had established headquarters there under Australian General Peter Cosgrove.

The arrival of thousands of international troops in East Timor caused the militia to flee across the border into Indonesia. Sporadic cross-border raids by the militia against INTERFET forces, particularly in the southern border held by the New Zealand Army, made it obvious that the militia had the support of the Indonesian military.

There was a major contact at Aidabasalala, 15 kilometres from the West Timor border, on 16 October 1999. In the action a covert reconnaissance patrol from 2 Squadron was repeatedly attacked in a series of firefights by a group of more than 20 militia. The patrol had been detected while they were establishing an observation post and were forced to fight their way to a landing zone. They were attacked three times over a one-and-a-half-hour period, and killed a number of their attackers before they were successfully extracted by Black Hawk helicopter. It was later estimated that five militia were killed and three wounded; there were no Australian casualties.

3 Squadron took over from 2 Squadron, and soon after their arrival some of the patrol members were ambushed while driving along a rough bush track and two of them were seriously injured. In the official release one trooper was shot through the side of the neck while another was hit in the leg. Both were evacuated back to Australia.

I spoke to some of the 3 Squadron boys after the operation, and they filled me in on the details. Apparently a group of suspected militia had been detained by the INTERFET forces and a troop from the squadron was tasked to escort the detainees back to the West Timorese border. A militia group had been tipped off about the planned route and had set up a hasty ambush on the side of the road near Balibo. As they entered the killing zone, the vehicles of 3 Squadron took small arms fire. Their drill was to dismount, return fire and fight through the ambush force. During this engagement Mark was hit in the shoulder/neck area. Ron was severely wounded in the leg and arm. The boys under fire had called up the squadron's Quick Reaction Force (QRF), which then moved up and conducted a sweep through the ambush site. A couple of militia fighters were killed in the firefight, and armoured personnel carriers (APCs) came in and assisted in battlefield clearance operations, including removal of the corpses.

Ron's battle wounds hit home to me. He was one of the young blokes I helped train as part of his reinforcement cycle and I worked closely with him for the first year. I heard later that Ron's leg was not healing easily and he had to undergo numerous post-op procedures to try to get the bones and tissue to mend back together. The ammunition used in modern warfare is absolutely lethal, and if it strikes bone on the way through a body then the bones will fragment and splinter into many pieces, and trying to reconstitute that damage is extremely difficult.

There was some stink from that contact about the guys who came in APCs and recovered the injured or dead once the contact was over. They loaded the militia bodies onto the vehicles and one of our men was accused of maltreating the bodies. Someone accused him of kicking them or some such thing. To me that's ridiculous. I know the fellow and he's a fantastic bloke, but he nearly lost his job over that. The army investigated it and dragged him through the coals. Eventually he was exonerated. He was just a really dedicated bloke and he may have pushed the bodies out of the way when he got into the APCs, but I would have too if I needed to get my blokes into a confined space.

As for 1 Squadron, we were busy preparing security assessments in preparation for the Sydney 2000 Olympics. We had been flying about the country conducting planning and hard training in the event of a serious security incident. We were scheduled to hand over the role of Olympic security to another squadron so we could deploy to replace 3 Squadron, as they were becoming fatigued.

When the time came, we flew by C-130 to a staging area near Darwin, where we met some of the departing SASR men and were briefed on our roles and tasks. My language course was a real asset and at one stage it looked as though I would be interpreting for the OC in the advance party, but plans were fluid and that didn't eventuate. However, it would prove to be invaluable on the operation.

We deployed in a Hercules to Dili's airport then on to the Dili heliport, where we were to be accommodated in a series of small Indonesian-built houses and offices surrounded by low concrete walls and topped with razor wire against militia attacks. It was sweltering hot in November, the midst of the wet season, with temperatures in the mid-30s, humidity around 90 per cent and daily downpours. The deployment was to last for three to five months, but we never got told how long we were going away for. When I left, Emily asked when I was coming back. All I could say was, 'I don't know, babe.' That was terrible.

We began to settle in. There were about a hundred of us, made up of three troops of shooters – Air, Water and Vehicle-mounted – and all the support: HQ elements, signallers, computer geeks, imagery specialists, medics and cooks. I found it interesting that the remaining 3 Squadron guys were quite comfortable in these surroundings. And they were cocky. It's the old story: you arrive somewhere and you're like the new kids on the block. Some were dead keen to get out and others were just as keen to stay longer. They'd had some contacts; they'd seen some action; and that's what they loved. They'd done a good job and there was a unit commendation for their combined actions.

Some were really helpful and others were more reserved, and some were sitting about sucking cans of beer. I remember seeing one officer with his feet up and a beer in his hand. He looked like he was in Bali having a holiday with his long hair and beard. He'd gone feral; and many were a bit like that.

I went inside and had a look around to see where we were going to put our bunks. For the first few days we had to share the space with L Troop until they left, and then we'd have the buildings to ourselves. There was ammunition all over the place, and they'd got used to living like that – a bit like *Apocalypse Now*. To us it was strange because we'd come straight from the barracks environment, where everything was controlled and you'd keep your firearm with you all the time. We'd ask, 'Where do you keep your long arm?' They would have it on their bunks. It didn't seem right, but these guys were winding down after four or five months and they were tired. They said, 'As long as you've got your pistol on your hip, you're all right.'

Conditions were fairly ordinary. We had showers with buckets on hooks. The shitters were Portaloos sitting in the tropical heat, so they were horrendous. The razor wire was pretty lame at keeping people out; so we did get a few locals climbing the fence and sneaking in to pinch stuff or maybe firing the odd round over the top. We had a lot of problems with feral dogs that would come in and pinch our tucker. You'd be in your bed at night and you'd hear this thing sniffing through your pack.

I was keen to get out from under the eyes of the head shed. You'd hear, 'Oh, how come Nev's not polishing his boots?' or, 'How come he's got a beard?' You just want to get away from all that. Fortunately, after a few days we got some intel briefs and were test firing our weapons before receiving some commander's orders. At the time I was the 2IC of my patrol, and my patrol commander was not yet in the country. A young captain was troop commander and the OC ordered me to take the patrol up into Eileu, which was the Falintil stronghold in the mountains.

The five of us would replace one of the teams that had been living up there for some months, interacting with the

Falintil soldiers and gathering information. It was a sort of 'hearts and minds' thing, helping them and fostering good relations so we could form a good long-term relationship since they would probably be the future commanders of the military and government of East Timor. They had all been corralled around Eileu because INTERFET didn't want them to be out fighting and complicating the situation.

To get to Eileu from Dili, we headed out of town and started climbing the escarpment. The mountains are several thousand feet high, and very narrow winding bitumen and gravel tracks make their way up the incline. It was probably a couple of hours' hard concentrated driving.

We didn't have our Long Range Patrol Vehicles (LRPVs) because it was a signature vehicle and someone would see that and straight away think SASR. They wanted us to be more unidentifiable, so we were provided with 110-Series Land Rovers, which we then modified to our own needs. We took the roofs off and placed machine guns on them. We had two of those for our Eileu patrol, one 4 × 4 and one standard army 6 × 6 that looked a bit like a utility.

When we arrived in Eileu, we spent our first few weeks living at an old abandoned set of villas and then moved to a prison about six kilometres outside the town. Eileu itself consisted of a few hundred houses on several streets. There was a medical centre and some stores. Most of the Falintil commanders were living there, and they looked to me like a bunch of bad boys who had come good. It was a feudal system and whoever had the biggest stick was a leader. Xanana Gusmão lived in an old Portuguese villa near the centre of town and the football oval. His was the flashest house; then on a sliding scale every other commander got the next flashest house in town. They all had reasonable accommodation. They didn't have electricity except for a generator if one was available. Running water was limited, and we used to deliver jerry cans of fresh creek water to two of the commanders' houses near our prison each day as a gesture of goodwill.

We were located in an administration building within the prison facility, which was about a hectare in area. There was a large wall and a couple of administration offices at an entrance leading into a central square that had housed prison inmates before it was commandeered by the Falintil as a barracks. By then the Indonesians had opened the gates and the prisoners were long gone.

We began to familiarise ourselves with the Falintil and also the other SASR patrols that were already there. You could see they were fatigued. Some were a little annoyed at our intrusion as I tried to wrestle some bunk spaces for my patrol. One soldier, Keith, got very angry when I asked him to move his stuff a few metres so we could get sleeping stretchers into the small cramped accommodations.

We were well supplied with fresh rations, meat, some vegetables, rice, clean water, generators and fridges to keep food. We were south of town, and there were two other patrols strategically placed within the town. We would feed information back to a central command point located in the town centre.

Each morning around 10 a.m. I would ride a quad motorbike or take a Land Rover to the town to have a meeting at this command centre, where we exchanged information and received any tasking. We would pass back information from our designated area, which included the ten Falintil soldiers at the prison farm, and also a kilometre or so from us the houses of some local commanders who were also surrounded by more Falintil soldiers.

Some of the commanders had tough-guy nicknames like 'Ular', which means 'snake' in Indonesian. These were the hard men of the Falintil. They were also a superstitious bunch, ranging in age from 18 to 55 or 60. I wondered how come the really young guys were commanders and figured they must have had connections or had committed some act of heroism. Of course they might have just had a special talent for getting guys to do what they needed them to do in a conflict zone.

Each of the soldiers would report to their own sub-commanders and each week their commanders would in turn report to Gusmão, whose house was their command centre. We were a small part on the sidelines of their command structure. What we were really doing there, as well as creating a relationship, was monitoring what they were doing and planning, and trying to maintain the integrity of the process.

It was a strategic plan and a good plan. Part of it was that they would eventually be disarmed. Very few of the Falintil had modern weapons. If you had a good weapon, then you had a good position within the ranks. They were always very proud to tell us how they had killed an Indonesian soldier and had pinched his weapon.

One of my tasks each day was to teach the kids English at the local village school. But because I couldn't speak Tetum or Portuguese, I had to use Bahasa Indonesia. Some of the older children spoke Indonesian and the headmaster would translate Indonesian to Tetum for the younger ones, or in his absence the older children would translate to the younger.

A motley crew of kiddies would turn up at the makeshift school each morning for a few hours. It was fantastic. I loved it, and I'd write out a lesson plan the evening before. We had a whiteboard but the school was just a thatched roof on posts buried into the ground on a grassy patch on the roadside. On a busy day there might be 20 to 30; when something was happening in town like a church event, then maybe one or two would turn up; but usually it was around ten to 15. I took over the role from the previous 3 Squadron bloke, who had established the routine.

All around that area they cultivated rice paddies. The locals were well established and it was a very fertile area.

They had bananas, cattle, goats and pigs. There was a river nearby, so there was a reasonable supply of water. It was a very nice little town and very scenic with probably two or three hundred people. As you walked down the street, you would see all these people milling around, heading to church or some social event. They were a very Catholic community.

As well as teaching school, one of the things I enjoyed was taking the patrol out to some of the more remote villages and setting up temporary aid centres. On arrival our excellent patrol medic John would provide treatment to the villagers, young and old. Occasionally our Australian doctor from the heliport would come up with us or on other occasions we were joined by the local non-governmental organisation (NGO) doctor.

On one occasion a mother of two children in the village asked us to visit her ailing husband, who had been ill for some time. John and I made a house call to a small neat home not far from the prison. On entering the dimly lit main room, we found a man in his forties lying in his bed, obviously gravely ill. He was extremely thin with his eyes sunken back in their sockets. A check on his urine showed the colour of black tea. John determined that he was most likely suffering from cholera.

The wife pleaded with us to help. We did what we could with our limited resources but two days later he passed away. The wife and children were left without any support mechanisms. Over the coming weeks I tried to provide them with some rice and other basics but I know they must have struggled to survive. This was a common story among these lovely people.

On another occasion Gaspar, the head teacher, asked me to come and see his sister, who was in labour with a child and was experiencing some complications. Gaspar said, 'She's been in labour for the past 12 hours and something is wrong.' In most East Timorese villages a family nurse will assist at the birth, but there was no such person here. Perhaps she had left the village or been killed. So I escorted him on a quad bike to his sister's house, which was a mud-floored tin hut near the rice paddies. I went inside to see what we could do to help. There in the humid 35-degree heat the partially clad mother-to-be was obviously in great discomfort. She was squatting in the corner in complete darkness. She'd been there like that all day without any help.

There was nothing I could do for her except get back on the quad bike and head the six kilometres into Eileu to try to find the NGO doctor. On the way I talked to John about it and he said she probably needed to be evacuated to a hospital. We located the doctor, a young Australian woman, and she jumped on the back of the quad. We headed back to the village with my rifle and her med kit swinging off our backs as we sped at 60 km/h along the dusty village tracks.

When we arrived, the situation was pretty much unchanged. After two hours we finally got things moving with the mother and managed to deliver the baby. For some reason the placenta would not come out. It was a medical condition, and I didn't follow it too closely, but there was a fair bit of blood. So the doctor and I organised for the NGO ambulance to come and take the mother and baby on the two-hour journey down to Dili hospital.

I heard later that both mother and baby were fine, and Gaspar came up to me later on and said, 'Thanks for all your help. We need a name for the baby boy. Can you give him a name?' I thought, Nev is a pretty crappy name for a Catholic kid, so I suggested Joshua.

13

'BRAVE LITTLE PEOPLE'

Some years later my old patrol colleague Guy visited the village and met Gaspar. He introduced him to Joshua, who was now a healthy young fellow about four or five years old. Those sorts of experiences give you a sense of responsibility and belonging. So when something like burns occur, it makes it all the more horrific. Even now, 14 years later, I get a bit emotional when I think about it.

We assisted medical teams treating people in remote areas, and we would treat kids with all sorts of illnesses and injuries. Sometimes they had been slashed with machetes; other times they even had gunshot wounds. Some of the wounds were shocking: terrible cuts to the back of children's heads and necks; on one occasion it looked as though they had tried to decapitate a child. And the wounds hadn't been treated properly. They weren't stitched so they were open, infected and seeping pus. We would bandage them up.

It was a very hot political situation back in 1999. International pressure had been mounting on Indonesia from other countries, including Australia, to force them to stop what they were doing in East Timor. There had been massacres in the cemetery after local elections, and I admit I don't understand the fine detail, and it's been a long time since I was back there. But when they annexed East Timor in 1975, they essentially turned it into another province of Indonesia.

At the time in Indonesia there was state control and overwatch all the way down to family level. There was central command from Jakarta in Java, and below that there were provincial commanders, and tied in very closely with that was the military. There was very little differentiation; you could be a general but you could also be a provincial leader. From provincial level there were sub-levels, and each level broke all the way down to each village and then into smaller parts of that village. Whatever went on in the village could be directly influenced by what happened in Jakarta, and whatever occurred in a village could be fed back up through the system to the highest levels.

It probably worked quite well in Indonesia. The system had its purpose and its place. But to the East Timorese, who hadn't been accustomed to such controls, this system was suddenly forced upon them after the Indonesian occupation. In each village and each town there were soldiers who helped establish the system and had a role to play in domestic security. That's one of the main roles of the Indonesian armed forces in Indonesia: domestic security. It's different in Australia; the military has no role in domestic security unless it's enacted in parliament, and it has very rarely been sanctioned in legislation.

However, in East Timor the Indonesian military would move about the villages and towns and talk to villagers in a leadership role, exerting their influence. When the Indonesian military were advised by Jakarta that they had to pull out, they decided, 'Let's just burn everything down that we've built up over the past 24 years; we've got nothing to lose.' And that's what they did. They slaughtered people and they committed horrible atrocities, rapes, stabbings, assaults and other mindless terrible acts.

I've worked with the Kopassus, and to me the Indonesians are like children; they have quite good soldiering skills for their nation's level of expertise. They are not very well equipped, but they are absolutely ruthless, and if they are told to do something and it's justified to them, they will carry it out. They will also go above and beyond that to do things that may be criminal. That dark side can come out of people in those times, and they are capable of some horrendous things.

The villagers and local farming families took the brunt of it. In some places it was catastrophic and obvious, and in others it had a limited impact. But across the tiny country you had the soldiers leaving together with a lot of pro-Indonesian people. And some of them would be staying as well. A lot of the local village leaders, the older men, were killed. We'd go into the village and need to speak to the leader and ask, 'Where is the village elder?' and some young bloke would come out and say, 'That's me.' We'd think, That doesn't sound right. How did you become the village elder? It turned out they'd killed the elder bloke because he was either pro-Indonesian or anti-Indonesian, depending on the village. The new leaders were out of control and the people were very scared of them.

We had to operate in this environment. Many people were still injured; they all knew someone who had been killed. They had lots of stories to tell us about the massacres and injustices that had been heaped on them by the military and pro-Indonesian militia. Our predecessors, 3 Squadron, had more exposure to it because they were there when the atrocities were still going on. They were trying to move the Indons and militia out, and we arrived when a lot of that had been done. But there were still many incursions back across the borders creating disturbances and killings, because the Indonesian forces still wanted to play a part and still wanted to create mischief.

On our medical patrols we might travel 50 kilometres from base. That's when we saw some of the injuries that have stuck in my mind. But I didn't have to go beyond the village to see some shocking sights. Eileu's small, understaffed and understocked medical centre didn't have a doctor; they just had nurses who volunteered. Whether they had proper training or they were just local people who had taken on that role I wasn't really sure, but they did an outstanding job.

My patrol would go down there and assist them. On any day they would get up to a hundred villagers seeking treatment for malaria, cuts and infections, even leprosy, and some other diseases that we never see in Australia. There were also tropical diseases, typhoid, cholera and those wounds. Children would have severe untreated skin conditions where their entire bodies were covered in sores or skin rashes, and often we would not have the medication to treat them.

The burns were what really blew me away. Most of them came from electrocution. Children would find wiring that had been ripped out of a wall, and it was harmless after they had wrecked the power supply. But when the people started to generate power again, they wouldn't know whether the wiring was live or not. The kids would be playing around with old wiring and next thing 'Zap'. The wounds were terrible. You'd see that the child may have grabbed the wire with his hand, but the charge had blown a hole in the back of his elbow.

These kiddies were lovely brave little people. A young girl about six or seven came to the Eileu medical centre when I was there helping. She had been burned by electricity and the joint at her elbow was fused together with scar tissue so that she could no longer extend her arm straight. The skin on her arm was burned away and each time she came in the volunteers would have to remove the old dressings, clean away the dead tissue and place new dressings on. This was a terribly painful process, and as each old bandage was peeled away, so came a layer of stinking burned skin and tissue. The poor child was in agony as the dressings were removed and then replaced. I would try to hold and console the children as the wounds were dressed and it was heartbreaking to see and to be unable to do anything for their pain. After a while a kind of calm numbness would take over as I saw case after case with similar burns and trauma. The thing that stuck in my mind the most was the screams of the children as we tried to help with their wounds.

The most we could provide in the remote areas was re-dressing wounds and providing basic medications like pain relief. If we were able, we would try to get them evacuated down to Dili for proper treatment at the hospital there, but getting more serious cases away to Dili was difficult because there was no public transport, so we'd have to ferry them ourselves, which often wasn't achievable; or they'd have to jump in the back of a five-tonne lorry with 40 other people piled in, bouncing around for hour after hour on the steep mountain roads down to the coast.

About 20 kilometres south of Eileu was a little village on the outer rim of a steep ravine. We visited that village a few times to offer the people some basic medical care, as they were in a terrible state. A great many of the children suffered from malaria, and John was adept at identifying the illness by now, as he had seen hundreds of cases. Among the most obvious signs were an enlarged liver or spleen as well as fevers. With severe cases we could arrange for a casualty evacuation (CASEVAC) back to Dili. One young mother had a baby that we helped to evacuate. The child was in a very bad way and I heard shortly afterwards that it had died.

We had some occasions where we had to deal with the militia, but I didn't have to fire my weapon at any of them. The threat was always there, and when we heard gunfire we would commence some defensive manoeuvres in our Land Rovers. On Christmas Eve 1999 I was out on patrol with our fellows down on the southern coast of East Timor near a village called Betano. Our task was to get to a remote area called Manufahi, which had not been visited by any INTERFET forces at that time due to its inaccessibility. The only way in was to traverse up a sandy riverbed from the coast for some kilometres and then cut across the land westwards towards the village. While we were driving north up the riverbed, suddenly the skies opened up and a tropical downpour began to swell the river waters. Very soon the dry sand gave way to floodwaters a foot deep inside our two Land Rovers. A couple of times we came close to disaster but eventually we reached a point where we thought if we left the river and headed due west we would strike the village.

This was vehicle-mounted work at its toughest, but we'd been trained for it. We roared out of the floodway and headed along rough tracks through several abandoned villages until, almost at last light, we came upon the small village of Manufahi. The people were shocked and frightened to see us at first, but after speaking through a young lad who had a smattering of English as well as Bahasa we were able to get the villagers to bring their ailing people out so they could receive some basic medicines.

By now we were accustomed to the numerous common diseases and illnesses, but often one or two would catch us out and we would be at a loss to provide any real treatment other than what John carried in his patrol kit. This occasion was no exception. While treating the village elders and some of the children, we noticed a young girl who the other children seemed to be poking fun at. She was only nine or ten years old but she had the most severe skin condition I have ever seen. Her entire body seemed to be covered in rough scaly skin similar to psoriasis.

John felt that in Australia – or most other developed countries – her condition would have been very treatable and would never have reached this shocking stage. He beckoned her to come in and, after a short examination, gave the parents, who seemed resigned to the child's condition, some skin lotion that might ease the suffering a little. We tried to convince them that what she really needed was a trip to Dili to the hospital for a proper diagnosis and specialist treatment. That in itself was a difficult task, as getting to the coast was challenging enough, let alone all the way to Dili on the other side of the island.

This dilemma was typical of my time in East Timor. On one hand it was one of the most satisfying and worthwhile operations I was ever able to be part of. On the other it was full of feelings of hopelessness at the conditions we faced in trying to assist the people.

We were still up in the mountains on 28 February 2000 when INTERFET handed over command of military operations to the United Nations Transitional Administration in East Timor (UNTAET). It didn't make much difference to our roles. By then we were getting towards the end of the deployment.

My last patrol task was to man an observation post for ten days on the border of East and West Timor. The post was high on a hill overlooking the border area delineated by a fast flowing river in a deep valley. On the valley floor near the river was an Indonesian Air Defence unit's position. At any time there were up to 15 Indonesian defence personnel at the base and we were able to observe most of their comings and goings. There was nothing of any note that took place, but the Indonesians' routine was scrutinised and recorded each minute in detail and passed back to HQ.

After months of being involved in the Eileu job with the Falintil and treating the ill in the mountainous regions, this mundane observation post was a real let-down. I wanted to get back to the mountains and continue the job of trying to make a difference to the sick and injured and teaching the children at the local school. But that was not to be, and soon afterwards we were sent back to Australia.

A New Zealand soldier, Private Leonard Manning, was shot dead in country on 24 July 2000, becoming the first combat fatality since INTERFET had arrived in September 1999. The contact took place in the south-west town of Suai when his patrol was attacked by a militia gang. Hand grenades and other weapons had been withdrawn from the Kiwi forces after the UN took over. We didn't have much to do with them because we operated as a discrete unit. But I heard that they rescinded that order after Manning's death. Two Australian infantry soldiers also died in East Timor in 2000: Corporal Stuart Jones by accidental discharge of a weapon and Lance Corporal Russell Eisenhuth through illness. No SASR personnel were lost.

I didn't really want to leave. There was so much more I felt we could do there. Coming home to Emily was a high on the one hand, but I also had a sad feeling that the work there was not completed. Soon after getting back to Australia, I considered discharge and took three months' long-service leave. It would take all that time of R&R to get the positive outlook back that I knew I'd need if I was going to stay in the regiment.

EMILY'S STORY V

Stuart's deployment to Timor was also a deeply worrying time for Emily. 'I didn't want to believe that he was going to East Timor,' she says. 'I remember praying and saying to myself maybe things will change tomorrow.

I was in absolute denial. When the day came, I put my brave face on, but deep inside I was very sad knowing that he might not come home.

'Stuart had given me this brown envelope containing his will the night before his departure. I still take a deep breath remembering that brown envelope. For me it was especially difficult because I had no family that were close by. My family live all over the world and my in-laws live over on the east coast, so there was really no one I could turn to for support. The little that I would hear on the news was the only source of information.'

Much of the time she spent writing letters to Stuart. 'They were precious moments,' she says, and all the more so because she was unable to talk about his mission to anyone except other members of the SAS community, and even they were limited in what they could say. 'We just learn to keep our mouths shut and for the obvious reason: the security of our loved ones,' she says.

It would be months before Stuart returned, and when he came home something in him had changed. 'At that time I didn't realise what it was,' she says. 'But there was constant patrolling of the house, locking doors. Any noise was a major factor.'

14

TO AFGHANISTAN

Those three months' R&R did the trick – at least I thought so at the time. I felt rejuvenated and ready to get back into solid work again. I still found it hard to toss some of the images of the young burns victims, but it was helpful to get back into our work. I was scheduled to undertake some sergeant's courses in the second half of 2000. And I was caught up in a new three-year training cycle incorporating the hostage recovery training roles, 'green' or war roles, and then counterterrorist duties in the third year. My 1 Squadron also received a fresh batch of men straight from the reinforcement cycle, and much of the year was spent around Western Australia getting them prepared for what was to come. So it was a busy time, and that suited me fine.

By the middle of 2001 I had completed all the courses I needed except the patrol commander's course, which ran for about seven weeks. In fact I had just started it when, early on the morning of 12 September, Emily called out to me, 'Come and see this!' We watched together as the World Trade Center towers collapsed. It was shocking to both of us, and as the story developed I found myself wondering if the Aussie SAS would have a role to play in America's response; and I could tell Emily was thinking the same thing.

At Swanny everyone was talking about it, and it wasn't long before I started to hear rumours of a deployment to Afghanistan. Of course the boys were itching to go. Civilians really don't understand the SASR mentality. These men train hard for a fight, and when it comes they want to be there first. They're a bit like football players at the grand final: they don't want to be on the bench; they want to be on the field. With professional soldiers, if you're not in the fight, then you're going to be restless as hell until you get there.

At work my colleague Blaine 'Dids' Diddams epitomised this warrior mentality. He was completely dedicated, very proud and keen to deploy wherever the fight should take him. In 1 Squadron he had served with his close-knit group in East Timor and the Solomon Islands. He had fought in Somalia, and many times returned to the 'Ghan until 2 July 2012. That's when he was killed shortly after inserting by helicopter into a landing zone in the Chora Valley. He was on his seventh Afghanistan tour.

Just after the Al Qaeda attack we weren't thinking about what bad things might happen. Our attitude was that you trained as hard as you could and that would minimise the risks of becoming a casualty. I bailed up the CO at a regimental meeting and asked – not very politely – if those of us on the promotion course could leave it to rejoin training with our squadron. He said he'd 'have a word' with the course senior instructors, and it worked.

We then sought the kind of terrain and enemy action that we'd be likely to face. Fortunately Western Australia has plenty of areas similar to the bare Afghan landscape, at least in summer and at low altitude. Winter in the mountains would be a different matter. We did live fire drills from vehicles and on foot by day and night. A small group of us also headed up to the Kimberley to conduct a forward air controller's (FAC) course to be able to direct aircrews to drop bombs and fire rockets onto targets as ordered.

After several weeks of build-up we flew out of Perth by C-130 to the huge US camp in Kuwait. Our LRPV six-wheel-drive vehicles had already begun arriving in country and we got to work preparing them for the operation. The camp was pretty plush, a bit like a small American town, with a mall that featured KFC, Burger King and a PX that reminded me of Kmart. We were allocated a huge aircraft hangar in which to stay and store all our kit.

After a few days of preparations at the base we moved our squadron vehicles by road at night to the El Al Salim

Airbase a few hours' drive away. There we were met by a big C-17 aircraft and we loaded up a troop's worth of LRPVs as well as all our battle kit. There would be several sorties to get all our men into Afghanistan on these leviathans.

As we approached the tail ramp of the massive aircraft, the noise from the engines was deafening. We were guided in by US loadmasters as we reversed our vehicles up the ramp. This was a difficult and stressful task, as it was hard to understand the loadmasters' American accents and unfamiliar hand signals as they tried to get our vehicles into the belly of the cavernous cargo area.

The squadron was designated Redback One, which I really liked, and the commander gave us our orders. We would be doing a tactical night insertion into Firebase Rhino in the middle of the desert at the southern end of the Helmand Valley. This would be done entirely without lights onto a dirt airstrip. I had heard of this firebase already in the news some weeks earlier when US Special Forces had parachuted in, captured it and established a small lightly defended airstrip. This was broadcast around the world, so everyone knew we were coming.

As we landed, we felt the hard impact that is common when pilots are using NVGs. As they applied the brakes, the back ramp began to open and a freezing cold blast of dust, grit and jet fumes smacked me in the face. Then, as the plane lost more speed, I could hear the loadmasters frantically undoing the straps that secured the vehicles to the aluminium floor. When the plane stopped, I could see forklifts at the exit ramp wrestling with cargo pallets; then I heard a loud crash as one of them weighing several tonnes was dropped by a careless driver. He moved it clear and we were given the command to exit the aircraft. The cold air was shocking after being confined in the artificial warmth of the C-17. We moved in low-range first gear as fast as we could to a position 200 metres back and to the left of the aircraft, where we rallied the vehicles and awaited further instructions.

Prior to the assault Rhino had been under surveillance by the US Navy Seals for several days. It was believed to be a drug-processing and storage facility and had a reasonably high level of security. The buildings were surrounded by a concrete compound two metres high. The 15 Marine Expeditionary Unit (15 MEU) assault force arrived in C-130s and captured Rhino on 25 November. Some C-130s were armed with mini-guns, a 105-millimetre Howitzer and a 40-millimetre Bofors gun, and could fly unseen some 10,000 feet (3048 metres) above in the night sky and provide pinpoint accurate fire onto the buildings and compounds they suspected were harbouring enemy combatants. So many of the buildings had holes in the roofs and ceilings where 40-millimetre high explosives had punched through, killing everyone inside.

In the middle of the compound where we set up camp there was a small mosque that was left alone by the US forces. We were housed in a large hangar-type shed with a concrete floor and sliding doors. It was about 50 metres long by 40 metres wide and as high as a three-storey building. Some marines had already set up in there. Many others were outside on the security perimeter, sleeping each night in their freezing fox holes; so we were among the lucky ones.

The marine commander, Brigadier General James Mattis, was a real old war dog who gathered all his soldiers and us SASR blokes together in the shed soon after our arrival and gave a speech. The marines obviously held him in high regard with their enthusiastic 'Hoo-aa!', which they shouted throughout his talk. The bit our SAS blokes liked most was when towards the end of his spiel he said, 'Above all else, look after your mates out there on patrol and don't let the enemy catch you by surprise. If threatened, kill 'em, just kill 'em.' The marines were like that, real gung-ho and quite different in manner from our blokes, who had a more reserved professionalism while just as keen to do the job.

The marines had lots of air assets and also the light armoured vehicles (LAVs) similar to the Australian military, as well as the ever-present Humvee 4WD. Outside the compound there were Apache helicopters and Black Hawks planted on the dusty desert ground. Every time something took off or landed, there was a total blackout as a huge dust cloud engulfed the landing zone.

As the base was so remote, everything had to be ferried in by cargo aircraft, and the airstrip was busy day and night as huge C-17s and C-130s landed all sorts of cargo, including water. There was no mess kitchen, just US 'meals ready to eat' (MRE) rations, and the shitters were an unusual affair with the blokes and girls (yes, girls in the marine combat roles) sharing plywood toilet boxes just outside the compound. I hadn't seen this set-up before but apparently they had been latrining this way for years. No showers owing to the lack of water, but the bitter cold made such a luxury seem ridiculous anyway. Our wash-up routine was a bucket each morning in which we could have a shave or just wash our faces.

At night there were regular 'stand to's summoning all of us to the perimeter fence with weapons readied as suspected enemy forces were spotted nearby. To see over the top, we would stand on crates or sandbags. This also happened when patrols went out or came back, so sleep was very irregular. One night as we all peered into the darkness over the fence, I could see helicopters landing and taking off and I could hear the gunfire of a C-130 firing mini-gun and 40 millimetre off in the distance. As I watched the phosphorescent whirl of the dust striking the chopper blades landing nearby, I could see one of the helicopters was struggling to land and also hear the engines howling. Then there was an almighty crash as the helicopter struck the ground and exploded into a fireball.

It all happened only a few hundred metres away and seemed surreal, like watching a movie. Luckily the pilots escaped but they lost two aircraft in the incident. The cause was dust blackout from the powerful rotor wash. The pilot loses his ground reference point and then smashes into the terrain.

EMILY'S STORY VI

As Stuart's departure approached, Emily felt a tightening of the nerves. 'The brown envelope came out again,' she says. 'I hated that rotten envelope. I would put it away and never look inside it. If I did, I thought, it would be a bad omen.'

Emily sips a glass of wine in the warm afternoon light.

'Afghanistan . . . such a horrible place,' she says. 'It's still very raw to me all these years later.' She had trouble sleeping, and this added to the emotional strain. 'I became very depressed,' she says.

At the time she was working for Senses Foundation looking after three men with intellectual disabilities. She would go to their house to make sure they looked after themselves properly by cooking their own dinner. She would do their finances, and their banking, and ensure they had packed their lunches, taken their medication and all the other necessities of a simple life. 'And when they had gone to bed,' she says, 'I would let myself out the door and come home to an empty house. That's when I would start thinking about Stuart

– where he was, what he was doing, what dangers he was facing.'

She had come to the Senses work after undertaking a course at Rocky Bay, in Perth's Mosman Park, a home for people with disabilities. Some were physically disabled and confined to wheelchairs others had mental issues, including dementia. It had earlier been a facility for quadriplegic children.

Since schooldays Emily had been drawn to psychology. Gradually this had been refined to a concern for children with autism and other intellectual disabilities. So when she saw just such a course advertised at Rocky Bay, she signed up.

'They teach you well,' she says, 'and at the end of the course I had to do a "prac" at Rocky Bay itself. These people are unable to brush their teeth. You have to do everything for them. I didn't want to do that. My specialty was autism, so I ended up going to work for Senses Foundation.' But even there she would have to wait until there was an opening for her preferred area.

The work with the disabled men filled the hours and had its compensations. But it was difficult to come home to an empty house. 'There were no suicidal feelings,' Emily says, 'I was just depressed. I went to the doctor and said, "I can't sleep," and he gave me sleeping tablets and antidepressants. He didn't talk to me or anything. I'm not a person of medicine. I didn't like to take it.'

As a young athlete she had always sought a physical solution to passing ills. She decided to use that strategy now. 'I joined a soccer team in Perth and played regularly,' she says. 'That helped. We trained three times a week and at the weekend we had competitions.' It was not easy to maintain the initial enthusiasm, since she was so much alone, so there were times when she pulled out. 'I go and then I stop and then I go again,' she smiles. 'But it helps.'

15

PATROLLING

In the early stages of this new conflict our role was ill-defined. Our Special Forces hierarchy had negotiated with the marines that we would head out on vehicle-mounted patrols, with the Americans in their LAVs and our lads in the LRPVs. This meant the whole squadron would be broken up into vehicle-mounted six-man teams. We knew it would be a learning curve for some of our blokes who were highly skilled in other roles such as parachute insertion and water and diving operations. And as expected it caused a few teething problems when they were caught out with simple things like operating in the sand with tyre pressures too high and continually getting stuck. It was embarrassing to have an eight-wheeled LAV pull out one of our prized LRPVs because the air operator had not lowered the pressure to suit the soft sand. But after some dirty looks and dirtier words all the boys became skilled at driving though the dunes.

On one such joint patrol we headed out as a troop with our troop commander Robbo leading our six or seven vehicles north into the Helmand River Valley. This was and still is a dangerous area, with many parts under the control of the fanatical Taliban forces. Robbo was a unique character in our unit, and initially our boys were cool towards him because of his caustic demeanour. He was a skilled air force fighter pilot and also a highly regarded forward air controller (FAC). He could fly a jet fighter and at the same time coordinate multiple jet aircraft to destroy targets on the ground. Just one of these tasks alone is a rare talent but combined it is a remarkable feat of multiple tasking.

Robbo was probably the best troop commander I would ever have. He was completely dedicated to the job and his boys in the troop. On one occasion while in Africa at the Mount Kenya Safari Club before Afghanistan, I heard some music coming from the hotel while I was out in the gardens checking out the wildlife, and went to check it out, expecting it to be a band or a blues DVD playing in the foyer. To my surprise it was Robbo tickling the ivories of the grand piano. That was just one of his many talents.

He would work till he dropped from sheer exhaustion, and had an amazing capacity for innovation. Later in the wars he was despatched on operations with the British Special Boat Squadron (SBS) in Iraq. Under fire, the British squadron commander was relieved of his position owing to a major tactical screw-up. I heard on the grapevine that the SBS had lost many of their squadron vehicles when they got stuck out in open ground and pummelled by enemy fire. Robbo was the next most senior officer and took charge of the squadron.

As our troop and the marine LAVs pushed through the desert of the Southern Helmand, we didn't encounter any opposition. We tried to remain clandestine most of the time by staying well out in the desert. We would occasionally come across small groups of men and boys heading south on small tractors or leading horses and carts. We questioned them but they told us very little. Dressed in black robes, they were usually armed with an AK-47 but would keep them out of sight. They knew they'd be no match for our heavy machine guns and Mk 19 grenade launchers. They would wait patiently while we searched their meagre belongings for any items that might reveal a hostile intent or a Taliban link. While they stood passively watching us, their eyes seemed to me to betray their true feelings of distaste or even hatred for us as infidels, invaders and possible puppets of an American regime. There were few smiles and it was obvious that life was harsh for these people. Later, I wondered how much hatred I would feel towards a foreigner invading my country and holding me at bay with his weapons while he searched my personal belongings. I would want to tear his throat out too.

At one stage we needed to cross the Helmand River and we searched for some time to find a suitable crossing point. This major watercourse tumbles down from melted snows far away in the mountains near the Pakistani border. The water is blue and clear and it flows fast. It is the lifeblood of the land, and along its banks and surrounding valleys there is a continuous ribbon of villages and farms. The buildings are almost all made from mud brick with small walled compounds around them.

The maximum fording depth of our vehicles was only about 90 centimetres, so we used our patrol motorbikes to scout the river's edge. We came across a local man on a camel who was also trying to cross the river. One of our patrol members approached him on foot and through sign language indicated we needed to cross the river in vehicles. He seemed more than happy to assist us.

His thin cotton clothing was completely unsuited to the harsh cold climate. He was wearing plastic sandals without any lining to keep his feet warm. I offered him some green army socks if he would show us where we could safely cross the river. He nonchalantly crossed on his camel, indicating a suitable path for the vehicles. We followed in our flotilla, with some of the motorbikes falling into the frigid water.

Once on the other side, with the motorbike riders trying to warm themselves and change their clothes, I kept my bargain and gave him the socks. He seemed over the moon with his new-found wealth and shook hands in thanks.

Then he went riding off into the desert and we never saw him again. This incident helped to emphasise to me the harsh reality of life in the Afghan desert.

On another patrol we needed once again to cross the Helmand River, this time near the village of Hazar Juft. It was just a dot on our maps but it had one unusual feature. It boasted the only concrete bridge across the river for many miles around. This was a well-constructed span about a hundred metres long. If we were to get over the river, we would have to approach it from the west, cross it and then drive through the township. Like many of the bitumen roads it had been built by the Russians when they occupied the country in the 1980s. As we stood some kilometres away from the village and surveyed its outskirts with our high-powered optics and thermal imagers, we began to identify the unmistakable outlines of heavy weapon emplacements on rooftops. It seemed that every second rooftop had a 14.5-millimetre Russian Dushka mounted and pointing towards the sky. Obviously these people were accustomed to trouble and were prepared for a fight.

Men could be seen standing about in their customary black robes and head garb with Kalashnikov assault rifles slung casually across their chests. We were on edge, and our US marine partners mounted in their LAVs were also cautious. The ubiquitous Hilux utility vehicles were parked all around, with people seated in the rear and bundles of RPG-7 rockets strapped upright like spears to the headboards.

These old beaten-up wagons were typical transport for both the Taliban and the Muj. They would trundle across the desert with up to ten men crammed inside.

We settled on a plan and advanced on the bridge. Our LAVs were up front with their light armour, with our patrol vehicles mixed in the column. We had decided to place two vehicles on the near side to provide fire support to the rest of the vehicles as we crossed. Once the first two cars were across, they would prop on the far side to provide additional fire support and then the remainder, at intervals of 100 metres, would rev up and cross flat out. This way we would minimise the chances of more than one LRPV or LAV being smashed at any one time by enemy fire.

As we got closer, the men in the village could see our plan and began to approach the bridge on their side. There was no open display of aggression; just calm acceptance and responses on their part. One of their utilities drove out from the village and onto the bridge. A heavy mature man got out and walked into the middle. He was unarmed and dressed as the rest of the locals were, but without the black robes. He began to beckon us with his arms outstretched. We stopped and watched, our weapons poised to fire, but we could see he was signalling a welcome to us from the village.

One of our interpreters, escorted by a few of our soldiers, moved forward and chatted with him. He was a village leader and he said he didn't want to see his people injured or the village damaged by more fighting. Our people explained that we needed to cross and that we were only interested in Taliban and not his village. After a few minutes we got the word from our troop commander that we would cross the bridge and proceed directly through the village and up into the hills on the far side.

We began to move again, pushing on slowly and deliberately, scanning our patrol arcs intensely as we went. The men in the village – a good few dressed in traditional black Taliban attire – didn't challenge us, but they stood and lined the streets, their unsmiling cold eyes drilling holes in the back of our heads as we rolled through their town. As we passed, I spotted a boy about 12 years old with an AK-47 slung across his chest like his father next to him. I watched with nervous interest as he began to raise the muzzle of the rifle, arcing around towards our vehicle. His father reached over and just as calmly placed his hand on top of the muzzle and pushed it down again. These people were steely hard, and sick of foreigners in their midst. They had been fighting invaders for hundreds of years, and killing infidels was as ingrained in them as breathing.

We got through unscathed, and from then onwards crossing through villages and populated areas proved to be the most hair-raising and tense times that we faced. Whether the men were friend or foe wasn't certain – and we could be staring at the most wanted man in Afghanistan but wouldn't know, as they all looked and dressed the same – and they all had those cold staring eyes.

Soon we began to patrol without the added security of our marine allies in their LAVs. In the lead-up to Christmas 2001 we prepared to move the entire squadron up to Kandahar, the traditional Taliban stronghold. This would involve a night and day road trip over several hundred kilometres north through the Helmand Valley and deserts then along the old Russian highway. We would pass through the city to the main airport, where we would establish a headquarters and new base from which to conduct all future operations. Along the way we would have periodic air support from US Apache and British attack helicopters as we approached likely areas of Taliban concentrations and townships.

The roads to Kandahar varied from good blacktop through to badly potholed areas and then to slippery gravel tracks. There were many abandoned trucks and burned out wrecks of cars and Russian military vehicles that appeared to have been destroyed by US forces.

Along the way we also passed many goods trucks that trundled slowly along on balding tyres at just a few kilometres an hour. Many of these ten-tonne trucks were decorated with bells and metal chains that hung from the cabin, so we called them jingle trucks. They were ferrying goods from Pakistan and Iran in and out of the country.

Our food for the journey and most of our time in the 'Ghan was mostly American MREs. They were packaged in small bags with a heat pack that could be activated by adding water, which was then placed alongside the meal sachet and quickly brought it up to a reasonably warm eating temperature. We also kept these water-activated heat sachets handy to heat up saline solution, which we all carried in case someone was wounded and needed intravenous fluids. Some of our other foods included Mars bars, high-energy milkshake cartons and extras we'd been sent by our families – especially Vegemite and decent-quality tea or coffee instead of the army ration-pack stuff. Some blokes even had cigars sent over. Most SASR blokes never smoked back home, as it would have affected their fitness, but when out on operations many (including myself) resorted to smoking as it was a small comfort on a freezing morning to be able to roll a fag or when you hadn't eaten all day, and it gave you something normal to do for a few short minutes.

En route to Kandahar we took regular short stops in the column to check navigation, grab a hot brew of tea or coffee or await an 'all clear' from our Apache helicopter top cover, which would scream overhead at 100 feet (30 metres) to scan areas for likely enemy ambush. On one such occasion while we waited and cooked up a quick billy of hot water, one bloke took the opportunity to go for a crap in a ploughed paddock on the side of the road. He found an upturned tree stump and went behind that to get a bit of privacy.

The local farmer spotted him and quickly rushed over to protest at this apparent outrage of the infidel crapping in his paddock. No doubt it was a terrible affront, and maybe bad form, but we stood there laughing our heads off at our poor comrade getting an earful from the local, unable to even take a shit in peace.

There was one strange moment as we passed through one of the smaller villages along the main highway. As we approached in the last light of a freezing cold afternoon, I scanned each side of the road from the driver's seat. As we sped closer to the village centre, I saw a young boy around ten years old run into the centre of the road and place something small in there. I couldn't make out what it was at first but I decided I would simply drive over it. Within a few seconds I was past, but as I passed I could see it was a small kitten jammed into the top of an open food tin. It was still alive and the child seemed to be playing some type of grizzly game to see if we would hit the animal in the can. Thinking about this later, I was struck by the reality of life in this inhospitable country, where children do such things that elsewhere in the world would be considered extreme forms of cruelty. Over here, life was very different and very cheap.

Approaching the outskirts of Kandahar at night, we again took a break from driving to get clearance from our early-warning teams, who had made it into the city earlier to scope out a safe route through. Once it came through, we moved forwards using night-vision equipment to drive and scan for likely threats. Local militia had set up many roadblocks on the way, and at each one we would stop briefly to get them to lift their blocks and allow us to pass. This was one of the most dangerous times, as these guys were an unknown quantity. On several occasions they raised their weapons in our direction as we stopped a few metres from them. This happened to one of my patrol guys in the front seat. The driver had limited time to respond in raising his own weapon to counter the threat, but our gunner Troy was on the ball and quickly swung the 50-calibre machine gun around to meet the militia sentry at eye level. The sight of the big muzzle in the half-light only a foot or two from your face would have been enough for anyone to completely lose their bundle. Troy described the sentry's face to me later, how he shrank backwards into the darkness, suddenly aware he was only a moment from a terminal blackout.

We finally reached the Kandahar airport shortly after midnight. As we approached the front gate of the massive, old, Russian-built, facility, I could see the US regular forces were already established at the main entrance. They were really gunned up, with missile systems mounted on the back of Humvees. We couldn't drive straight in, as the guards had placed heavy concrete blocks across the entry way. They needed to make it very difficult for a vehicle-mounted bomb or improvised explosive device (IED) to be driven into the base. It was so constricted that our vehicles could only proceed one at a time, and we had to do numerous multi-point turns to successfully negotiate the barricade.

Once inside the airport our column of LRPVs was guided by the US forces to a compound, which was to become our patrol base for the next four months. We were allocated a low line of office spaces facing the compound centre. Each of our patrols was allocated one office in which all members would set up a small sleeping stretcher. It was so crowded that we slept shoulder to shoulder; but that was only on the rare occasions that we were allowed to sleep there at all. In the coming months we would only spend a few days at a time at the patrol base and always in frenzied preparation for the next job.

16

JOINT TASK FORCE 106

After a night's sleep in our new base we sat down to a hot breakfast for the first time in weeks. The US had set up a small mess facility and mobile camp kitchen a few hundred metres from our office-cum-dormitory. The food was typically American military, with grits and other unfamiliar dishes, but it was steaming hot. We made the best of it, as we knew we'd only get the occasional hot breakfast; from now on it would be mostly the American MREs. This we ate in combination with our own Australian rations as well as others that we could trade with the Coalition forces nearby.

The base itself was a combined civilian and military airport with old Soviet-era aircraft and military stores all over the place. Our predecessors there had been the Taliban, who set explosive devices for us under their welcome mat. Over the next few days there was a constant series of explosions as US bomb techs destroyed these crude devices with their own explosives. These explosions sounded like rocket or mortar attacks and continually set our nerves on edge.

In our compound were various other Special Forces groups, including Dutch, German, Canadian and American. We were jointly known as Joint Task Force 106. However, Special Forces guys invariably like to work as a discrete force, so we tended to keep to ourselves.

We got to make our first contact back home to our families in Australia by email. We would not get a phone call until Christmas day, but around the base at Kandahar airfield the Americans had a couple of areas with computers where we could go and send some emails and later on make a phone call. The squadron also had a couple of computers that we could use but they were painfully slow as the satellite link was not the best. As there was always a line of blokes waiting to send emails, we would sometimes miss out, but at least communication was available. In February we got to watch the screen and see a delayed image of our partners back home in Australia.

Talking to Emily by email was a rare pleasure. The internet connection was slow and often cut out, but we got to talk almost in real time, and this made Em's life a little more bearable back in Australia worrying about where I was. We weren't allowed to discuss operational matters, so conversation was limited to what was going on back home in Australia and the outside world. Also I could ask her to send me things like tea and coffee, chocolate and magazines to read.

At Christmas we had a direct phone call, but that day I was sick as a dog. I had picked up a dose of giardia, a waterborne infection caused by a microscopic parasite that's found worldwide, especially in areas with poor sanitation and unsafe water. The symptoms are abdominal cramps, bloating, nausea and bouts of watery diarrhoea. I spent that day in my sleeping bag and the rest running to and from the toilet. Some cooks were brought in to make the blokes some traditional roast chicken and naan bread. Russ brought me a bit and it was the best I'd ever had, although I didn't eat much. Most of the night was spent sitting on the shitter in minus 10°C. I thought I was going to die. I'd picked it up from dust infected with the bug during LRPV driving through villages where raw sewage flows onto the tracks and is then lifted up in the dust.

After the first mail runs arrived in country, there were great piles of stuff for the boys, which their caring mums, wives and girlfriends had sent over in boxes. One of my favourites was Vegemite and SAO crackers. Another thing I loved was hot salami, which was great energy food to help you stay warm on bitter cold LRPV forays through the desert nights. Cigarettes, cigars and 'rolly' tobacco were high on the wanted list as well as extra cold-weather clothing such as woollen beanies and socks.

The Australian Army had a very limited range of cold-weather gear at that time. The last serious cold-weather operation that Australia had sent troops to was the Korean conflict. Prior to departure we had called in the mountain warfare guys and asked them to come up with a list we could buy off the shelf in outdoors shops around Perth. I had done some mountain training also, and we soon came up with a wish list that included tents, jackets, thermal underwear, Gore-Tex coats, boots, socks and fuel stoves. There were more than 60 blokes to fully kit out, and once the local stores had been emptied we bought the rest from interstate.

One item of gear close to every soldier's heart is quality boots, so we were all given a short list of mountaineers' boots from which we could choose two pairs. I got a set of Italian leather and Gore-Tex hiking boots that turned out to be okay, though most blokes went for a set of Scarpas. But no matter how expensive the boots, we all suffered terribly with ice-cold feet out on patrol. At one stage the Americans would offer us rubber boots, which slipped over our existing footwear. These were ridiculously large but we wore them as they relieved our miserable condition when the temperature on the ground was below minus 10°C. One of our patrol members, Guy, was about 195 centimetres tall with big feet to match, and the only set available for him was a huge white pair that made him look like a scary bearded Ronald McDonald.

One of our first trips out from Kandahar was to send a vehicle-mounted patrol to the foothills of a high spur of the Hindu Kush, an 800-kilometre mountain range extending from northern Pakistan across into central Afghanistan. We had been tipped off by the US Special Forces that there was a Taliban training camp hidden up there. Our squadron was tasked with an assault on the encampment and clearance of any enemy forces. As the camp was well hidden in extremely steep terrain, we decided to pre-position a mounted patrol as overwatch to provide essential information regarding the Taliban movements leading up to our assault.

The patrol was led by Matt, a strong member of our squadron who had been a friend of mine during our selection course. He had made good progress through the ranks and was now a patrol commander sergeant renowned for his consummate professionalism and also for his dry wit, which sometimes put others offside. But I definitely respected him for his tenacity and the OC knew he would get the job done. Our troop under Robbo, with Russ as my patrol commander, was given the task of inserting Matt's patrol by LRPV. We would carry them and their heavy packs in our six-wheel drive vehicles (in addition to our own patrol members) as far as we could to reduce the amount of walking they would have to do to get to the overwatch position.

To survive in the sub-zero conditions for several days prior to our squadron assault, they needed to carry additional gear to sustain them. This made their packs incredibly heavy. In fact another friend of mine, Shane – a huge man who was part-Aboriginal part-Native American – fractured a vertebra carrying his 90-kilogram pack, webbing and rifle up that mountain, and it would plague him ever after.

Another was Sam, who was closer to my stature, and who sat in the back of my vehicle at the start of the journey. After many hours of slowly coaxing our heavy LRPVs through rocky terrain during a freezing night, we eventually reached a point only metres from the steep mountain base. The six mountaineers dismounted and commenced to unload their packs from the vehicles. We jumped down to assist them. Mark and I lifted Sam's pack, and it was so heavy we feared for his welfare. Just getting the packs up the mountainside would be a feat in itself.

In the darkness just before dawn Sam leaned forwards as Mark and I positioned his pack on his back, and strapped and adjusted the load. As he stood upright, I heard the groan as he accepted the weight. Quickly the lads came together and then moved off up the sheer slope. We would not see them again until after the assault four days later.

While Matt's patrol made its way to the summit and relayed information on the enemy, the remainder of the squadron readied for the assault. The patrol and troop commanders prepared their orders and us 2ICs in each patrol did all the administrative work. This included: sourcing ammunition, water, rations and specialised equipment; booking intelligence briefs; test firing weapons at the range;

and liaising with signals staff to book signals briefs. And that was just part of it. From the time the warning order was given, the 2IC was usually the busiest person in the patrol.

On this mission we would be using quad bikes as well as LRPVs, and we would be inserting via helicopter. As always we would travel by night, land the helicopters several kilometres from the target area and move across country in the vehicles to establish our assault positions. My task with another patrol member was to ride a quad bike with a trailer carrying a mounted 50-calibre machine gun on a tripod. We also had to carry all our personal equipment and packs as well as hundreds of rounds of ammunition. This made the trailer very heavy and tough to handle.

The helicopter insertion using American Chinooks went off without a hitch, and from the dark and dusty landing zone we moved slowly with the other patrols towards the target. When we reached a point close to the target, we split up to head to our various positions. We had been advised that US Coalition aircraft had dropped Joint Direct Attack Munition (JDAM) laser-guided bombs onto the camp a day or so earlier, so we were expecting that there would be plenty of damage to the facility on our arrival. We were also advised that there were numerous caves and bunkers throughout the target area and these would need to be cleared during the assault.

As we approached slowly in the last few minutes before first light, the terrain became increasingly steep and rocky. This made it really difficult to ride the quad bikes, especially with trailers. When we crossed the steep slopes, we had to stand on one side of the bike and lean into the hill to stop it from rolling over. Just as the sun started to rise above the horizon, Mark and I reached the summit of a small hill overlooking the Taliban facility. Creeping up to the top of the hill, we expected to contact Taliban at any time, since their position had a commanding view of the area. We saw signs of destruction from Coalition aircraft, with bits of debris and documentation strewn about the area. Just in time I saw a landmine wedged between two stones. I gave it a wide berth.

Time for the assault was closing fast, so we had to hurry to get the machine gun and tripod off the trailer and lined up on the target area. We then added the traditional ammunition belts to those already on the weapon. We made it just in time for the opening salvos of the assault.

A ground force of US Special Forces, Afghan soldiers and our squadron swept up through the area from the south into the centre of the camp. Other teams had already been positioned up the valley to cut off fleeing Taliban forces. My job was to aim the weapon a few metres to the front of our formation and engage any threats to our men. I had to provide close cover while ensuring I didn't hit any of our own troops. That was the biggest risk, particularly since there were Afghan anti-Taliban forces mingled in with our attacking force.

The assaulters fired high explosives into the caves and threw grenades into the dugouts. We could see the small teams of Aussie, Afghan and US troops moving from bunker to bunker and to cave entrances. We could also see the massive craters peppering the ground in the valley above the caves from the Coalition aircraft the day before. Some of the bombs and rockets had apparently been ineffective and many caves were still intact. But many of them would have collapsed under the tremendous force of the bombs striking directly above them.

As the sun rose, we began to get a better view of the scene. We could also see where Matt and his patrol had been hiding out thousands of feet further up the mountains. The clearance was basically unopposed, and only a few Taliban fighters were detained, although anyone hiding in the caves would not have been found after the explosives collapsed them. I walked down into the camp, where I could see the trenches that had been laid out in a zigzag pattern to provide maximum protection to the Taliban.

The ground was littered with documents and I found some photographs of bearded men holding up the severed heads of their victims. Whether they had been taken at the facility recently I didn't know. But it showed me the brutality that these people could inflict upon another human being. Those images would stay with me forever.

I heard over the radio that John's patrol had had a heavy landing in their helicopter upon insertion. Apparently it had broken some of the landing gear and the chopper had to be recovered after the assault. Luckily no one was injured and the patrol vehicles were still able to conduct their mission. The pilot was a woman who would later be killed in another action in which we were involved in the Shah-i-Kot Valley.

Over the coming weeks and months we conducted many similar tasks searching for Taliban strongholds and training facilities. We had limited success, and some of the boys felt that the targets we were given were less than priority jobs. Whether or not this was the case, the lads were doing their best to perform well in difficult circumstances.

One long-range patrol was particularly challenging for our troop. It was a reconnaissance of the valley far to the south and east of Kabul. We needed a squadron patrol base for a resupply, so we secured a thin perimeter around an old remote Russian airstrip. This we nicknamed Patrol Base Bess. The airstrip was a kilometre or so long and had a few small mud-brick buildings on its outskirts that we could use to conceal a few of our vehicles. It was now February 2002 and winter was at full strength. With our open-top vehicles and each of us dressed up like 'Michelin man' with multiple layers of clothing to try to keep warm during the long nights, we really had to concentrate to stay alert, as the temperatures and wind chill plunged to minus 30°C.

While C Troop pushed from our patrol base towards the east and the mountains close to the border with Pakistan, B Troop had located a massive arms cache only 30 kilometres to the east of Bess. They had been busy for a day or so prepping explosives so they could destroy the hundreds of tonnes of ammunition, high explosives, mortars and landmines as well as old Russian T-72 tanks that were strewn about on a small hilltop close to a sprawling township. My patrol under Russell was tasked to resupply the troop with more explosives, as they didn't have enough to complete the entire blow in a single event.

That morning the temperature was the coldest we had experienced to date. The boys put on every layer of clothing they had before setting out from Bess east towards B Troop's location. Along the way it began to rain, and then the rain turned to snow, which turned to slush. We had to stop continually to make sure the boys weren't getting frostbite. On one of the stops the boys took a photograph of our vehicle, which was covered with white ice and looked like it was stuck in a huge deep freeze. Icy stalactites hung from the bar work and ice covered everything in the car.

To keep warm, we drank hot coffee from a flask, and at every stop we would jump up and down and run around the cars to try to keep the blood flowing through our frozen limbs. After several hours we approached the outskirts of the township where the boys had found their ammunition cache. We could see the small hill, which was no more than a few acres of high ground jutting up from the plains. On top were the outlines of anti-aircraft guns and the turret of a tank. We drove up the hill to the summit, where we met the other troop members, including my friend Sal, who had been buying naan bread from the locals and passing it out to some of his colleagues. He generously offered our patrol some, which we greedily ate.

While we passed the explosives to B Troop, I looked around the fortified position. There were underground bunkers that were open and full to the brim with all manner of ammunition. We were all well aware of the danger of mines, so every step was calculated. Because of the dangers, Russ minimised our time there, and we then headed back to Bess two hours away.

When we arrived, we were greeted with the shocking news that Sal had stepped on a small anti-personnel mine. He had been treated at the time by medics and evacuated by helicopter. He had lost part of his foot. Sal would spend the rest of this tour in and out of hospital back in Australia. He was at the squadron's homecoming back in Perth but his injuries eventually led to his discharge from the army, and I haven't seen him since that time.

Apparently his CASEVAC delayed the explosion, and we were back at Bess when they ignited the blast. A huge mushroom rose like a nuclear cloud high into the air above the distant township some 30 kilometres away. Several seconds later we heard the explosion as the sound carried on the frigid desert air.

A few days later we also heard the terrible news of Andy Russell's death.

EMILY'S STORY VII

The day Andy Russell was killed – 16 February 2002 – was Emily's birthday. She saw the report of the unnamed casualty on the nightly television news and telephoned the regiment. She couldn't get through. Then one of Stuart's SAS mates, 'Danno', called and he told her who had been killed.

'I was devastated!' she says. She knew Andy, and that made it personal; but the possibility that it had been her husband came crashing home. 'It is really hard on the families when you see on the news someone has died and you don't know if it's your loved one,' she says. 'I didn't sleep much at all; I would just go to work and come home and sit and watch the news. And I cried lots!'

The one consolation was that when Stuart was back at base camp, he was able to call her via Skype. 'It was great to have the internet and be able to speak and see Nev via video link,' she says. 'But he looked so different and so very skinny, with a bushy heavy beard and he had severe giardia. It needs to be treated with a strong course of specialised antibiotic. But because there were no pathology labs where Nev was working in Afghanistan, it took a while for it to be diagnosed and he suffered a great deal until it was properly treated by his medic John. Even now he still has stomach problems from the old infection.

'I was mentally, physically and emotionally out of whack. I went and saw the doctor and he basically handed me a script for antidepressants. It would have been nice if the doctor had listened to why I was down and maybe refer me to a psychologist. It was like those pills were just going to fix me. I don't think so.'

Emily was suffering the classic symptoms of a form of PTSD herself: anxiety, sleeplessness, hypertension; and there was very little she could do about it. She tried self-medication by opening a bottle of wine and drinking alone in front of the television set. But the emotional relief was fleeting and the side effects disproportionate.

'I know that watching the news was not a good idea but it was the only source of information that I had,' she says. And she was unable to share her fears and worries because of the nature of Stuart's work. 'It's difficult for the wives of the regiment. There wasn't much really that you can talk about to let some frustration out because you always have to watch what you say. I know I kept away from a lot of social gatherings for exactly this reason.'

17

CASUALTY

Andy Russell's death hit the whole regiment hard. He was a great bloke and a top soldier. When I heard about it, I was out on patrol not too far from where the tragedy occurred. We were patrolling to the south of the Helmand Valley close to the border where Iran and Pakistan meet, and we had linked up with a group of about 15 Afghan militia. We found them in a small village when we interrupted their lunch as they sat out in the open around a large blanket spread over the ground. They were eating rice and some meat as well as the usual hot sweet black tea. They also had a type of unleavened bread.

They invited some of us to sit and eat with them and share their meal, which we did. Of course we were cautious and aware that we may get sick from eating their tucker, and most of us at one time or another did get sick. But after months of rations and dehydrated foods it was extremely tasty, and I especially enjoyed the goat's milk yogurt that they used to flavour the meal. Our troop commander Robbo thought it might be a good idea to have them tag along. They were mounted in old Japanese Hilux 4WDs, and by patrolling with them we got to see them closer; they didn't improve on acquaintance.

On one occasion a strange relationship became apparent between a younger man and the leader. At night while we patrolled our perimeters on foot, the Muj would usually maintain a sentry well within the perimeter of ours, keeping watch while his comrades slept. Our sentry, Mark, could see what was going on because we had a thermal imager, which is very powerful, and could clearly see objects several kilometres away even in pitch darkness. Mark said that during the night he watched the senior commander get up and leave the back of his utility. He appeared to be disturbing and maybe molesting the younger man, and the following day the young man fired his weapon on full automatic into the air to vent his frustration. They had a saying: 'Girls for babies, boys for sex'. We didn't understand their ways, but it put us all on edge about the Muj and added to our concerns about how far we could trust the leader.

As we pushed through the barren desert, we came upon the rotting carcasses of large fish about 60 centimetres long lying out on the desert sands. This was very surprising, as the ground was parched and very flat. A few kilometres further along we saw small wooden boats lying on their sides in the dry sand. Where was the river or lake? Checking our maps, we could see the area at certain times was completely inundated, a little like Australia's Lake Eyre. We skirted it to ensure we didn't get bogged.

The patrol became a complete farce, as they expected us to be their hosts and provide them their fuel as well as tea at mealtimes. We ended up on a wild goose chase after they provided some really dodgy intel. However, there was one highlight. We established an observation post close to the three borders at the corner of Afghanistan, Pakistan and Iran. From there we could watch the activities of the Pakistanis in the high mountain range to our south and simultaneously the Iranian border stretching along a series of fences to our west. We had been looking at the routes any Taliban supply trucks were utilising into and out of Afghanistan from these bordering nations. The intel gathered showed just how porous the borders really were, and how anything could be moved in and out of Afghanistan from any neighbour.

After completing the task, we again moved north and set up a troop lying-up place (LUP) in the lee of a series of small creeping sand dunes slowly making their way northeast across the pebble-covered desert. As usual I put my dusty sleeping bag next to the driver's side wheels of our LRPV, dug a small hip-hole, lay down, then tried to sleep. I could hear the ever-present threat of the drones overhead watching us and searching the surrounds. It was supposed to be reassuring to have their extra eyes providing overwatch, but it put our nerves on edge.

Fortunately we had acquired a US Air Force special operations guy, Jess, who called up his command on the satellite comms advising them of our exact location so they could confirm us as friend and not foe. He was a young bloke from Hawaii who was great to have along on patrol, as his communication skills and easy way of coordinating air support was invaluable. Jess was a character, and often bore the brunt of much piss-taking from his Aussie friends.

It was the following day after we had moved further north and stopped at an LUP that we received the news over the radio that one of the patrol commanders from A Troop had sustained fatal injuries after his LRPV had struck a mine just ten kilometres to the north of our position.

The boys were numbed, as Andy was so full of life it was hard to imagine that he could have been killed. News also came that Fred the 2IC and the gunner Picko on the same vehicle had sustained minor injuries. Apparently, when the explosion struck, Picko had been thrown some metres from the cupola of the LRPV and landed nearby, relatively unscathed. Fred had been in the driver's seat and was lucky to survive, as the bullbar had peeled around and struck the metal just near his legs. Fred had been advised not to move when he saw Andy lying injured nearby, but had ignored the risk of further mines and calmly treated Andy by tying his trouser belt as a tourniquet around his leg to stem the blood. An American pararescue-jumper (PJ) med team had bravely been flown in to assist, but to no avail. Andy's injuries were terrible, and he was kept alive only a short time before he succumbed to the trauma. I believe one of the US PJ medics who had assisted later died in the Battle of Anaconda. Coming on top of Sal's injuries, the effect was to drive home to us that nowhere was safe in Afghanistan. Death or disabling injury was waiting around every corner.

During the nights at Patrol Base Bess the temperature would plummet to around minus 15°C. To counter the bitter cold, we put up two- and three-man tents. They provided a basic level of protection from the biting winds. It was a risky solution because it reduced our ability to hear approaching threats but really there was little choice – the alternative was hypothermia and frostbite. All our drinking water froze in the night, including our plastic 20-litre jerry cans on the vehicles. In the mornings they would be solid lumps. To remedy this I would sleep with a water bottle in my sleeping bag. Body heat would keep it in a liquid state so I could have a drink when I woke up, but it was just like sleeping next to an ice-cold water bottle instead of a hot one.

Our equipment was affected. Our weapons and machine guns would be coated in a thin layer of frost and ice. Mud would freeze into icicles as we drove through puddles. Batteries would give out after just a few short hours of use. Any area of skin would get frost nip if left exposed, so you had to be completely covered from head to foot when driving in the vehicles. The ambient temperature alone was not the worst of it. Our LRPVs had no heaters, windscreens, roofs or doors, so as you travelled at night the wind chill would take the temperature down to minus 30°C.

Most worrying was that our LRPVs would not start or run correctly, and this could leave us exposed to the enemy. We quickly figured that the diesel fuel in the dual tanks had become so cold that a layer of paraffin sludge was forming, causing the fuel systems to block up. We noted that each morning the locals would light a small fire on the ground under their trucks' fuel tanks to get the juice flowing for the day's journey. We couldn't do this due to security and time constraints, so we needed to come up with a better plan and fast. We were literally sitting ducks without our capacity to move quickly.

After some discussion with headquarters the command came over the radio that an aerial resupply would deliver aviation fuel to us. They had chosen JP8, which was not diesel but closer to kerosene, and it wouldn't be affected by the low temperatures. We were concerned about how our vehicles would cope with this highly flammable liquid designed for jet aircraft. But when it arrived by C-130, we quickly drained the hundreds of litres of diesel out onto the ground from the LRPVs' two large fuel tanks and then refilled the tanks with it. We also cleaned the filters and lines by bleeding them and hand pumped the primers with the JP8.

Then, with a certain trepidation, we started them up. To our surprise and pleasure they ran even better than they had in normal conditions. The US mechanics had warned us that the JP8 would cause the engines to run hot and might reduce their life expectancy. That was not our top priority; we just needed them to do the job then and there. Once the fuel had been changed, we could again focus on the job at hand, which was searching for the Taliban.

We spent a few more days at Bess and met some of the local tribesmen. Their alliances were sketchy at best. They seemed to have some control over the local area and claimed to be Muj. I think anyone who had a gun in that environment would use it to maintain authority, and they would make allegiances with whoever they could to protect their position. Most were headquartered at a disused Russian power station near a dam about three kilometres away, but they moved about much like us in small groups or militias in their dilapidated Hilux utes. Whether or not they were our friends or enemies was hard to tell, and we didn't trust them. But at times we were able to sit down with them and drink tea, which seemed to be one of their favourite pastimes. If we were lucky, one of them would speak a little English, but usually we could only communicate with them through an interpreter. Simple jokes and gestures were usually the best way to break the ice and get on friendly terms with them. To me they often seemed childlike in their humour, gossiping and giggling among themselves about something that we could not understand.

They were very interested in our equipment, our vehicles and especially the weapons. They, of course, had their own weapons, generally Soviet Kalashnikovs, variations of the AK-47, and RPG grenade launchers. And on some of their vehicles they had mounted a 12.7-millimetre heavy machine gun and even multi-barrelled anti-aircraft weapons.

Their lives were simple and harsh, and they appeared to survive with the very barest of essentials. Even in the coldest winters their clothes were just thin cotton long shirts and cotton pants, and their feet were clad in open sandals. To them we must have seemed completely overburdened with our masses of specialised equipment and cold-weather clothing. They usually slept on thin mats with a blanket on the cold earth or concrete floor of a mud hut near that dilapidated Russian hydropower station.

They ventured out each day when the weather and fuel permitted. They seemed to be as wary of us as we were of them. We never saw any women with them, though they told us that some of them had families with children. Our main reason for building a relationship was simply to gather intelligence on the areas we were about to visit. But even then we took nothing as gospel.

Late in our deployment we received word that the entire squadron was to move to a new patrol base near Kabul, where the US and Coalition forces were establishing a command centre at Bagram Airbase. We mounted our vehicles and commenced the long road move in the dead of night northwards from Kandahar along the main highways and heavily potholed Russian roads towards the ancient capital of Kabul. We were already fatigued after nearly four months of operations and the drive up in midwinter was long and cold.

Upon arrival we hoped we would be able to get our heads down for a few hours' rest, and when we finally rolled in we were allocated a large aircraft hangar near an airstrip. We parked our LRPVs and met up with a few squadron members who had arrived the previous day. They told the boys to have a rest, as most were walking zombies, but we had only a half-hour's kip before we were hauled out and headed to a new operation to the east in the high mountains bordering Pakistan. A concentration of Taliban had been detected there and they would be targeted in a massive assault by Coalition and US aircraft, Special Forces and local Muj.

The men were disappointed at not being able to rest longer but also excited by the prospect of a new battle. We knew that part of the country. It was where my patrol with Russ as the patrol commander had inserted a month earlier up that steep mountain valley to try to get eyes on the target area. On that occasion our troop moved by night as far as we could along mountain trails, past dark villages until even our LRPVs could no longer take the steep terrain.

Our patrol split from the rest of our troop and moved by foot to a point around 10,000 feet (3048 metres) high, where we were assured that given the right weather conditions we would be able to view the villages in the Shah-i-Kot Valley where Taliban forces were believed to have gathered in a big concentration. We departed the main troop harbour with our packs just before the sun rose ready to spend a full day trying to get eyes on. As we climbed higher, just the six of us, the weather closed in and it began to rain; and as we climbed still higher, the rain became snow. The snowflakes were like big feathers that felt ice-cold on your skin and then instantly melted to soak down your neck and into your warm underclothes. After two hours of trudging we eventually came to a plateau and moved across to its north-eastern edge, where we felt that once the weather cleared we would be able to see the target.

We concealed ourselves behind jagged boulders with two men at a time on watch, and used our powerful zoom lenses and camera equipment to try to get a bead on the activity below. We took turns trying to peer through the clouds or resting, eating and sending back radio communications to keep our headquarters updated. But after a few hours the weather hadn't changed and we began to feel that our efforts would be in vain and that we'd have to return without anything valuable to report.

As I peered into the fog and drifting snow, I suddenly saw the clouds part and we had a glimpse of a green valley surrounded steeply on all sides by high mountains. In the heart of the valley there were ploughed fields with rivers and creeks and numerous mud-brick compounds and small buildings. On some of the lesser peaks on the flanks we could see men dressed in black robes digging pits. Guy quickly aimed his camera lenses to snap some images before the weather closed in. At the same time Troy, our sig, sent messages of what we were seeing back to higher command. At one point through the binoculars I was lucky enough to see an old Russian BTR 40 armoured vehicle moving quickly between vegetation in the far distance near a village.

The Taliban were obviously well aware of the capabilities of US drone aircraft and satellite imagery, and were trying to hide from them. I could also see soldiers carrying rifles standing in front of buildings. This and other intel we immediately relayed back to HQ. They responded asking if we were in a position to call in an air strike. Luckily I had done that basic air contact officer's course in the Kimberley and advised Russ that we could do the job if needed. All the boys were excited now. Minutes later a second signal came through telling us to get out of the area; we had to be at least 30 kilometres away by 6 p.m. that day. We were disappointed that we wouldn't be around to see the action. But it was clear that something really big was planned. Shah-i-Kot would never be the same again. The Battle of Anaconda was about to unfold.

18

THE HAMMER AND THE ANVIL

Moving 30 kilometres in itself would be a difficult task, as it had taken us almost four hours to walk from the troop harbour. We frantically packed and prepared for a forced march back down through the valleys to rendezvous with our troop. We had to continually look to the rear, the flanks, the front and up above for any threat. Eventually we made it back to the relative safety of the troop harbour but there was no time to rest. The troop commander quickly briefed us to be ready to move within minutes back to our old Russian airstrip at Bess about 120 kilometres away.

I was hot and sweaty from the march downhill and absolutely starving, so I quickly opened a cold tin of Australian rations and wolfed it down. I needed energy for the drive back through the cold night and rain. Soon we were snaking our way down the mountains and west towards the plains. In the darkness I had to use NVGs and periodically I'd see a flash of infrared light illuminate our column from the US C-130 gunships flying high overhead. We had special panel markers across the bonnet of each vehicle to reflect an indicator that we were friendly and hopefully avoid being fired upon.

The road back was steep and rough but we moved at speed. At one stage I felt the car drop from under me as we hit a deep pothole and the front left tyre blew. We rolled to a stop to carry out repairs. By now my whole body was chilled to the bone, and the sweat on the inside of my clothes and coat had made me hypothermic. As I lifted the spare tyre onto the vehicle, I felt a sharp pain in my back.

After the wheel nuts were tightened and the tools were packed away, I found I could no longer stand straight but was hunched over staring at my boots. The combination of the cold and the pain in my legs and back meant the rest of the journey was the toughest I've ever had. I continued driving for a while but I couldn't see straight, so the troop commander told me to take a break and jumped into the driver's seat. It was freezing cold, one of the coldest nights I could remember, and as we raced through mud puddles the water spray quickly solidified into icicles hanging from the bar work on the car.

After what seemed like hours of bouncing and wincing through the pain, we came upon Bess and the rest of the squadron, who had set up a few tents in anticipation of our arrival. Some of the lads helped me out. Our medic gave me some anti-inflammatories and painkillers and then helped me into my sleeping bag, where I stayed until the following morning.

The squadron commander allowed us to sleep in until 7 a.m. My back now felt a little better and I was able to stand up relatively straight. Apparently the information we had gathered had been vitally important to the Coalition forces and was being used to help formulate an intelligence picture for the upcoming battle. For his part in the effort our patrol commander Russ received a commendation.

It would be almost four weeks before the US high command gave the order to attack. It would be a classic 'hammer and anvil' operation, with US and Muj forces coming in from the north as the hammer and a US Ranger Company inserted by helicopter into the valley as the anvil. On the eve of the battle they moved us overland from Kandahar to Bagram, where the squadron recon party was holed up in a giant hangar. We only had time to get our heads down for a few minutes before we were shaken awake and told to mount up to head into the mountains where we had been a month earlier. We were tired, but still dead keen to get into the action, so we quickly dressed in all the clothes we could find and headed out through the heavily mined verges and potholed roads towards the Shah-i-Kot Valley.

Our task was to cut off the Taliban fighters who were squeezed between the hammer and anvil and had fled our way from the attack. We arrived the following day in good weather and set up our cut-off position some five kilometres west of the entrance to the valley. We assumed our regular troop defensive perimeter on a low hilltop with interlocking heavy weapon arcs. We had a commanding view and were perfectly positioned to take on fleeing forces or reinforcements heading into the fight. We were also somewhat exposed, so I set to work digging some shallow shell-scrapes or foxholes in case of a mortar attack. My patrol commander Russ thought this was unnecessary, but humoured me by letting me dig most of them myself with the help of Troy and Guy. Luckily the ground was soft, so it didn't take long to have enough cover for each of our six members.

We spotted an SUV moving swiftly towards our position en route to the valley. We despatched two LRPVs at full speed to stop the vehicle and, if necessary, destroy it. But when he saw us coming, the driver turned and headed flat out back the way he'd come. It was too late and our lads had them. Luckily there were no shots fired, and the occupants turned out to be a load of journalists. They were very lucky not to have been engaged by our machine guns. Among them were a woman and a couple of men who seemed annoyed we'd stopped them. We held them for a couple of hours and eventually handed them over to US forces to be escorted away.

Suddenly a massive bombing raid smashed high explosives into the valley and surrounding hills. We could easily see the American and British war planes – B-52s, F-15s and Warthogs high above – dropping their deadly payloads onto the sheer mountainsides where Taliban fighters were dug into caves. We watched their bomb-bay doors open with a mixture of awe and terror as the bombs fell away from the fuselage. Since the B-52s were at such a great height, it was difficult to tell where the bombs might land; sometimes they would appear directly overhead and the falling dark specks seemed to be heading straight towards our position. When they struck the ground, we would first see the dark plumes of smoke, and several seconds later hear the staccato thunder, as they exploded in quick succession.

After an hour or two waiting at this cut-off position, I noticed an old man in the distance among the rocky gullies slowly approaching our location on foot. I wondered what he was doing walking about alone in such a forbidding and dangerous place. When he got within 50 metres, I grabbed some food rations out of my pack and took them out to him. I could see that he was unarmed and posed no threat. He was very thin and appeared around 60 years old, was dressed in rags and carried little except a cloth sack with his meagre possessions. I offered him the plastic bag of rations, and he seemed over the moon with gratitude. After that I motioned him to leave and he wandered slowly away back into the low hills and valleys.

Late that afternoon we were listening to the radio chatter over the satellite comms and could hear the US pilots talking between themselves, Special Forces on the ground and higher command back at Bagram. The ground unit had sighted some vehicles to their south that appeared armoured and were possibly Taliban. Plotting their position quickly on our maps, we concluded that they were viewing *our* position from further up the valley. Immediately we contacted the unit and told them in no uncertain terms that we were in fact a Redback unit and not Taliban. This showed how easy it was for friendly forces to be attacked by mistake. We were always on edge, and whenever we made a short stop we always spread out a big Aussie flag on the ground near our vehicles so that we might be identified better from the air. I'm not really sure how effective this would be if viewed from an aircraft flying at 20,000 feet (6096 metres) at 800 km/h, but anything was better than nothing. There were, of course, other checks and balances that had to be completed prior to destroying a target with air strikes, but we did not want to test that system. At night we could not see the planes or smoke from the impact, but rather the flash and sparks as the ordnance struck the hard granite and stones of the mountainside and produced a hail of burning hot shrapnel.

That evening a new task was radioed through to our troop commander Robbo. We quickly gathered about the vehicles to listen to his orders. We were to move closer to the battle zone and establish an observation post on high ground. This would split the squadron. A Troop would remain down in the valley as cut-off while C Troop (us) would climb a high point a few kilometres further east to be able to see fleeing Taliban. We could then direct A Troop onto them.

We moved before dawn along a wide rocky riverbed in our LRPVs and then split from the other troop and headed up great buttresses of jagged mountainside. After several hours of slow travel we located a sheltered saddle between two high points and circled the vehicles into a defensive position. Russ and I then climbed up a steep ridge line to find a suitable observation post. Once we identified a good spot, we called the troop commander on the hand-held radio to advise him to send the remainder of our patrol up.

It turned out to be a great vantage point, and before the ground battle commenced we were able to direct A Troop onto small groups of men on foot, mounted on donkeys and sometimes on vehicles. The vehicles were the most difficult to stop, since by the time we had alerted the cut-off force to their position they had usually fled into one of the small mud-brick villages to the south-west and were almost impossible to identify. Once they saw our LRPVs closing on them, they made a beeline towards an inhabited area.

While straining my eyes through the spotter's scope, I experienced a strange situation. Out to the north-west a man dressed in black approached a donkey that his wife or daughter had placed out in the desert several hours earlier. Suddenly and very gently the scope began to sway left and right away from the focus point. Initially I thought I had bumped it with my hat, but then realised we were caught in an earthquake. The scope swayed and the ground silently moved for around ten seconds. The rest of the patrol looked stunned, not knowing if it might come again and shake us from our precarious perch. It didn't, but it was the first time I'd ever experienced an earth tremor.

We remained on task for several hours, staring through our binoculars and telescopes trying to pick out any movement far below. When Russ took over the spotter duties and I decided to rest my sore eyes, he became agitated that I was not assisting and this led to a clash between us. This was not very professional on my part. It was just pent-up frustration at being stuck so close together for so many months, and I told him to find himself a new 2IC. After a few minutes things cooled off and we again focused on the task at hand. Just before dark we were relieved by another patrol and came back down the mountain to get some much needed sleep.

Before first light we were all awakened by the bombardment further up the valleys. We gathered again for a brief from Robbo. A US CH-53 helicopter carrying troops had been shot down by RPG and small arms fire as it approached its landing zone. One of our B Troop patrols was already in situ calling in air strikes onto enemy positions as they attacked the survivors on the ground. Matt's was the patrol up on the mountain top. They were mountain-warfare trained and were able to see along one side of a ridge and valley but couldn't see the other side, so we deployed as a troop minus a single patrol left to secure the vehicles. We climbed up to an elevation of about 10,000 feet (3048 metres) to assist Matt from a different vantage point and to call in air strikes on the enemy below.

To get some of our gear up there, we took several quad bikes that could be cached at the bottom of the steeper sections until needed for the return trip. The climb was a hell of a challenge. We had to cover almost seven kilometres as quickly as possible over steep and rough ground along valleys and over several spurs get to the foot of a very steep peak. Then we had to scale it hand over hand with our heavy packs dragging us down. In the final 200 metres we clawed our way to the top of a narrow saddle between two rock pillars. Some guys were struggling and had to be helped over the last few metres of the almost vertical climb.

Just prior to reaching the top, I was able to look across to a far hilltop about two kilometres away and see three or four men dressed in snow cammo fatigues lying prone on the snow-covered ground. This was obviously Matt's patrol, and they were definitely doing it harder than us, as we at least had numbers if something went wrong. They had been there for a couple of days, and had to lie still for many hours to remain concealed from the enemy.

Finally we could look down an almost vertical pitch 300 metres to the valley head below. US and other Coalition forces – the 'anvil' – had congregated to go toe to toe with the Taliban. I dug a shallow terrace into the side of the rocky ground so that a couple of our patrol could share it as a rest place. At the summit some 20 metres above, there was a narrow plateau from which the troop commander could direct aircraft mini-gun fire, as well as rockets and bombs onto enemy targets. This close air support commenced immediately we reached the summit and continued on all through the night. Robbo, Matt and Russ stayed up while some of us caught a few hours' rest. Robbo was probably the best FAC in the Australian Defence Force (ADF), as he had written doctrine on it for the air force, so he was invaluable in this situation. All through the night the 2000 pounders and mini-guns roared, and sleep was almost impossible on the stony cold and sloping ground. Some of the biggest shells hit just over the edge of our mountain-top hideout and we felt the shockwave, saw the massive flash and heard the hot metal rip the air overhead.

As dawn approached, we were able once again to see the situation clearly below, including the remains of at least two helicopters that had been destroyed where they had landed under heavy enemy fire. We could also see the US ground force's positions and occasionally caught sight of scurrying Taliban fighters moving between small mud buildings or along ridges as they manoeuvred for positions to engage Coalition troops.

The sky overhead was alive with aircraft all hours of the night and day. One minute it was a predator unmanned aerial vehicle (UAV) droning slowly around 3000 feet (914 metres) above. Next we'd see a stream of B-52s fly in from thousands of kilometres away. Then it was Warthogs farting their deadly hail of 30-millimetre cannon fire down onto the rocks and ridges below. F-15s circled higher still and occasionally screamed down below the safe threshold to deliver a JDAM and then screamed upward again, sometimes followed by the snake trail of a surface-to-air anti-aircraft missile that the Taliban had somehow obtained.

When the jets caught sight of the incoming missiles, they would immediately deploy a myriad of brightly coloured flares of glowing light designed to divert the heat-seeking missiles from their exhaust trails. It was a fantastic, terrifying and awe-inspiring display, and I wondered how anything could possibly survive the terrible onslaught as high explosives struck their targets and jagged hot metal shrapnel flew at supersonic speeds across the rocky frozen ground.

We remained in that high vulnerable position for two days, with our troop commanders and PCs continually calling in air strikes on the valley floor. After a few hours on day two we were advised that our troop would be relieved of our duties there and A Troop from 1 Squadron would take over. They would be slightly better equipped to cope with the cold and would bring equipment to sustain them for a few days. Our job was done and we would make the long freezing trip by foot and then LRPV back to Bagram.

Soon we saw the soldiers of A Troop at the base of the hilltop making their way hand over hand up the steep pass leading to our position. I would be one of three blokes to ride the quad bikes back down the valley to liaise with our vehicles. The remainder of the troop would walk beside us and provide security along the way. I was not pleased with that, as I knew how vulnerable riders would be to anyone who wanted to take a pot shot at us. But someone had to do it. For the last two hours on that hilltop I had been up in the second observation post location, which was about 40 metres higher than the main element of the troop and was totally exposed but offered great visibility down into the valley on the eastern side of the spur. Despite the danger it was a great place to be. The sun was out that morning and the sky was clear.

It felt as though you could almost reach across and touch the massive mountains just a kilometre away. They were higher than the one we were on, and any Taliban sniper worth his salt would be able to pick us off from there. I kept my head low to avoid silhouetting against the granite slabs surrounding us.

Finally two blokes from Paul's A Troop climbed the last few metres to our observation post. We gave them a warm welcome and a briefing. Now it was our turn to move out, so we said goodbye and climbed back down to the troop camp, threw our packs on and began the steep descent of the mountain. At the foot of the steepest section I recovered one of the quad bikes concealed under some vegetation and rocks. We loaded it up with the packs of those who were carrying injuries so they would have an easier time walking the more than six kilometres back to the vehicles. Then we moved as a troop along the ravines and creek beds to our vehicles.

Patrolling with locals in the Helmand Valley.

A meeting with some village elders.

Two local villagers.

Our patrol commander, fighting the cold.

On the side of the highway out of Kandahar.

A camp on an airstrip built by the Russians.

A patrol lying up in the mountains in the eastern part of Afghanistan.

I'm in the middle, facing away.

The remains of a Russian helicopter – still there at Bagram Airbase.

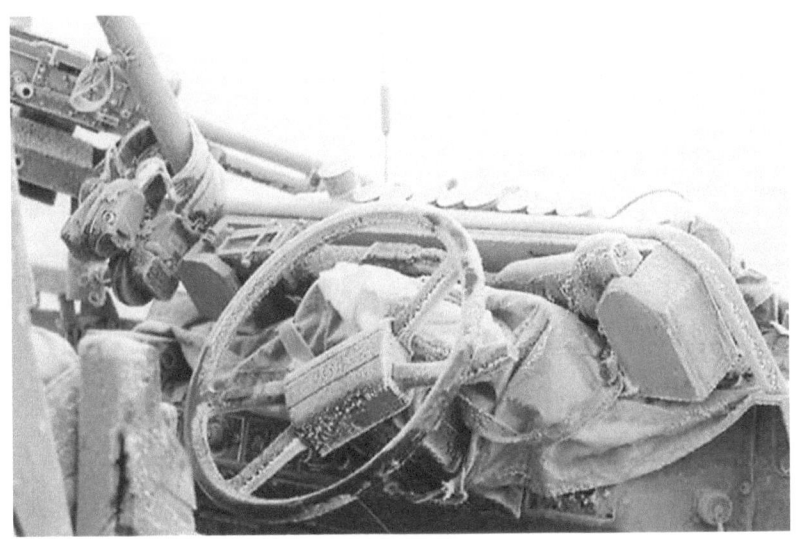

A frozen vehicle.

A goat carcass – donated by local villagers – being prepared for cooking.

The first meal after Operation Anaconda – I'm on the left.

An underground weapons cache left by the Taliban.

Outside the weapons cache.

An air strike in the Shah-i-Kot Valley.

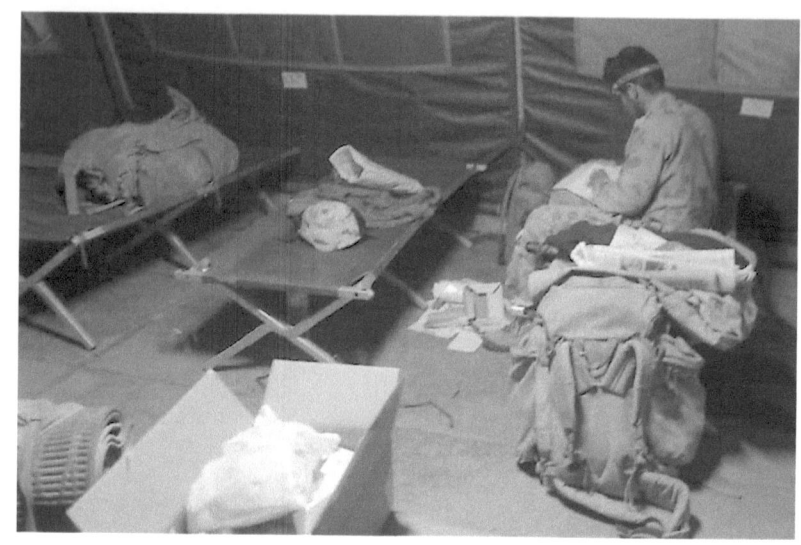

Reading mail from home.

Coming back from Operation Anaconda.

19

AFTER AFGHANISTAN

Two hours after we left our position, we heard over the radio that Paul's troop had engaged two enemy combatants as they approached up the spur. Apparently they had decided to take an unconventional route out of the valley to escape the terrible bombardment that had been raging for days. Paul sighted them 100 metres away as they made their way towards his position. He told me he engaged them both with his M4 and struck one of them square on. They retreated back over the edge of the spur and were not seen again.

When we finally made it back to the vehicles, we put on all our cold-weather gear for another long hard drive back to Bagram. I was tired but I remember well the last few kilometres as we drove into the airbase. We must have been a wild-looking bunch with our long, crazy, windblown hair and thick beards. There were some media about as we reached the huge hangar where we'd slept so briefly a few days ago on our way out. We were greeted by the CO and some of the other staff from 1 Squadron Headquarters. It had been a whirlwind of activity, the highlight of the entire trip to Afghanistan.

We were all tired, but a hot meal was offered and we were told to go into the mess in a hangar across from ours. I washed my face and dried my beard so I wouldn't look quite so feral. I could see a line of US soldiers waiting at the bain-marie while the cooks loaded up their plastic plates with hot food. To my great surprise they saw us coming and stood aside to let us all through to the front of the line. It was a small gesture, but one that the boys of C Troop really appreciated. It was the US soldiers' way of saying, 'Thanks, fellas, and welcome back.' They had heard about the job that the Aussies had done to support their troops on the battlefield and were letting us know that it meant something to them.

Bagram was just a haze for the next couple of days as we waited for the remainder of 1 Squadron to come back in from the field. It took a while but finally A and B Troops made it to base.

Then came the night I stood out on the freezing tarmac smelling the hot kerosene exhaust from the C-17 and trying to block my ears from the high-pitched roar of the massive engines as we loaded all our equipment into the cavernous back end of the great machines. After five long months our operation in Afghanistan was done and we were bound for Kuwait for a week or two before another long air trip back to Australia.

It seemed to end so suddenly after the long non-stop combat activity where we couldn't relax for a moment. We'd lost a top soldier in Sergeant Andy Russell to a landmine and almost lost another, Tristan, who was badly injured when he stepped on a mine. But we'd acquitted ourselves well, and in the circumstances the casualties could have been a lot worse.

In Kuwait we had time to rest and try to return to some form of normalcy. I found that I slept every day for most of the day, only getting up to go to the mess. Most of the other 1 Squadron blokes were the same, and it must have looked odd to the incoming squadron to see everyone in bed asleep in the middle of the day, every day. We were exhausted from the long ordeal, and this was the body's way to recalibrate itself.

Whenever I went to the mess, I found myself deliberately walking on the concrete and not allowing myself to step onto the gravel or dirt. I was still subconsciously trying to minimise the risk of stepping on a landmine.

We all had to have some sort of psychological interview, which was part of the established processes for returning to Australia after operations. We had it after Timor as well. Most blokes spoke very little – just the bare minimum to get through it as quickly and as painlessly as possible. I'm sure the psychs knew that we just went through the motions and told them the answers they needed so as not to raise a flag. There were questionnaires to fill in, and most of us just ticked the boxes to avoid raising any alarm. I didn't want to sit down and discuss things about operations with someone I hardly knew and who would be judging me on what I said to them. Just tick no, no, no on the questionnaire; just answer no, no, no in the interview so I could get the hell out.

On the plane back to Australia I was nervous about seeing Emily again after so long away. We were told our return would be a big deal, with pollies including the PM John Howard coming over to see us arrive at Swanbourne. That was okay, and I think the boys appreciated it. But for me, seeing Emily waiting there in the hangar was quite emotional, and I gave her a long hug. She was very emotional as well, especially when we saw Tristan in a wheelchair welcoming all his comrades home. He had been flown back a few weeks earlier to receive treatment for his injuries.

We were all given a month off to have a break and take our families away for a holiday or try to resume our normal routines back in Australia.

Looking back, we were ill-equipped on that mission. The army should have been aware that our fuel was unsuited to the cold. We shouldn't have been placed in a situation where we were sitting ducks when our fuel lines clogged up. And we weren't really prepared for what faced us when we arrived. It was kind of like the Wild West. Everyone had a gun, even the kids. There were ten-year-olds walking around with Kalashnikovs hanging around their necks. In some towns there was a Dushka heavy machine gun on every third or fourth building with a guy sitting behind it. But that's what they're like; it's a feudal place where there is constant fighting between towns and clans. They had been doing it forever.

As you drove through, your eyes would be like dinner plates and you would direct your rifle at any threat. It was a very foreign environment for an SAS unit to be in. We wanted to be unseen, but there we were the centre of attention. We could have easily been badly knocked about; it was terrifying and it would have been a living hell if it had turned loud. It didn't happen, but you'd see the hatred in the eyes of the men and also the children.

I recall one of the towns we went through. It was close to Kandahar and it was called Lashkar Gah. Once we got to Kandahar, we had to travel through it regularly. It was kind of a No Man's Land; every time you'd drive through, you'd wonder if you'd make it without being shot at. If there was an opportunity to kill a foreign invader, they would take it, but they picked their battles wisely.

Emily and I were now living in our own house in Perth's northern suburbs, which we bought in 1997. We just stayed home. I didn't really want to go anywhere; I was just happy to be back in Australia. We may have had a short trip away on a weekend, but nothing big.

None of us knew it yet, but our rest would be a brief one and a time of reflection before leaving for a new theatre of conflict: Iraq. However, before that I was lucky enough to get another trip to Hereford to spend time with 22 SAS, and on this occasion we were going back to Africa to train around Mount Kenya for a couple of weeks.

I'd done some rock and mountain climbing in Australia, and when we got to Africa most of the blokes went off to do a vehicle-mounted training exercise. But because I'd had some experience in mountaineering, they assigned me to the mountain troops. So while the mobility guys were doing live fire shoots and training in the desert, I was climbing on Mount Kenya, travelling across glaciers. I just got lucky.

We did two weeks up around 15,000 feet (4572 metres) on Mount Kenya and it nearly killed me. I went as far as 16,200 feet (4938 metres) but did not go to the summit. However, three weeks at that altitude really took the weight off, and when we came down to the military camp at Nanyuki at around 6000 feet (1829 metres) it was like being turbo-powered by the rich air.

After three or four weeks' hard training, we had some time off. Most of the guys wanted to go to the coast and have a couple of days there, but I thought, My in-laws live in Kaptagat; I'll hitchhike over there and see Emily's mum and dad. When I mentioned it, the CO said, 'Why don't you go and talk to the chopper pilot and see if he'll take you?' So I had a chat with him. I told him the village where they lived, pointing to a dot on the map, and said, 'They've got a blue roof; can you take me there?'

Being a Brit Special Forces aircrew, they said, 'Yeah, let's go.' So they jumped in a Gazelle helicopter and flew us from the base of Mount Kenya, down through the Rift Valley and over lakes filled with flamingos, up an escarpment on the western side of the valley, about 9000 feet (2743 metres) high.

As we reached the far side of the rift escarpment, I heard the pilot say, 'This is gonna be close.' It looked to me like we were going to hit the mountains but we just got over with metres to spare. The helicopter nearly didn't make it; we were literally skimming over the trees as we approached the village. And then they were flying around looking for a blue roof. I was the only one in the back with my feet out the door looking. Finally they said, 'Mate, we can't find it. Why don't we go to the nearest airstrip and we'll drop you off there?'

So they took me to Eldoret International Airport, which is pretty small, and they pulled up on the strip and I got out with my little backpack on and I said, 'Thanks, fellas. See you later,' and went looking for a taxi. I saw a man near a matatu (minibus) who looked like Emily's father, James, and sure enough it was. They were very happy to see me and I had a great visit.

What I didn't realise at the time was that the Brits couldn't take off again. At over 7000 feet (2134 metres) above sea level it was too high up; the helicopter couldn't get off the ground at that altitude. They had to get out a C-130 and tear the thing down and stick it in the back of the plane. It must have cost them $200,000 but I got a free trip to see the oldies. I only found out about this when I got back to base.

After that I had a really busy year in 2002 doing promotion courses in the eastern states, and I was keen to spend some quality time with Emily, so was not really ready for or expecting the Iraq deployment. Our OC Paul gave us a heads up in December that we might be going to Iraq if the Coalition decided to invade. The reason, as I understood it at the time, was the threat of weapons of mass destruction (WMDs). That's since been proven wrong, but that's what we believed. Our job would be in the western deserts denying Saddam Hussein the capacity to launch his scud missiles towards Israel. We would also be passing on any intelligence and generally creating mayhem for the Iraqi military when time allowed. But that would be down the track.

The call-in came during the Christmas break. OC Paul gathered all the boys into the squadron Q store at our Campbell Barracks HQ. That could only mean one thing: Iraq. It started out informally with a few promotions, including mine from corporal to sergeant. We then went through some likely scenarios regarding a squadron deployment to a third country bordering Iraq. At the time it was a secret as to which country we would stage from. It turned out to be Jordan, and the reason for the secrecy was their sensitivity about being seen to be supporting the West.

Our 1 Squadron command group would deploy first to set up a base and begin battle planning and preparation to receive the remainder of the squadron. I was part of the command group with the other patrol commanders, the squadron commander and operations staff as well as some logistics and intelligence guys. The remainder of 1 Squadron, including C Troop with the remainder of my patrol, would arrive a couple of weeks later.

My patrol consisted of five blokes, all specialists in their respective fields and with lots of previous operations under our belts. We were a tight crew and had served in patrols together from East Timor through to Afghanistan. My 2IC was Shane, a sharp operator who could lead my patrol in a heartbeat if needed. Troy was our scout and had previously been our patrol signaller in East Timor as well as operations in Afghanistan, a really strong bloke who could be counted on in tough situations. Greg was the patrol signaller and as a bonus was also fully qualified as an FAC with the same level of operational experience as Troy. We could rely on his skills to call in Coalition air strikes on enemy positions. Dutchy was our medic and was the patrol intellectual. He looked like a bit of a bookworm and sometimes wore black-rimmed glasses in the field but had a great sense of humour and was the brunt of many light-hearted gags for his efforts.

Last of all was Tony, the C Troop sergeant. He was to be allocated to our patrol until the troop operated together, when he would resume his role as adviser to the troop commander and take charge of all troop administration, including ammunitions, rations and resupply. Until then he would be crew gunner on one of our two LRPVs. Tony was always really laid back and was pleased to be relegated to patrol gunner while in our patrol.

We had two LRPVs per patrol, and there were three or four patrols of five or six men in each troop, preferably six so that we could have three blokes in each vehicle – a crew commander, a driver and a gunner on the 50-calibre machine gun or alternatively a Mk 19 40-millimetre grenade launcher. The crew commander in the front passenger seat also had a 7.62-millimetre Mag 58 machine gun with a range out to around 800 metres. The 50 calibre was accurate out to 1800 metres or so. Shane, my patrol 2IC, manned the crew commander's seat in our second patrol vehicle.

The LRPVs were six-wheeled, highly modified and purpose-built Land Rovers. They weighed about four tonnes unloaded and had a capacity for an additional two tonnes of equipment carriage, which made them quite heavy. They had almost 300 litres of fuel storage and could carry as much ammo as you could jam in the storage areas. We also carried

Javelin missiles, an 84-millimetre Carl Gustav anti-armour weapon, all our personal weapons and M4 rifles, and each man had a pistol strapped to his leg, belt or chest rig.

The command group flew out a week later with our destination Jordan's capital, Amman. We sat in the Amman air terminal waiting for our bus and trying to look unobtrusive, but it was obvious that we were together on a mission, as we all looked the same and had similar large black-wheeled carry bags. From there we were whisked away in a bus to a remote airfield and military facility called Al Jaffa, which was a few hours east-north-east of the capital.

The US forces were already there when we arrived. We had a small compound to ourselves with climate-controlled tents borrowed from the Americans. Each patrol was allocated one tent. It was pretty good there. The mess was walking distance away. There we would meet many US Special Forces guys plus a few others who I knew from 22 SAS in the UK. No one told the others what we were doing, of course, but it was generally friendly and the tucker was plentiful.

In the period before the rest of our men arrived from Australia, the command group spent hours looking over maps, getting briefed and planning various scenarios for the battle. One of my tasks was to look at a likely insertion point for my patrol's two vehicles reaching well inside Iraq a few days before the ground war would start. I had real reservations about this, as I felt we would be vulnerable as a patrol and be better off as a troop formation to take on the might of the Iraqi forces. But I busied myself with the task and other patrol commanders did the same.

To my relief the plan changed and we would now insert across the border as a squadron minus one troop via a vehicle-mounted push. Our freefall troops would insert a day earlier by helicopter with their vehicles and push deep into the Iraqi western desert to get eyes on the area of operations (AO) and be able to observe and report on the main access routes during the start of the invasion.

Jordan was really cold and at night the temperature would plummet to below minus 5°C. The days were generally sunny and quite comfortable. We would be moving and working at night, so we were preparing for a chilly operation; hopefully nothing as cold as the 'Ghan though. This time we would be issued with better quality cold-weather gear, which we called puffy jackets, as well as bib-and-brace overalls also made of soft material.

When the remainder of the squadron arrived, we welcomed them to their new accommodations and briefed them all on the likely battle plan. Our time then became very hectic as we commenced battle preparations. The LRPVs had to be fully kitted out with ammunition, food and fuel, water, camouflage nets and specialist equipment. As well we had to re-zero all the weapons with their night-laser and infrared-vision equipment.

We also had to get some of our final inoculations against various deadly diseases, including biological weapons, that we might be exposed to while in Iraq. They included the regular ones like cholera, typhoid, measles, mumps and rubella, but also some really nasty vaccinations against plague, anthrax and smallpox. These required a series of three vaccinations to build up immunity and made many of the men quite sick. We were warned of the possibility of a severe reaction and, in very rare cases, death. Luckily our reactions for the most part were akin to flu symptoms, with a nasty blister appearing on the skin at the injection site. I did hear of one fellow who refused to have one of the inoculations. He was promptly sent back to Australia and would not serve in SAS operations again.

20

FIRST INTO IRAQ

With fellow patrol commander Russ I was assigned the job of selecting a suitable route for our squadron's hazardous dash from the border crossing to the western boundary of our AO, some 250 kilometres out in the bare, treeless, western Iraqi desert. This was tricky, as we would have to dodge enemy positions and inaccessible hilly terrain to arrive within one period of darkness. If we crossed the border at midnight, we'd have only six hours to reach our objective. And we needed to be in position before the main invasion so we could cover the two principal roads east–west through Iraq: Route 10 and Highway One.

Our planning was mostly carried out using aerial photos and a computer program similar to Google Earth but with much better resolution. Our biggest difficulty was avoiding all the military establishments and armoured units of the Iraqi Army that dotted our intelligence maps.

Once we had agreed on the route, we decided that near our AO my patrol would split from the squadron and establish a food and water cache that could be a means of survival should any of our blokes become separated during the coming battles. After that we would rejoin the squadron and be prepared for further tasks as they developed.

The lads were all really keen. We spent a few days in the Jordanian desert conducting shake-out patrols and practised the various skills we would need for the real thing. One of the most important was 'break contact', which meant if we were attacked by the enemy we had to get out quickly. This is normal for a small reconnaissance patrol force, as we would not have the firepower to take on major enemy forces without additional support from our troop or squadron. If we encountered any armoured vehicles, our two-vehicle patrol would engage and then quickly withdraw to a position to utilise our anti-armour weapons. We became very quick at doing this, but it would later bite me on the arse in combat.

The training culminated in a squadron 'live fire' assault on a mocked-up enemy position built of plywood at the base of a hill in the middle of nowhere. Just prior to the training assault we bumped into the 4 RAR Commandos, a newly formed Special Forces unit from Sydney. They had turned up in the area without adequate cold-weather or sleeping gear and were now freezing. They would later assist with security after the capture of the gigantic Al Asad Airbase.

The live fire assault was an absolute ripper, with the entire squadron in 20 vehicles advancing into contact in extended formation across the open desert at night. It began in the early evening and the sight of all the LRPVs speeding across the desert through NVGs and making brief stops to engage their targets was awe-inspiring. Tracer 50 calibre rounds and Mk 19 40-millimetre grenades cracked past and smashed into the target area. The crump, crump, crump as the Mk 19 rounds struck their targets really got the blood running. Realism was a priority and the risks were quite high, but we loved it.

Once on the mock enemy position B Troop dismounted from their vehicles and swept through on foot to clear the structure of enemy. My patrol simultaneously secured a position on the left flank and provided fire support. Troy, our scout, was keen to destroy one of the buildings with an 84-millimetre round, and was about to fire when I stopped him. The B Troop lads were already advancing on foot and I didn't want to risk a fragmentation injury to anyone. He let me know his displeasure but we didn't need to be one bloke short for the real thing when it came.

We then made the long dusty night drive back to Al Jaffa. The training was done; now we would be fighting the real battle. The intelligence picture was developing, and we were eventually given the green light to move to a forward staging base. As usual we moved at night, and when we reached it we knew the invasion was imminent. It was really cold and we were jammed into small army green tents with sleeping stretchers shoulder to shoulder.

We completed final maintenance and prep on our patrol vehicles. Then came the order to move again, this time almost to the border. We started in the late afternoon and while moving along an otherwise deserted road we pulled up, and on Paul the OC's command we test fired all the squadron's weapons out into the desert. This was the most spectacular test fire I'd ever seen – more than 20 combat vehicles and their crews all getting their rounds off simultaneously: Mk 19s, 50-calibre machine guns, Mag 58 machine guns as well as personal weapons and pistols. Everybody wanted to make sure their weapons worked, as we knew there were no more rehearsals from now on. The next rounds would be at the enemy.

After that we continued east towards the border. We drove late into the night along dusty tracks to avoid being seen. At one stage we stopped for a navigation check and I must have nodded off. I woke minutes later to find all the guys in my car had done the same; the vehicles in front had left without us! I woke everybody up and tried to call the convoy on the radio but they couldn't receive us, so we pushed on following their dusty tracks in the sand. We caught up after a few minutes and I got 'what for' from the boss for letting the convoy get separated. The SSM, Steve, was far more understanding and just said, 'Okay, let's go.'

Once again we pushed on through the dark, with me feeling guilty that I'd almost jeopardised the operation before we started. We drove into the following day and eventually came over a small rise in the undulating terrain to see dozens of American camouflage nets set up across the landscape, all concealing men and their vehicles. We had made it to the final step-off point.

Directions came from higher up for our patrol to set up camouflage nets to conceal our presence from any prying eyes. The threat of Chinese satellites observing us and alerting the Iraqis was real. We huddled under the nets and tried to get a little sleep. Some time that afternoon SSM Steve came over with some gear. He said, 'We've got stingers.' These were infrared homing surface-to-air missiles, shoulder launched. You beauty. He gave us a 'soldiers' five', or really brief talk, on how to operate them to shoot down enemy aircraft if they attacked us. This was a relief, as until then we had no means of defending ourselves from above.

Later that night we packed up and moved forwards in moonlight. Again it was really cold, and when we stopped we could make out some small buildings nearby – the border posts manned by the Jordanian military. A few hundred metres east was the crossing point and the earth berms – mounds of dirt about seven metres high to provide some limited defence against an enemy assault. They had been constructed to limit access by vehicles like ours.

We were not alone. An American Special Forces battalion would go through after our squadron, and they were waiting nearby. One of our patrol commanders had been involved with the plan to get our LRPVs over the berms, and it was decided that a company of American soldiers would dig a trench under cover of darkness just wide enough to drive our vehicles through. The American Special Forces units would then split from our convoy and move to the north, and then cut east towards Ar Rutbah, the first big city over the border in Iraq. We were advised that other US SF teams had been involved with coercing some of the Iraqi border guards to leave their posts so we could get in undetected. That must have been a scary job.

A funny event happened that night. The Jordanian military had placed a liaison officer, who we called Major Abdul, with us throughout all our previous training in Jordan to keep an eye on us and report our movements. This bloke was often seen strutting about looking very important. We just stayed friendly and cordial to him, as we suspected he had not been advised of the real reason we were approaching this close to the border. He thought it was just for training. Then the boss finally let the cat out of the bag and said, 'You better go away now,' but not as politely as that. We could hardly see him for dust as he legged it from the column of vehicles towards his mates in the border posts nearby.

It was early in the morning of 19 March 2003, and until then I had thought that diplomacy might avoid the invasion. But I knew for sure it was on when OC Paul quietly slipped around to each of our patrols huddled around our freezing vehicles. He told us that the decision to invade Iraq had been made by the president of the US, George W. Bush, supported by our own prime minister, John Howard, and other Coalition leaders. He said that our plan would now proceed and we would indeed be privileged in that no other Australian forces had invaded a foreign country since Anzac troops assaulted the beaches of Gallipoli. To top it off, my patrol with my LRPVs in the lead would be the first combat force to mount the invasion.

I felt high as a kite on the adrenalin of that moment and nervous thoughts were racing through my mind. Would I do a good job? Would I see Emily ever again? It was too much to contemplate. We started the vehicles in unison on Steve's command and began to move the short distance towards the border.

I had some serious butterflies in my guts. We reached the earth berm and the OC on the radio just said, 'Go!' Away we went to invade Iraq. There were a few US soldiers standing around in the dark watching as we drove over the earth mound. Some of them saluted. I was scanning like crazy with the Mag 58 machine gun trying to identify any threats. I was also worried about the risk of landmines, which I had become phobic about after my experience in Afghanistan. But we got through without incident.

Simultaneously 1 Squadron's A Troop was inserting by helicopter with their patrol vehicles crammed inside. They didn't quite make it across the Jordanian border before a Chinook broke a fuel line and had to land in the desert while the other helicopters circled above waiting for quick repairs to be made. They got moving again and flew A Troop deep inside Iraq, getting eyes onto the main east–west routes. On the way out one of the same helicopters would run out of fuel and be forced down in Iraq. A search and rescue team would be deployed to recover the crew and aircraft.

We had made it into Iraq without any shots fired, and began to shake out into our squadron formation, which was two single files of around eight to ten vehicles, my two patrol vehicles leading the way on the left side and Russ leading the right side forwards. As we moved, I was able to view our navigation system and see that we were on track with the dull green glow of our checkpoints on the screen. This was great, as it showed we were able to move at high speed over the desert at night. We were really getting along, around 70 to 80 km/h. It was totally dark and I could only see the vehicles to our flanks and rear with the use of my NVGs, which made everything appear as shades of green. The squadron was spaced out over about two kilometres behind us when it came over the radio that a truck and bus were approaching the centre vehicles in the formation from the south. By then we were up on a small hill and starting down the far side, still bearing east, so I swung our vehicle around to observe our vehicles behind us and we were ready to provide fire if required.

The enemy vehicles must have been moving at some speed, as they quickly passed through the gap in our convoy without knowing it. Once through they must have got wind of it, as they sped up and high-tailed it north. The command came over the radio from OC Paul: 'Stop those vehicles!' It was like a red rag to a bull, and streams of tracer 7.62 millimetre, incendiary 50-calibre machine-gun and 40-millimetre grenade arced across the night sky and smashed into the bus and truck. The tracers would have been invisible to the Iraqis as they were infrared, but for us it was like cracker night when I was a kid in Sydney.

We had a great vantage point from the hill, but we didn't fire, as I could see the lads were easily dealing with the situation and our rounds would have to pass over the top of our guys. My patrol was okay with this and enjoyed the show as much as I did.

At the end of it the B Troop lads stopped the bus and truck, provided some first aid to some of the bus passengers, who were border-security forces fleeing the scene, and sent them away on foot. The truck, which was loaded up with weapons and ammo, was destroyed by an air strike organised by our squadron.

I heard later that the command group back in the Coalition HQ in Qatar, where they were watching it all on satellite and listening to the contact, were freaking out. Here we were in contact within 45 minutes of our border crossing. They thought, Holy shit, what's next? But we loved it and the adrenalin was keeping us primed for the days to come.

That first enemy contact was a real ice breaker. As a fighting element we could now see how effective the assault formation and weapon systems were and how formidable we could be against a ground threat. The boys were riding high and more confident than ever that we could deal with whatever came our way.

We continued east, quickly closing the distance on the western edge of our AO. There were a few hiccups when we came across difficult terrain, and we simply adjusted the route. At some point before first light, when we were close to our AO, my patrol broke free from the main column to head out and establish a cache of food, ammunition, water and equipment concealed for later use. We had a predetermined location on the end of a small hilltop. By the time we reached the area, it was first light and we set up an LUP; then Shane went up the hill on foot with two others to conceal the cache. It didn't take long. After that we pushed northwards to link up with our troop who had established a position closer to Highway One and Route 10. The other elements of the squadron were nearby. As soon as we linked up, we were told to rest for a while.

Then came a new mission. The OC had convinced higher command that a large communications facility on our route should be assaulted, cleared and rendered useless. It was getting towards afternoon, so we all set to work preparing our equipment for the job. He told us that the enemy had access to chemical warfare, so we donned our MOP 3 chemical protection suits and kept our gas masks strapped to our belts just in case.

My patrol's task was to move along the eastern boundary fence of the huge compound and provide fire support to the main element – B Troop supported by Russ's patrol in LRPVs. They would use wire cutters to breach the perimeter fence and move northwards clearing all the buildings of enemy inside the perimeter. The other patrol in C Troop would do the same on the western perimeter fence.

The plan was good, but our layout of the perimeter fence was incorrect. This would cause some minor issues a little later in the evening. The idea was to remain fairly silent until we needed to engage with weapons. By then, hopefully, we would be on top of the Iraqis.

While moving our vehicles into position for the night assault, we received continual updates from our observers on the radios giving us information on enemy movements. There was plenty of activity and we could see some lights in the main buildings at the northern end of the compound. It was really difficult to see the perimeter fence but eventually we found the south-east corner and began to move slowly forwards paralleling the remainder of the troop. It didn't take long till everything got noisy. Somewhere in the compound the B Troopers began engaging enemy mortar positions.

We could hear our patrols on the other side engaging with 50 calibres and Mk 19s. As we looked north along the perimeter, we could see enemy soldiers running outside the fence line and diving into weapons pits. I told Troy on the gun to engage the pits, and he put fire towards the area, but his NVGs were only good to a couple of hundred metres and I'm not sure how effective the fire was. It then became difficult to identify targets for him. I had hold of the thermal sights that picked up heat signature and I could easily see what the bad guys were doing. But I realised that instead of being where we should be, we were actually opposite our brothers in the other patrols and potentially in their fields of fire. This was due to the layout not being as we had been led to believe in our orders.

I heard some explosions just to our rear. Shane in our second car was further back and said they were our boys' Mk 19 rounds landing just behind us. I was busy trying to get our gunners' 50-calibre rounds onto the enemy pits to our front, so Shane got on the radio and warned the other squadron members not to engage our position and he marked his spot with an infrared glow stick. That put an end to the incoming friendly fire ... and just in time too, as he later said that the frag was smacking into the tailgate of his LRPV.

By this time the Iraqis had had enough of being pasted. A bus appeared about 300 metres to our front leaving via the gate and heading towards Route 10. Our lads engaged and I saw the telltale signs of sparks and flash letting me know they were hitting their target. The bus miraculously got away but I doubted it would get too far with the damage it sustained.

One of the B Troop lads in the building clearance party who was much closer to the bus said when the ammo struck it looked like the inside was a disco with a strobe light flashing on and off and the soldiers looked like they were dancing – no doubt trying to avoid the incoming rounds.

Once the squadron had cleared the compound, we linked up with the other vehicles and high-tailed it eastwards towards Baghdad and deeper into our AO. As we departed, I heard the sound of explosions behind us. Initially I thought that mortars were being fired at us from the enemy at the compound. It turned out that US warplanes were using their ordnance to destroy what was left of the communication facility. It felt good to know that we had their full support overhead.

After that we again split up. C Troop, including my patrol, crossed north over the main highway and would now push to the east clearing our AO and searching for scuds. B Troop would do the same on the south side of the highway. I decided to try to get the higher ups to agree that all the 50-calibre guns have thermal weapon sights to provide a much clearer picture at ranges where the infrared couldn't reach. I never knew if this eventuated but I later passed my views on to Defence staff in post-war interviews on lessons learned in the battle.

21

'AS CLOSE AS POSSIBLE'

We pushed slowly eastwards in troop formation for hours, and I was feeling really tired now. We hadn't had a decent sleep in days. As the sun rose, we let the troop commander know that we needed to stop and get a couple of hours' rest. He was keen but it was difficult to find a concealed location in the flat desert. Eventually we came upon some old mud walls about 60 centimetres high that were once the walls of a house. It was the best we could find, so we set up a troop perimeter, lowered the camouflage nets and put hessian over the vehicle tops to reduce their outline. From a distance they would look like Bedouin tents. We put a sentry on each gun, then sent the other men to sleep.

The lads were so exhausted they just collapsed and were asleep in seconds. I decided to man the sentry position on our 50 calibre first, hoping I could rest a little later. The boys didn't complain. It was really hard to stay awake, and the sun was up now.

It seemed as if we had only been there a few minutes when I got the surprise of my life. I scanned my weapon arcs to my front and then for some reason I looked across the arcs of the patrol to our left. I could see Steve in the gun turret there and also, about a kilometre off in the distance over his shoulder, I could see two Iraqi armoured vehicles with gun turrets pointing at us. I had to look twice, but I had no doubt. I could actually see inside the barrels of their main guns as they fixed on our location. They appeared to have lots of equipment tied to their sides as if they were carrying looted gear from the last town, which was probably Ar Rutbah.

I yelled, 'Tanks!' as loud as I could. The blokes shook themselves awake. My driver Greg got the LRPV engine running as other guys madly threw their sleeping mats into the back of their vehicles and jumped in. We pulled the cars around into a fire position so we could bring all our weapons to bear on the enemy. Then our training took over and we broke contact away from the direction of the enemy armour as we'd practised so many times in Jordan. The rest of the troop followed suit, some probably wondering what all the fuss was about.

About two kilometres later we halted in defensive formation and the lads with the Javelins prepped them ready for action. I jumped down off the vehicle, as I could see the camouflage hessian skirts had become tangled in the axles and wheels of the cars in our haste to leave. I cut them away with a knife and left them in the desert.

The troop commander got his FAC to call in aircraft to locate the armoured vehicles but they couldn't find them. Now the adrenalin was going again, and so were we. From that point onwards whenever we pulled up into an LUP we prepped the Javelins for firing before we rested. We also never put hessian skirts down again. To this day I still get ribbed about this incident, as some blokes just didn't see the armour and reckoned I was hallucinating.

That evening we had our first major breakdown. While repairing the vehicle in the darkness, we learned that the Coalition was about to launch the main assault across the desert into Iraq. We had been there for a full day, and now the US warships out in the Gulf were going to initiate the battle with the launch of hundreds of Tomahawk missiles. We knew the US Special Forces who had crossed the border with us and then headed further north had been really busy as well. In the far distance we could hear the sound of their High Mobility Artillery Rocket Systems (HIMARS) raining hell onto enemy positions. Sometimes we could see the missiles as they tracked into the sky and on towards their destination.

We heard some dull droning sounds and looked up to see a Tomahawk cruise missile pass just a few hundred feet over our heads. First one, then two, then many came droning along on their way to Baghdad and other targets. One must have had a faulty jet engine as it coughed and spluttered its way across the sky. I looked at the other blokes and hoped it wouldn't land on us, but it just kept on coughing and spluttering its way to the horizon.

The breakdown that night turned out to be minor, and our mechanic Greg, and Jason, managed to sort it out in quick time. Good thing, too, as we would have had to reload all the equipment to another LRPV and destroy it with explosives if we couldn't fix it. We couldn't leave anything for an enemy to kill us with later. In fact the vehicles had been holding up well under the heavy loads and difficult conditions. They were old Land Rovers we received back in the early 1990s. They'd been fully overhauled numerous times and had many modifications that made them more capable than when they first came into service. We really grew to love them, as we spent all our time living in and around them in the deserts of the world, where we had operated over the past year or two.

Over the next several hours we continued to search our AO and eventually we linked up with the squadron. The boss had decided he would set up an observation post off the highway for the night. We were all pretty tired, so we sat up in pairs looking towards the road with thermal binoculars while others slept. There was some traffic heading west towards the Jordanian border. The vehicles were difficult to identify from our vantage point, but we could see they were belting along at high speed trying to get away from whatever was happening in Baghdad.

Apparently that night some VIPs from the Russian Embassy were fleeing the Iraqi capital. Our lads stopped some of their vehicles, as we suspected there might be high-value targets on board. They were none too pleased with being delayed, but we were just doing what our mission dictated and eventually they were sent on their way. What we were really looking for were Saddam's regime members and high-ranking officials of the Ba'ath Party.

Over the next few days we detained many people along that highway. Some had great loads of American dollars in their possession. Many were sent back the way they had come. Many were suspected insurgents who were coming in from Syria in buses. It was quite obvious who they were, as they had bullshit excuses for wanting to go to Baghdad and they were all young men of fighting age. Whatever powers had sent them must have known they would be going to their death.

By then OC Paul had a bold plan. His idea was to gradually push our AO eastwards towards Ar Ramadi, a city of almost 500,000 about 110 kilometres west of Baghdad. Along the way we would deny the enemy access to the western desert. We were only a small force but we could move very quickly and trick the regime into thinking we were far more numerous than the reality.

'AS CLOSE AS POSSIBLE'

One of the major hurdles on our journey eastwards was 'Kilometre 160' (KM 160) as we called it. This was a town located where Highway One and Route 10 came close together. It was a major centre and a stronghold of the Iraqi military. From a distance it appeared as a dusty town with low-lying buildings stretching for a kilometre or so along the highway and a very tall communications tower at its eastern end.

Before getting too close, Paul wanted to check out some military outposts that stretched northwards from the town for about 30 kilometres. We had heard these were a ring of military checkpoints to provide early warning to Baghdad should an invasion force come from the west. We moved up on one and from about a kilometre out some of the lads identified enemy movement around a few buildings. We were keen to get among the action again but Paul pulled the squadron back out into the open desert. He had a better plan.

That evening he gave us our orders. This time my patrol would again separate from the main body then push as close as possible without detection to get eyes on KM 160. Simultaneously the main body of the squadron would assault the outlying command post from the north pushing the forces back into the stronghold. From there the town could be devastated from the air using Coalition air strikes.

I was restless knowing my patrol would be out on its own again and possibly an easy target for a company of Iraqis.

In the very early hours of the following morning we headed out – my two vehicles and one other patrol of two who would escort then leave us once we got close to the chosen site. It was really clear and very cold on our approach to the town. About five kilometres away I figured that was as close as we'd get before we were spotted, since the terrain was completely flat and barren. Our big advantage was that we could disguise ourselves to look like Bedouins from a distance. But if they came within two kilometres, our cover would be blown and we'd have to fight and withdraw.

I had eaten some bad rations the day before, and when I stopped the vehicles I immediately jumped out and ripped off about ten layers of clothing to take a shit. I was really desperate as I'd been holding back for hours trying to be tactical; but all decorum was gone now as I squatted metres from the car in full view of my laughing patrol. In the rush I didn't realise I'd dropped my cold-weather bib and braces under me and now they were covered in shit. This was too much for the rest of my patrol and I received no sympathy. When I finished cleaning up a bit, I took my knife and cut the braces off the only decent cold-weather clothing I had. For the rest of the day the blokes called me 'shitstraps'.

Once the fun was over, we got to work lightly camouflaging the vehicles. They were parked together head to toe so we could use the machine guns in all directions. We stayed very close to the vehicles in case we were seen and needed to react quickly. The sun was starting to get high now and we set to work observing KM 160 and passing the information over the radio. After a while our HF link with the squadron became weak due to atmospherics, so we started using the satellite communications system to pass information directly back to the special operations command centre (SOCCE) in Jordan. This link was much clearer but it meant they had to relay any information between us and our squadron HQ who were busy clearing the military outposts.

About an hour into our set-up we started to see major enemy movement at KM 160. Greg spotted about 150 enemy soldiers on the western end of the town moving around dug-in positions. I looked through the spotter scope to check it out and saw what he was talking about, but it was beginning to get a little hazy as the daytime temperature rose. About this time we were starting to feel very vulnerable owing to the open terrain.

Off to our east we spotted dust clouds moving north towards where we knew the remainder of our squadron was busy conducting clearances. We could see small trucks and SUVs moving at speed three to four kilometres away. This indicated to me that either they were going to engage our squadron or they were about to flank our position; and that would leave us exposed. I discussed this with the blokes and we decided our best defence was to attack. Our objective was to engage the 150 enemy soldiers we had identified. I figured this would take their minds off any offensive action towards us. I got Greg, our radio operator and air-traffic coordinator, to knock out a nine-line 'close air support mission'. This message format was used by Coalition forces to get a ground target destroyed by Coalition jet fighter/bombers. Within minutes we had F-15s in support overhead. Greg began talking to the US pilots, who had some trouble with his Aussie accent, but the first bombs came down within minutes. They landed close to where we needed them but were not as effective as we wanted. He got them to come in again and again, each time dropping 2000-pound (907-kilogram) high-explosive ordnance onto the outskirts of the facility where we'd seen the enemy soldiers.

News came over the radio that our squadron was also in contact with enemy fighters to our north. We could hear the explosions and see huge clouds of dust in their direction as they also coordinated air strikes against enemy positions. Around this time we were told that a top-secret bomber was overhead and that it would drop a 'daisy cutter' on the KM 160 facility. Our patrol would call it onto target. The daisy cutter is a 15,000-pound (6804-kilogram) bomb. It would clear a 600-metre radius of buildings and any personnel in the open, as it was designed to do in the jungles of Vietnam.

However, the powers that be changed their minds. By now it was becoming too difficult owing to dust and heat haze to effectively view the target area, so we began plans to link up with the squadron. We waited until after dark and then, using NVGs, moved to a map location the squadron had provided. We closed in very quietly, talking on the radio to let them know we were coming. We were met by Steve our sergeant major and OC Paul on arrival and it was warm welcomes all round from the boys. They all had mad stories about the day's events and the desperate battle they'd had with the enemy.

Milo, one of the patrol 2ICs, told us how they had advanced into contact with the Iraqis' fire striking the ground all around them and the RPGs exploding in air bursts but too far back to be effective. Others said a Javelin missile had been super effective in completely obliterating an enemy SUV. Milo said the missile was fired when both sides were firing, but when the Iraqis saw the smoke trail coming their way they just stood and waited to see what would happen. After it hit and took out their vehicles, the wind went right out of their sails and the battle was essentially won. I felt like we had missed the best action by being away at our observation post.

I later learned that when the squadron heard us calling in air support, they were worried we would be lost to the enemy, but they could do nothing to help us as they had their own fight to deal with. One of the guys that day had done very well engaging a mortar tube with his sniper rifle and also firing a Javelin missile and destroying an enemy vehicle full of soldiers. Apparently his actions had helped turn the tide of the battle, and he was later awarded a Medal for Gallantry. He would forever be known in the media as Trooper X; to me he was just a good mate.

A funny story came out of this day's events, which we kept from the squadron OC for some time. After the battle our troop commander and John were rummaging around and found a Soviet-era anti-armour weapon. One of them picked it up and an unfired rocket slid out one end. It fell to the ground, ignited and shot off a short distance before exploding. A piece of fragmentation came back and hit our troop commander in the arse. Somehow he managed to get first aid and keep it all quiet for fear of looking like a dill for such a silly mistake. The blokes gave him no sympathy and laughed at his misfortune.

The following day the squadron, with my patrol included this time, made a stealthy approach towards the KM 160 facility, but this time from the east. Along the way we checked out the final outposts of the enemy close to the township. As we moved slowly forwards, we could see SUVs a few kilometres away on our flank. They seemed to be shadowing us as we moved through the desert. Whenever we sent a couple of vehicles towards them, they would disappear into the dust and haze. We suspected they were Iraqi forces using civilian vehicles to monitor our movements and pass on information about our unit. After a few failed attempts at catching them, we eventually trapped one. Seeing no chance of escape without being fired on, the driver decided to stop at a Bedouin tent.

The tent's owner must have been surprised, but when we too arrived the Bedouin offered us no useful information on the strange visitor. We all must have been strange to him and his family. We approached the driver of the SUV very cautiously with guns levelled. He was dressed as a civilian and appeared to be carrying no military paraphernalia. We studied his passport but saw no reason to detain him longer. We were later told that the insignia on his documentation was Ba'ath Party membership and he was one of the bad guys. He was very lucky that day.

That afternoon, as the squadron closed on KM 160 from the east, we were severely hampered by a ferocious dust storm. The sky turned to a deep brown, then red, and visibility dropped to just a few metres. As day became night, we couldn't see the vehicles we were travelling with. We decided to circle into an LUP. Normally the spacing for this type of LUP formation is around 50 metres between patrols but the conditions meant we had to put the vehicles bumper to bumper like the wagons in the old western movies.

Sand and dust permeated everything. Our mouths and eyes became sore and gritty. Ears started to fill up. To breathe we needed to cover our faces with a cloth. We got into our sleeping bags to catch some rest. The inside of a sleeping bag is a very nice place when you're tired and miserable in a dust storm. But the dust storm also had the effect of negating the ability of Coalition forces to provide aircraft support to us should we need it. Eventually the storm began to abate and we moved on again. Then it began to rain. It damped the dust and turned all our clothes and faces a muddy red.

It was about this time that our squadron got good visibility on the north-eastern side of KM 160. It was not much to look at, but the huge communications tower stood like a beacon and that made it an excellent target. Then one of my patrol members noticed that our surrounding area was littered with rocks that appeared to be painted. He said, 'Maybe we're in the middle of an Iraqi Army range impact area used to sight in their tank armaments.' He had a point. I immediately advised OC Paul, who didn't appear concerned. But I was all for getting out of there.

Then I spotted my first Iraqi landmine. The ground was completely barren and windswept. Possibly the mine had been buried but was now completely exposed. It was round and green and about the size of a dinner plate. It was designed to destroy or disable vehicles. We just drove around it and kept on going.

The OC was very aware of the enemy we had sighted from our observation post the day before. So he moved the squadron to a position a few kilometres north of KM 160 and we called in F-15s to attack the communications tower. The first bombs landed near the base and threw up huge amounts of dust and smoke. That was enough for the Iraqis.

We could just make out a couple of vehicles departing the compound near the tower, hightailing it east towards Ar Ramadi and Baghdad. Just in time, too, as the second bombs detonated almost close enough to blast them up the road. Our A Troop located further east along the highway would later hit some of this fleeing enemy with another Javelin missile.

One of the US pilots indicated that he was able to see numbers of armoured vehicles on the ground. As we couldn't see them from our position, we couldn't direct strikes onto them. And despite our proximity to the target area, we were no longer able to identify large numbers of troops on the ground as we had a day or so earlier. Apparently the Iraqis had used the dust storm as cover to bug out back to Baghdad. I didn't blame them. From our position some five kilometres away when a 2000-pound (907-kilogram) high-explosive bomb hit the deck, we first saw the strike, a few seconds later came the blast wave, which felt like soft wind or a light earth tremor, and some seconds later came the sound. To feel a blast wave at five kilometres is daunting; but then you realise that at a few hundred metres anything in the open would be torn apart by that wave of energy and shrapnel. After we dropped the initial bombs on KM 160, the Iraqis must have realised the terrible destruction to come and got their men out. Wise move.

I did hear from a Bedouin we questioned a few weeks later that some Iraqis had been killed by the bombs my patrol had called in, and the casualties had unfortunately included the town's doctor. I had no way of knowing whether that was true or not, but it gave me much grief to think I may have helped cause the death of a caregiver.

22

TOWARDS BAGHDAD

After the second series of strikes on the site our squadron commander decided we should sweep through the town to clear it of enemy. Personally I was not too keen on our relatively small group of Special Forces soldiers doing this. It seemed a task for a larger force of regular infantry, and we would probably take casualties if we went ahead. As it turned out, I didn't need to worry as the next morning before the sun rose we again moved into position, this time as a troop formation, and our FACs coordinated a further huge series of air strikes on the site. American B-52s unleashed their bombs and their detonation was like rolling thunder through the target area. They also ignited oil and fuel storage depots and created a black plume of smoke that hung around for several days.

That day we did move by vehicle through the town, but by then it was in ruin. The communications facility, which was once heavily reinforced concrete buildings surrounded by two-metre walls, had taken several direct hits and the roof had collapsed. Walking on top of the wreckage, I wondered how many soldiers were underneath. I heard some noises coming up through a hole in the rubble and broken concrete slabs. I looked down and saw a couple of black furry balls moving about. I reached down and grabbed a puppy, which I took back to our car, stupidly thinking I could somehow look after and save it.

It was dumb, but at the time it seemed the right thing to do. It was cold and shivering, so I wrapped it in a length of hessian and put it on the aluminium floor of our LRPV. The rest of the patrol named the dog 'Bomber'. It must have been around two months old and its mother was nowhere to be found.

That night we moved further to the south-east to a more remote and secure position to lie up for the night. We were now moving as a troop formation while the rest of the squadron had split away with similar tasks to conduct.

At mealtimes, or when there was a break in the action, we usually heated up some small bags of US MREs. We sat about the patrol vehicles while those on sentry duty manned the 50-calibre machine guns scanning the horizon for enemy. We also heated up some water for coffee or tea and sat around chatting. I tried to feed little Bomber but he wouldn't eat, as he probably hadn't been near people before, or maybe he was still in shock.

That evening the temperature dropped dramatically to below freezing and although he was wrapped in the hessian he began to whimper. To stop his noises, I placed him inside the top of my sleeping bag despite the fact that he had fleas. This didn't stop his cries and I became worried he would give our position away. After a while I couldn't take the noise anymore as security was our biggest concern, especially at night. I quietly gripped his little body in my hand with his head in the other hand and throttled the poor little bugger as quickly as I could. As I increased the pressure around his neck, I could feel his little body struggling to break free and get breath. Eventually he became still and I knew his fight was over. I took a shovel and dug a small hole a few metres in front of our vehicle and buried him there. I felt awful for doing that, and even today I still hate that I did it. Sometimes such things can have a big impact on us.

The next day we linked with the squadron to establish a rolling roadblock eastwards along the Route 10 highway. We pushed a patrol along each side while other patrols rolled up the road. As we came across a vehicle, the front road patrol would search it and its occupants while the other patrols would roll past and take over the lead. It was good in theory but once we stopped a vehicle it took longer to deal with it than anticipated and this bogged the column down.

As my patrol took its turn on the road, we saw a small red sedan fast approaching from the east. We aimed our weapons at the driver and motioned for him to stop and get out of the vehicle. He seemed confused or terrified at being bailed up by a fierce-looking bunch of bearded foreigners and he would not get out of the vehicle. Since I was in the front crew seat, I dismounted from my car and approached the driver's door, all the while gesturing him to get out. Meanwhile I kept my finger poised over the trigger and the safety catch switched to fire on my assault rifle so I could engage in an instant. Since he wouldn't get out of the car, I reached in to grab him and drag him out by his shirt front, but this was not successful, as he was not just big but really overweight. When I grabbed a handful of his wavy black hair, he became more cooperative and made it to the pavement on his knees.

While the lads covered him with their weapons, we conducted a quick search of his car and boot. Nothing was suspicious and no firearms were discovered so we let him go. Others followed and when we released them they looked confused and fearful. I seriously thought that they believed we would kill them.

Seeing terror in people's eyes is not pleasant. Sometimes it comes across as arrogance, frozen immobility or even smiling compliance. On one occasion another patrol member, Fred, was tasked to cover some detained unarmed soldiers while the rest of his patrol searched the vehicles. These guys were obviously regulars, as they were in military uniform, but with no insignia. When ordered or motioned to sit on the ground, one poor fellow, down on his stomach, reached forwards with his arms and placed his face on Fred's boot to kiss his feet. He was absolutely terrified and believed we were about to shoot him. Another patrol member who was closer said he'd pissed himself. We had no intention to harm him, as he presented no threat without a weapon, so once again we let them go after our interpreter gave them some stern words about not resisting any Coalition forces they might come across.

We later made a bit of a joke of this to Fred, who we accused of enjoying having his feet kissed a little too much. It seems cruel, but in that situation it helped to relieve the tension to make light of even the most awful circumstance.

Many of the high-value target interdiction (HVTI) tasks were conducted in broad daylight, where we were very vulnerable to enemy attack or vehicle bombs. So we were always on a hair trigger and nervous as hell of anybody we might stop on the highway from Baghdad to Jordan. To add to the difficulty, we were all severely fatigued, especially in the first two weeks of the campaign when we were constantly on the move.

As a squadron we then set up a roadblock on the main Highway One. It was similar to any multi-lane freeway in Australia, with a guard rail running down each side and a centre median strip. The only difference was that traffic travelled on the right-hand side instead of the left. Initially my patrol was placed out as flank protection on the south side on a small rise, allowing us to see for many kilometres each way and provide early warning. We were manning our 50-calibre-gun turrets about 50 metres from the rest of our patrols, who were standing on the highway stopping traffic and conducting searches. Our job was to give them cover as well, but this was always tricky as we had to aim at the threat vehicles while not fragging the backs of our own men.

We rotated through short rest periods and ate, smoked or chatted to relax. That was when I heard shots ring out from the direction of the road crews. It appeared that one of our blokes fired at an Iraqi vehicle to force it to stop. They were not accustomed to being stopped on this route and didn't expect to see us, so they tried to bully their way through. It didn't work. Others turned around and headed back the way they came. They often appeared proud and indignant that these people – some dressed in shorts – were delaying them in their travels.

I was out in the road centre when an Iraqi taxi approached from the west heading towards Baghdad. I raised my left hand and motioned the vehicle to stop while I pointed my M4 assault rifle directly at the occupants in the car as it closed on us. I could see at least two men inside with their customary red chequered headscarfs. It slowed but failed to stop, and it seemed that they might try to push through.

Our orders were clear: letting anyone through would expose our troops further back to a threat. I fired two rounds directly into the front of the vehicle and it immediately came to a smoky hissing stop. I did this almost without thinking; it was a purely instinctive reaction that we'd practised thousands of times in our training.

The occupants were dragged out and quickly questioned by our blokes with the aid of our interpreter. They were two middle-aged men intent on travelling east, and we had destroyed their car. They argued and waved their arms and let us know they were very unhappy. Why they didn't just stop I'm still unsure, but they risked their lives in not doing so. We eventually told them to move on and the last I saw of them they were pushing their broken taxi east along the highway.

The ability to fire instinctively and without hesitation like this is something that we train for continuously in SASR. The difficulty is not pulling the trigger; it is knowing instantly when it is justified and what to aim at when it happens. While in Iraq, we were tasked to go into many buildings searching for enemy. The blood rush starts just before the assault and continues throughout. It is this adrenalin that feeds you to do extraordinary things and push your body even when injured. When the action is over, it can take several hours to come down, but when you do exhaustion hits hard.

By now much of our food, water and ammunition were heavily depleted as well as our stores of Javelin missiles. We had been busy as a squadron and as individual troops over the first two weeks of the war and we needed to be resupplied.

The OC gathered the squadron far out in the desert away from any habitation. A detailed resupply list was radioed through to our logistics guys in Al Jaffa. Some of the gear we requested must have seemed unusual – cans of Coke and chocky bars, boxes of cigars, and for me it was rolly tobacco. SSM Steve was responsible for coordinating resupply and Aussie C-130 crews dropped it to us via parachute.

We returned to our various tasks. A Troop and B Troop operated further east along the highway closer to Ar Ramadi. Several of their contacts with the enemy resulted in capturing enemy persons of value, and destroying several communications facilities and a huge weapons and ammunition storage site. Some kilometres away towards the east we saw the explosions and the glow of burning buildings. It was spectacular and we could hear the small explosions as primary charges set off larger stores of high explosive. Smoke plumed out across the still, cold desert sky and lingered like a dark blanket even after the sun rose the following morning. The B Troop boys were busy again.

We had now reached the easternmost point of our AO. OC Paul was keen to push on to Ar Ramadi, where Coalition forces were bogged down in negotiations with local leaders to try to secure a peaceful surrender of the town. Our senior hierarchy would not allow us to go further east, so Paul looked to the north of our AO for more targets of opportunity. One of these was the facility at Kubaysah.

Located around 20 kilometres north of the highway, Kubaysah was a massive cement works in the middle of the desert. Its towers and silos from a distance looked like some medieval castle. The facility covered several square kilometres and contained roads, housing, plant, holding yards and even tracked railway systems to move the raw and processed material in and out. It was a major asset to the Iraqis as it supplied cement for roads and building material to much of the country.

We were unsure of the strength of enemy forces guarding it, so Paul split the squadron into smaller groups to conduct reconnaissance from several directions to establish threats, defensive positions, troop locations, escape routes and access points. Then he called the patrol commanders in to give squadron-level orders. The PCs would then adapt the orders into tasks for their respective patrols while the team members were flat out preparing ammunition, cleaning weapons, making explosive charges, eating, resting and any number of other tasks that had to be undertaken before a battle.

The task given to my patrol, Charlie 3, was to move to a small facility located about two kilometres to the southeast of the main works. I needed to establish just what this small compound was and see if there was any advantage in using it to gather more intelligence about the structure of Kubaysah. After discussing this plan with my patrol, we decided to go straight up to the front entrance, with each vehicle providing fire support to the other. Our hope was that a show of force would be enough to discourage the few security personnel we believed were at the compound from opening fire. But if necessary we could bring to bear our two 50-calibre machine guns and two Mag 58 machine guns onto any resistance. Fifty-calibre machine guns are a very effective means of discouraging an enemy; the rounds can punch holes in concrete and steel, and ours included Raufoss ammo, which has an explosive and incendiary component.

It was around mid-morning when we parted company with the squadron, who were holed up in a small oasis with date palms and a few small abandoned structures just five kilometres from Kubaysah. Other patrols left at the same time to conduct their respective reconnaissance tasks. We skirted around the back of some low undulations to avoid being seen and continued until we were only 30 metres from the front entrance, with both cars parallel and 25 metres apart. All guns faced the target area. We could see a guardhouse just inside the front entrance on the right-hand side. On the veranda of this were two guards with an AK-47 leaning against the wall.

They didn't raise the weapon, so I led an assault team of four men to clear the building while the other patrol members manned the guns. The building was basic inside with just some cooking items and chairs as well as another AK-47 with a few loaded magazines. The Iraqis were very compliant. They were men in their forties, and if they'd known the nasty surprise we had for them they would have legged it off into the desert. First we questioned them through an interpreter and learned much about the Kubaysah cement works. We discovered that the main reason they carried weapons was to stop other security forces from the works from stealing whatever was available. Most men in this part of the country carried some form of weapon to protect themselves and their families from their countrymen, a bit like the lawless old west. We detained them and decided to use them on our approach to the main Kubaysah facility to warn the forces that secured it to give up their arms and avoid any unnecessary bloodshed.

Naturally we kept them in the dark about this and took them back with us to the squadron. Once they were seated comfortably in front of our commander and an interpreter with hot tea and food, Paul broke the news to them. They instantly became very agitated and animated and spoke nervously to each other. The interpreter let us know that they thought their own Iraqi security forces at Kubaysah would surely kill them.

At mid-afternoon we received our final orders and were ready to conduct the assault. In 14 vehicles we moved across the desert slowly to avoid creating a dust trail that would be seen by the Iraqis. About a kilometre from the eastern gate of Kubaysah we changed formation into two parallel extended lines, all guns facing towards the security forces at the entry point. My patrol was on the right forward flank. We were now in sight of the front gate and we could see movement on the road that led into the area. Now we increased our speed and listened to commands on the radio from Paul ordering us to stay in formation.

About 200 metres from the gate we came to an abrupt halt facing the security forces. No shots had yet been fired. We then sent the two Iraqi security guys we had detained off on foot towards the command post near the front gate. One of the local commanders came out to meet them and I could see them discussing something very animatedly. But then came the real surprise that clinched the deal. From our rear I suddenly heard the deafening roar of two jet fighters closing on us. Within an instant they were overhead and screaming past the facility. Then they circled back, and this time when they arrived overhead at around 200 feet (61 metres) they cracked the sound barrier with a mighty sonic boom that shook the ground and air for kilometres around. It was so loud that the years of settled dust on the cement works' conveyors and towers fell in cascades to the ground. I was initially convinced the pilots had dropped live ordnance onto the facility. But this was not the case, and it was really Paul's plan all along.

It was a completely successful ploy, and from that moment the Iraqi weapons disappeared. They had very quickly hidden them in wall cavities and behind cupboards. We had one hell of a time finding them as we searched and cleared all the buildings and workshops. It was a massive task, as there were multi-storey buildings, conveyors and scaffolds 20 metres above the ground. There were silos 60 metres high, and roads and railway works to clear. It was exhausting and took more than two hours before we reached the rear perimeter gate and guard station. This we also cleared, and inside we discovered more weapons, which we took away.

Eventually we all linked up again, still on a high from the excitement of the clearance and success of the task. Brief orders were given that the squadron would now move west, out into open desert country, where we could once again establish a secure night perimeter and get some rest in preparation for the next big job. As we moved out across the desert at high speed with the sun just starting to dip onto the horizon, it was a surreal experience to look out from our position on the far left flank and see all 20 LRPVs moving around 85 km/h over dead flat ground side by side. It was a great feeling to know that with such a force we could eat and sleep well that night without fear of an enemy force trying to disturb us.

Strength in numbers... for a soldier there's nothing quite like it.

23

'MOST DIFFICULT MISSION'

Living in and around our LRPVs over such a long period meant that strong bonds developed between patrol members. This was one of the real positives of the experience for me. Procedures are always important for security, and if we weren't moving at night we were resting, sitting in observation or manning the guns. This way a bloke would usually get at least five hours' rest.

Mealtimes were the best part of the day, and we would usually fire up a billy of boiling water for brews and an MRE each. Then we'd sit around chatting quietly. In the mornings the last gun sentry would wake the rest, and slowly we'd roll up our sleeping bags, stash them in our 'Alice packs' (the US backpacks we used) and secure them to the vehicles. Then we'd sit quietly until the sun was just above the horizon. This was called quiet time, and we used it to listen for any sound of enemy forces.

'MOST DIFFICULT MISSION'

Going to the toilet in a flat desert landscape was completely without any privacy. Basically you'd let someone know you were going for a shit, walk a short distance downwind, dig a small hole with a shovel and go in the hole. It was often windy, so you'd have to be careful that the toilet paper you carried didn't blow away. A trick was to use it then place a small stone on it to keep it in the hole. You'd fill in the hole with the shovel and leave no sign that you'd been there.

One time our patrol 2IC Shane was sitting between the cars having his morning brew and chatting with Troy, Greg, Tony and Dutchy. I thought I'd play a trick on him since he was always whingeing that I didn't go to the loo far enough away from the vehicles. As he made a deal out of it, I always made sure that I went where it would annoy him the most. I decided this day that I would pretend to go just in front of the cars. I took a piece of toilet paper and rubbed it on the dusty front of the car to make a dirty mark and then, checking the wind direction, let it blow towards Shane happily enjoying his coffee. I couldn't have wished for a more effective outcome, as the wind lifted the toilet paper and gently dropped it into his mug between his feet and under his folding chair. His reaction was priceless. He called me every name under the sun to the delight of the other patrol members, who were in on the fun. After a while I let him know I was having a lend of him. Jokes like these helped alleviate the daily tension and fatigue.

After the Kubaysah clearance we needed to get an extension to our AO approved from higher command to allow 1 Squadron to push further north. This would allow us to approach the massive Iraqi Air Force base of Al Asad, which was sure to be heavily guarded. It was about 20 kilometres from Kubaysah, but the terrain on the approach would be very difficult, with dry creek beds criss-crossing the area. The airbase was only ten kilometres from the mighty Euphrates River, and many villages and small towns lined its banks.

A Troop was ordered to establish an observation post on high ground to the south-west of the base about two kilometres away where they could see most of the south side of the base. The rest of the squadron joined them a few hours later just on last light. By then they had identified enemy forces on the base as well as many aircraft on the ground. In fact they'd called in US air strikes, and when I arrived with C Troop we saw the massive explosions as laser-guided bombs – including 'bunker busters' – smashed onto their targets. Their bunkers were used to protect parked aircraft, and there were others shaped like pyramids about 20 metres high that concealed huge underground command and communication areas. These centres were completely self-sufficient, with radio-communication rooms, filtered air equipment and power generators so commanders could coordinate their air assets while war raged above. Unfortunately for the Iraqis they had been built some years ago, and new technology made them vulnerable to attack. The bunker busters would penetrate deep into the concrete and steel, and a delayed explosive charge would then detonate and completely annihilate anybody inside.

I had witnessed similar devastation before when mounting operations from damaged Kuwaiti airbases prior to heading off to Afghanistan. All these air strikes were very accurate and hit their marks. Our role was not to damage key infrastructure unnecessarily. In fact we were told to preserve it if possible so that some new Iraqi government could use their resources again. So after some hours of calling in air support the decision was made to cease the strikes. By then we figured any threats had been neutralised. Now it was our turn to get involved at ground level.

That evening OC Paul once again gathered his patrol commanders together. We were given orders for a squadron-size vehicle-mounted assault and clearance of the entire airbase. This was to be our biggest and possibly the most difficult mission of the entire campaign. The base was massive and there could still be large numbers of enemy forces concealed inside. Our troop commander then delivered his orders and we busied ourselves with preparations for the assault at first light.

The plan was to split the objective into sectors, and each troop would assault and clear their designated areas. At the same time we would cover each other in case of enemy resistance. We would move first by vehicle then dismount and clear buildings and infrastructure before remounting and moving to the next designated area.

That night no one had more than a couple of hours' sleep. We roused ourselves well before the first light. C Troop would move along the main access route to the facility one patrol at a time so that we always had stationary vehicles covering as we approached. A and B Troops had similar tasks but would approach from different directions so we could saturate the target area simultaneously if required. Smaller groups were tasked with providing overwatch so they could coordinate air support if necessary.

On signal using NVG's we moved silently and slowly to reduce our dust signatures, then as the first rays of the sun lit the sky we replaced the NVGs with dust goggles. Each crew member's headset crackled with commands as we jostled along giving coordinated tactical support to each other. Suddenly we spotted enemy forces outside the compound and near the front entrance. Our gunner Troy gave the thumbs down and readied the 50 calibre for action. We immediately informed the troop commander but he was hesitant to engage because he didn't want to go noisy this early in the assault. My patrol boys were annoyed as hell as they wanted to kick arse hard and fast, but we stuck with his plan and continued to push forward.

At the front entrance there were some SUV vehicles moving and I heard some 50-calibre fire from the other troops directed towards that area. They had seen personnel with weapons near shipping containers and engaged. We entered the main gate but the enemy had fled inside. The gate had a Mig jet fighter mounted on a pedestal just outside and a huge sign board of Saddam Hussein's image. The gate and guard post were slightly damaged from air strikes or looters but it was easy enough to get through. The area was built around a natural watercourse with copses of trees and date palms scattered about and painted road edges. The base grounds were well constructed and had been meticulously cared for. Roads led off from the entry point into the centre.

We moved cautiously along or parallel to these bitumen roads heading to our first objective, the command bunkers. We approached caterpillar fashion, with one vehicle in the patrol stationary providing overwatch and ready to fire and the other vehicle moving from one position of relative cover to the next. That LRPV would then take over the fire support role and the first car would move up. This continued until we arrived at the first bunker or building to be cleared.

Assault teams dismounted and moved to an entry point, then simultaneously blew the doors and cleared the building room by room. Clearances were very fast and two men stayed together to support each other while another two cleared separate areas within the building. Normally we preferred to have at least a four-man team on building assaults but due to the size of the buildings and concrete bunkers we had to break the teams into the smallest sustainable grouping.

As we cleared each room, assaulters would call out 'Clear!'. This would let the others know they were ready to move on to the next objective. Most were for accommodation, communications equipment or generators and machinery. Others within the bunkers were briefing rooms with chairs, tables, map displays and projector equipment. All appeared neat and tidy but had not been used for some time. At no time did we encounter enemy forces and there were plenty of signs that looters had been collecting anything of value. This had probably happened after the initial bombs had fallen and most of the soldiers had fled.

We continued to push on with clearing structures, continually keeping radio and visual contact with the rest of the troop and squadron vehicles. On one occasion we entered a huge hangar probably used for aircraft maintenance. It was made of corrugated iron and steel that provided no protection from air strikes. It had taken a direct hit through the roof and the bomb had then smashed onto the concrete floor 25 metres below, leaving a big crater. Pieces of the floor had been thrown up and through the thin metal walls, turning them into tattered ribbons of hanging steel. Much of the roof had then collapsed into the building. Nothing would have survived that strike. Surprisingly I didn't see any bloodstains, so I can only imagine that the Iraqis had already left when the bomb hit.

We also discovered an Olympic-sized indoor swimming pool that was fully intact, although the water looked a bit too green for a swim. Then there was a small mosque, undamaged, but all the internal fittings had been taken away. A natural spring fed the ablutions fountain, where devotees would have washed their hands and feet before entering the mosque.

Later in the day my troop was tasked by OC Paul to clear any enemy forces from the western perimeter. Dust clouds had been seen in the area and we suspected enemy vehicles were moving about there. We drove back out then turned north and drove along the outside of the fence line, LRPVs spaced abreast in extended line formation as we expected imminent enemy contact. When we came over a slight rise, we were able to see a small cluster of brick buildings in the distant afternoon haze. We could also see men moving about in green uniforms and what looked like a truck. Some of our cars immediately engaged with the 50-calibre machine guns, and ammunition strikes could be seen near the buildings. We continued to close the gap without further engagement but lost sight of the enemy in the low ground. When we regained visibility, I saw a vehicle speeding away from the area. We eventually reached the buildings and cleared them but found no enemy, just a few locals who had moved in to steal whatever they could.

We decided not to pursue the enemy as they were moving quickly and we were far from the security of the squadron. It would be too easy to be drawn into a trap and ambushed. We found lots of old ammunition and some food and cooking supplies but little else. It appeared that some of the security forces who had fled the bombing had occupied this small cluster of buildings outside the fence. They probably didn't want to abandon the area completely for fear of retribution by the Iraqi forces still moving about closer to Baghdad.

We made our way north through the facility to the airstrip. The runway was about 3000 metres long and would have been able to handle almost any aircraft. There was a tall control tower with a big administration section at its base. We cleared it and occupied it ourselves as the squadron HQ. From high in the tower we could view a large part of the facility except for areas to the south where we had initially entered the airbase. The squadron rendezvoused at this point and deployed all patrols to establish a thin perimeter in a rough circular formation. This was to be our own mission control.

Soon afterwards we received intelligence that there might be a counterattack from forces in a small town to the east – on the banks of the Euphrates – that we called Little Baghdadi. It would probably happen that evening, so we prepared to hold our ground. As it turned out, nothing eventuated that night and we soon established a routine around the air-control tower. Most of our time was spent defending our turf from looters.

The airstrip had been badly damaged by the 2000-pound (907-kilogram) bombs gouging massive craters, but we reckoned it could be repaired and become a valuable asset to Coalition forces. Our troops set about getting old machinery lying around the area back into working condition. A massive D8 bulldozer that we saw at Kubaysah was resurrected by some of our lads and slowly driven the 20-kilometre journey across the desert. It did the job, and over a couple of days the airstrip was able to land a C-130 or perhaps even a B-17 cargo aircraft. During this time other patrols maintained security around the area and took the opportunity to go looking for hidden Iraqi jet fighters cached in the desert and nearby hills and wadies.

It appeared that the Iraqi Air Force had anticipated the devastation that was to come and had taken the clever step of hiding most of their aircraft out in the desert camouflaged under nets and tarpaulins. The squadron managed to locate at least a hundred, ranging from Russian Migs to Chinese and Russian helicopters. Most were very old and it is doubtful if more than a quarter would have actually been able to get off the ground let alone be a real threat in combat. Our job was not to destroy them but defend them from looters. We spent a lot of time keeping them away by firing warning shots over their heads. This was pretty ineffectual, since they just waited till we left the area before returning to grab anything of value.

We managed to locate many Iraqi field artillery pieces and anti-aircraft guns on the hillsides. Most we simply turned over with our vehicles to make it difficult for any enemy force to use them against us. Many were still loaded with high-explosive rounds and some went off when we moved them. Luckily no one was injured but one time someone came very close to losing his hand.

We were out in the desert a few kilometres from the airbase and had gathered a variety of the heavy weapons we had found around the base. We also had a lot of ammunition. Most of the stuff was Russian or Chinese and the OC wanted the lads to have a test fire of all the different weapon variants. I was given the job of safety officer and tried to coordinate the exercise so no one got hurt.

One was a link-fed 40-millimetre anti-aircraft gun that resembled an old Bofors gun. The blokes were using 'guessametrics' to figure out how to fire it and Milo was trying to feed the rounds into the mechanism. Suddenly two rounds shot off accidentally while his hand was in the feed area where ammunition is dragged into the breach. The gun stopped firing immediately but his fingers were stuck in between the cartridges. Had the gun continued to feed and fire, he might have lost his hand. I told them to leave that weapon alone but soon afterwards when my back was turned they were at it again and eventually managed to get it firing accurately down range at a few old vehicles we had dragged there as targets.

Other tasks over the final few weeks in country involved patrols to remote areas of our AO. On one we came across a missile range where parts of an old scud were scattered about the desert. Closer to the airbase we discovered a huge storage facility of weapons and explosives. There were hundreds of thousands of tonnes of ammunition. Much of it was mortars and artillery but there were also brand-new missile systems still in their packaging. Some were about six metres long in large wooden crates.

We spent all day breaking padlocks on shipping containers in the storage areas trying to locate those phantom WMDs. Thinking back, we really should have been more careful, as we had no protective clothing or respirators with us when we searched the massive stash of deadly equipment. Later specialist technicians came into the facility and spent long hours sifting through all the ammunition, identifying each item in an attempt to locate a WMD.

None were found.

24

AFTER IRAQ

On Anzac Day 2003 we were still in Al Asad, where, in typical Aussie fashion, we commemorated the anniversary that means a lot to all Australian soldiers, especially the SASR. The lads all piled up on one of Saddam's command bunkers near the control tower in a formation reminiscent of that famous photo of the 11th Battalion on the pyramids in 1914 before they left for the Dardanelles. This was a deliberate act by our OC and SSM, who knew a good photo opportunity when they saw one.

We enjoyed a game of two-up with some of the Iraqi money we had found and we had a barbecue. I was in charge of barbie duties and I used a Russian survival axe I liberated from a Mig jet fighter survival kit to flip the snags, burgers and steaks. Some of the top brass and pollies from Australia flew in on an Aussie C-130 to shake hands with the blokes, and it turned out to be a really memorable day.

Shortly afterwards word came through that our task at Al Asad was completed and US forces came in to secure the facility. It later became the largest US airbase in Iraq. The squadron was airlifted back to our old base of Al Jaffa in Jordan, which we'd left some weeks earlier but which now seemed like a lifetime ago. There we spent days cleaning and de-servicing our equipment, weapons and vehicles in preparation for the return to Australia.

On this occasion there was no media fanfare; we returned to the barracks at Swanbourne to meet our wives, girlfriends and children, along with many brass and politicians, who were always happy to greet the SASR blokes. It was great to be back home and without a single serious casualty. That was almost unbelievable given the hazardous combat tasks we'd been engaged in. Some weeks later we had a big ceremony where campaign medals were given out at a parade and members of 1 Squadron were presented with the Unit Citation for Gallantry, which had never before been awarded. My old mate Trooper X received a Medal for Gallantry to add to his collection.

My patrol and the rest of the squadron had little time to rest on our laurels. We were to take over the CT role as soon as possible and we needed to prepare for that so that another squadron could rotate back into overseas operations.

EMILY'S STORY VIII

'Iraq was emotional because everything was on television,' Emily says. By now she had pursued her ambition to work with autistic children by completing a TAFE course as an education assistant. The practical element was conducted at Lansdale Primary School and she so impressed the principal that she offered Emily a job there the moment she graduated.

'They were very good people,' she says. 'I was a special-needs assistant working with kids with autism. This was the area I'd wanted to be involved with for ages, so it was a small ambition realised. And when Stuart was in Iraq, the faculty looked after me; they called me to see if I was okay, and the support they gave me was very, very important.'

Then at last he was home. That was a huge emotional relief. But there was a catch. 'I always had the feeling that part of him was still back there, still caught up in the experiences of war. It's as though my husband went to war but he never really came home. I can't help it; that's how I feel. He came back injured and it takes a long time to heal.'

They tried to have a baby. It took a while, but in 2004 along came Kenzie. 'She was the light of our life,' Emily says. 'I think it helped Stuart to cope. He's very strong, so much better now than when Kenzie was born.

'I tried to help by getting him to talk about what was troubling him. I knew it's something I really shouldn't do because of the nature of the job but I'm not going to regret it because I would try and get information from him, to give him some way to release it. I would pester him but I'm not one of his mates; I wasn't there; so he couldn't really tell me. But I am his partner and I get frustrated because I can't get him to speak to me.

'When he's hurting, I want him to tell me what it is that's hurting him. But that's the most difficult thing for him. It's getting better, but it's a very slow process. However, the best thing is that he is a wonderful dad, absolutely wonderful.'

•

Little Kenzie was born in Subiaco Hospital. Emily had suffered some complications during her pregnancy but I was around at that time so I was lucky to be there for the birth of our daughter. She was very healthy and everything we could have hoped for.

It was really a highlight for me, as Emily and I had wanted a baby for some years. That was a turning point in my life and I figured the foremost purpose for any man was to be a good father to his children. Everything else would be second to that from now on. However, by that time I was not in good shape.

Soon after our squadron's return from Iraq, we took over the CT role. My job was the troop's training sergeant, otherwise known as the 'Charlie One One', the senior training officer within the troop. This was a big task with a lot of pressure, as I had to ensure that training each day developed and improved the troop's capability to deliver a CT solution for any security threat that might strike Australia over the coming year. As a unit we were very busy and travelled regularly to all parts of the country conducting preparations for any imaginable eventuality.

These included: an operation out of Darwin with the navy for ship-launched assaults on simulated terrorist strongholds on land; helicopter operations over on the far north coast; and regular training in our Western Australian facilities not far from Perth.

The PTSD was making its presence felt. On training exercises as a team leader I found myself treating it exactly as if it were the real thing back in Iraq or Afghanistan. I felt real anxiety and cold fear even though I knew it was just training and the bullets fired were not fired towards me or just paintball or blank simulator cartridges. I became very angry when critiqued over any issues and responded aggressively to my colleagues. This had the effect of isolating me from my mates, and that only added to the pressure. My sleep was severely affected and it got to the stage where I would only sleep a couple of hours each night. I found my stomach was sensitive and painful, and I couldn't drink or eat things I usually enjoyed.

Finally I decided that I didn't want to be promoted above my rank of sergeant. The whole idea of taking on new responsibilities was just unacceptable to me. I bottled it up for a while but I knew I'd have to tell my boss, OC Paul, and one day when he was arranging courses that would promote me to the next level I could keep it to myself no longer. That was when I blurted out my decision, first to the sergeant major Steve and OC Paul, then to the RSM, and was told in that phrase I'll never forget that I no longer had 'employability within the regiment'. That's about the time when they gave me a couple of weeks off on sick leave and I started on the medication.

I later came to realise that my illness was causing me to make poor judgement calls, and that whatever happened it would have been a fast track out of the army for me anyway. But I also realised that there were traceable reasons for my condition.

From around the time we returned from Iraq, I had been the emergency action (EA) commander once again. This had been the case since I'd been a lance corporal – the team commander frequently was off doing courses, so on the training deployments to Canberra or Sydney or Townsville I'd take over his role. And I think it's just too much for one person to be at that tempo for so long. You're worried about your blokes. You're worried about your performance and making sure that everything works properly. You're on the range three or four days a week and you're running through high-risk live ammunition and high-explosives scenarios several days each week if not every day.

Things got worse at home. We were really struggling. At the time I was self-medicating with alcohol and drinking far too much beer when I was at home. We had the new baby so we were both getting up three or four times a night anyway. So it was pretty difficult. Emily had her own issues and she was struggling too. And at night I was hypervigilant, patrolling about the house.

As soon as I started taking the pills, I put on a lot of weight – up to around 85 kilograms from my normal weight of about 76. Other effects were that I tended to be lethargic, as if I'd taken a sleeping pill. At first that medication really knocks you out. After that you're able to work but probably not at the same capacity. At the time you don't realise it; you think you're doing fine. You sleep but it's probably not proper sleep.

After the sick leave there was a period where we finished CT team exercises and went on to green roles – bush warfare. We went up to Lancelin in the dunes north of Perth and I had to run a range shoot. I remember bumping into OC Paul and he said, 'All right you're in charge of the anti-armour weapons at the range shoot.' So I set up a template, put out certain things, a lot of steps to make sure it was safe to go. And then we had a big squadron anti-armour shoot where we were firing rockets and heavy weapons. We were staying at the navy hut there for a couple of nights and he said, 'How are you going, Nev?'

I said, 'Good, good,' and somehow we got to talking about that medicine. He knew about it and I said, 'Yeah, I'm still on it.'

He said, 'What?' He didn't know. He must have assumed I'd stopped taking it. It wasn't long after that that I was no longer in the sabre squadron. The reality was the unit couldn't have an operational patrol commander on some antidepressant medication. It was just taking too much of a risk considering what could go wrong.

I accepted the transfer from my beloved 1 Squadron to the training squadron. A lot of the blokes would regard this as a bit of a demotion because everyone wants to be in a front-line sabre squadron, but for a few years I had actually wanted to be a part of it. I'd been in the sabre squadrons for a long time – from 1992 right through to 2004 – and I thought it was time for a change. Also I enjoy the instructor's role and I suppose that was reflected during my time in East Timor when teaching those kids gave me such satisfaction.

Because the regiment was involved in two wars, there was terrific pressure on the training area to get the boys up to standard for their combat duties. We were running courses for close-quarter urban combat. It's one of the more difficult courses within the regiment for new reinforcements to get through. It's very demanding. You've got to be very weapon aware and you've got to develop weapon-handling skills to a very high standard; and you have to be extremely accurate using short-barrelled weapons. And our standards were completely unforgiving; we were always trying to stretch the envelope. The courses would go from five or six in the morning to five or six at night – back-to-back for six weeks at a time. One course went for three months. But at least in the training squadron, while you were very busy for much of the year, there was a period when it was mainly administration.

I wanted to be there; I enjoyed that aspect. I wasn't going away on extended operations so I could focus on being around the family. We did have a few short deployments to Malaysia and Thailand for training Special Forces overseas; then we had a very busy period when we had to train new guys for the reinforcement cycle. But it was a good time. I enjoyed it.

But I was drinking way too much. That was the time I had a big fight with the bloke next door. So while I was enjoying it, everything really wasn't hunky dory. It's not till you look back that you realise what was going on.

I also became aware of another factor that possibly played an important part in my condition: traumatic brain injury. It affects people who are frequently exposed to explosives, from IEDs to the smaller detonations we use in training exercises. The first time I was on team in 1994 with 3 Squadron, I became the method of entry (MOE) explosives operator. My role was to build explosives charges to open doors, blow through walls and cut into steel compartments. There were big explosions very close by, and my team would run around through the door or whatever I'd blown open and I'd run in behind them.

You knew you were standing a bit too close when you'd be dazed by the explosion for up to ten seconds after the charge. But you still ran in because it becomes a reflex action after so many times. There might be three or four teams, and you'd be trying to blow the charges simultaneously with them entering at different points to saturate the target area, getting as many guys in there as possible in the shortest period of time while anyone inside is basically traumatised by that initial shock. It makes them temporarily disorientated so we can engage them.

Time and again you'd be inside the fireball. The things that stopped you getting badly injured were your double hearing protection, body armour, helmet and fire-retardant suit. I tried to use the hearing protection every time but sometimes I'd forget the outer ones. Partly that was deliberate because in a close-combat situation you have to be able to hear what your mates are shouting or you could find yourself in the line of fire. But I must have done hundreds of those over a period of ten years, either as the MOE operator or as a team member. On top of that, a couple of times I was blown up and had fragmentation injuries. You put all that together and it's got to have serious effects on the brain.

I was on that medication for about two years. They changed the mix from time to time. Once Professor Kosky had seen me two or three times, he handed me over to the unit psychologist, who was a major at the time. He was pretty good, a young fellow. He was trying to keep me operational at work without telling too many people. So he was trying to do the right thing for my career but probably not the right thing medically. And I don't blame him because at the time I really wanted to be with the regiment.

However, by 2006 I had come to the end of my tether. I put in my discharge notice and, because I'd done my 20 years, I took a couple of months' long-service leave. I used that time to look for work outside.

I was still taking the medication, but the moment I got out I went to see my GP, who happened to be an ex-military medical officer. He said I needed to get my weight down, so I just went off all medication. I didn't ask anyone; I just went cold turkey and stopped.

I saw the weight starting to come off. I wasn't coping too badly without the medication. I think it's got its good points but plenty of bad ones; it's very addictive, especially the sleeping pills. When it kicked in, my extremities would feel like stone. My hands and my feet were like lead weights and the sensation would slowly creep up my body until I was gone. When I first started taking the medication, I thought, This is great; I should have done this years ago. But my cholesterol started going through the roof.

I had the option of seeking a medical discharge, but there's a bit of pressure from inside the army against it. So I just took regular discharge and went looking for a job. I bounced around between a few different things. There was a place nearby that did defensive driver training around Australia and overseas. They wanted a training coordinator, so I went and did that. I lasted about two weeks, but the stress was just killing me. I was mostly sitting at a desk on the phone asking people to come in for appointments or to reschedule course sessions, and just couldn't do it. So I just walked away.

I did a lot of reserve time work at Swanbourne. They always need people in the regiment and I'd go down to the mobility cell two or three days a week teaching vehicle-mounted skills for about six months. But it was just filler. I felt okay going back. Everyone there was my best mate. You could come and go. You've got freedom but you're also hanging out with your good mates, and every now and then we'd go and do a bush trip somewhere or do some fast driver training round the race track and I enjoyed it. I still enjoy that today.

But it was no substitute for a proper job, and I was determined to somehow get myself back on an even keel. That was when I decided to give the coppers a go.

25

PROVIDING SECURITY

I had a couple of mates in the tactical response group of the Western Australia Police and I thought my training might work in well with their skill set. So I applied and was accepted in the trainee course at the Police Academy. It covered procedure, law, weapons, unarmed combat, computers, filling out reports, court briefs, the whole deal. It took eight months but I reckon we could have killed it in three. I did all right; I got the Dux award and I enjoyed it.

The money was not good; I was down to about 50 grand a year, which was really difficult for Emily and the family, but I had my Defence Force pension and that topped it up a little bit so we got through okay. Then they posted me to Wanneroo station, which was great because it was so handy, just round the corner from where we lived. I was there for seven or eight months but I started to get disillusioned with it.

The police mentality was not what I'd been accustomed to. In the SASR you're always looking after your mates, but the police mentality is to do the dirty on your mates so you can move up the rungs a bit quicker than the next bloke. It's cut-throat. Also I had gone from being a sergeant down to the lowest common denominator and that was really difficult. Blokes ten to 15 years younger would be talking down to me and they didn't have a clue about what I had been doing.

We went to a drug bust and I was given the role – which usually goes to the most junior guy – of looking after the property they'd seized. You have to process it, bag it, weigh it and go through this long process. It took me about two days to complete and I thought, What am I doing here? This is terrible.

That weekend I was taking Kenzie for a walk in the park and I got a call from a mate, Steve, saying, 'Nev, we need a security adviser for AusAid in Papua New Guinea. Do you want to go?' I said, 'How much are you paying?' The answer was about $14,000 a month. I talked to Emily about it and she was keen, so we said, 'All right, let's do it.'

The AusAid deal is that the Australian Government has a support package and they send officials from different government departments in Australia to be placed in the same sort of role in Papua New Guinea as an adviser to try to foster good government. It seems to work okay. They get paid a lot of money and are probably happy to get out of the Australian office for two or three years.

The trouble was that Emily had a misunderstanding of what it would be like, and I really should have known better. But we went up there on a contract for six months. Emily was two months pregnant with Jonathan, our second. Steve had said they wanted me there a couple of weeks after I got out of the police. So we basically packed clothes in a bag – ours and Kenzie's – flew via Brisbane, where we had to get visas, and then up to Port Moresby.

Steve picked us up at the airport and took us to the international hotel, where the company who was running the show had their offices. He introduced me to some of the staff. Judith was running the office and Steve was a subcontractor for them to provide security for AusAid. They are a big service company. They had the contract to look after the administrative requirements including housing, vehicles and most of the other things Australians would need in Papua New Guinea during their three-year posting.

After the introductions we sat around the pool and had a chinwag. By this time Emily was tired as we'd been 14 hours on flights from Perth, so she went up to our room. I followed a bit later and we settled in. The hotel was okay, nothing special.

Next morning my job was to go downstairs and get a rundown on what was going on security-wise for all the officials. We had about 30 officials all round Moresby, and in the outer provinces there were probably another 20 and then all their families. All up you're looking at 50 to 60 people. My role was to be the security adviser to ensure that they were safe. It also had a bit of occupational health and safety thrown in, so if you saw something that didn't look right you'd alert someone in the company.

Unfortunately I was a bit hamstrung in my role because as security adviser you have to be fairly autonomous to give accurate reports: to tell AusAid, which is based in Canberra, what the real situation is and what needs to be done to fix it. The chief administrator who looked after some of the facilities up there, like the accommodation for all the officials and the multi-storey buildings that they leased, was also the overseer of my reports. His name was Gavin, a great big bloke in his early sixties, an ex-policeman. But if I found fault with any current arrangements, he felt it would reflect on him. He was supposed to forward my reports to Canberra, but if he didn't like them because they undercut what he had already put in place, he would either not forward them or he would just disagree with them and undermine my recommendations. So it was just a horrible situation to be in.

Nevertheless I enjoyed the job – travelling around the provinces, going out and meeting officials and getting their side of things about their accommodation and vehicles. It was very interesting. Then I'd make obvious comments on how to fix things. It wasn't hard. The hardest thing was dealing with people such as Gavin, because everything I did he saw as pulling the rug out from under him. Basically I was saying that all the stuff that he'd done up to now was not up to speed. If I found a fence with holes in it, I'd say we need some new fencing. He would say there's nothing wrong with that fence; I put it in and it cost me a million dollars last year.

It was just a really crappy situation and I let AusAid know. The AusAid director would come up from Canberra every few months and I just told her, 'You can't run it like this and get an accurate representation because the security adviser needs to have a level of autonomy so he knows he can do what's right and not be worried about other people.'

We soon moved out of the hotel. Basically Emily became a prisoner in our home and I wish we had been advised better. Before we left, I asked Steve if we would be able to get some better accommodation – a fairly nice house and a decent standard of living. He said, 'Yeah, you can get that for 3000 to 4000 kina a month.' Well, it was about double that. So about 60 per cent of my wage had to go on rent, and while we were there the Australian dollar went through the floor, so that didn't help. In 2008 it dropped to about 60 cents. And costs were inflated because of the mining industry moving in.

We had a few security incidents. When you arrive in Papua New Guinea, you hear all these horror stories, and a lot of them are true. Some of the expats who work there, usually in the mining industry, would mix with the locals – the girls in the nightclubs (or even the boys in the nightclubs if they're like that) – and that could lead to trouble. On one occasion a bloke who lived on another hill just across from us invited a boy around; something went wrong and he was found dead in his apartment the next morning. There was all hell to pay over that. But fortunately he wasn't under my watch.

There was another lady, an Asian who was married to an Australian. Someone climbed up on a second-storey balcony and said to her, 'I'm gonna fuck you and then I'm gonna kill you.' And he punched her in the face and knocked her on the ground. He thought she was unconscious and then, as he was going through the house looking for stuff to steal, she ran and jumped off the second storey. She survived with minor injuries. Someone called the police, he did a runner and the local security contractors came around to look for him.

The security are often worse than the criminals, but they managed to track this bloke down and they chased him over streets and buildings and through backyards until they caught him. I spoke to the manager of the guys who caught him. I used to see him on a weekly basis. He told me the guy was in a bad way by the time he arrived on the scene. One of his guys had picked up a stone and was going to hit him, and he said, 'Stop! Don't do it like that, do it like this,' and he kicked him and broke his arm. The bloke was covered in blood. They wanted to show him to the lady so she could identify him but the blood was covering his face. All she'd see was a red thing. So they put him under a tap and then took him over and said, 'Is this him?' and he's pouring blood. It's brutal. I reckon the security guys actually were hoods before they were employed. Some of them have got a gunshot here, a knife scar there.

We had some other minor incidents – lots of burglaries. And when you drive around Moresby, you always keep your windows up and your doors locked. You don't stop for anybody. You stop at lights but you have to be prepared to drive away.

A lady who was driving from the airport after dropping her husband off hadn't locked her car door. As she went around a corner, she had to slow down and someone opened the door and went to jump in the car. Luckily she was able to speed up and instead of him getting in the car he fell out on the road. If he had made it into the car, well, you hear these stories of what happens to people and they're awful; they're raped, gang-raped and even murdered.

There was another incident at the local supermarket where we shopped. It's like Fort Knox, with a razor-wire fence all around and about ten security guards. Once you are inside, you are fairly safe. An expat lady was in the car park and a local lady came up and said, 'My car's broken down just up the road. Can you give me a lift up there?' The Aussie woman said, 'No I won't, but I'll ring someone and they can assist you.' The local woman said, 'No, no.' She was adamant. 'It's only just up the road.' Then she pulled out a knife in the car park under the watchful eyes of the security. Luckily the expat woman just refused and the local backed off; but if she'd gone with her at knife point the local would have taken her car, taken her possessions, and at the very best she would have left her at the side of the road. These sorts of things happen regularly.

Another incident was more a safety issue than a security one. A bunch of about ten officials wanted to go and do part of the Kokoda Trail. For the first five or six kilometres, from Ower's Corner, you can do that in a day and come back again. I thought that would be okay as long as they used a reputable company, and one had been recommended by the Australian High Commission. So up they went, but that night a big rain storm came in, the river came up and they couldn't get back across the river. Late that night I got a phone call from one of the officials who had come back early and managed to cross the river before it rose. He said, 'I'm back but the rest of them are still out there.'

All hell broke loose. It was just a nightmare. That night I was trying madly to ring the company that was organising the trip and no one was contactable. They had no satellite phones, no radios, nothing. It was just some bloke who had put an ad in the paper saying, 'I'm a good guy, I'll take you up there.' Someone had looked at it and no further.

I went into the office and stayed there all night. I wanted to go out to Ower's Corner and help but I had to stay and coordinate, so I sent some security guys. The High Commission had also sent some security guys but they'd gone to the corner, turned around and come back and said, 'There's no one there.' So our company went up and they hung around there all night and no one came back. The next morning our security walked down to the river, which was starting to come down, and we found them. It turned out okay but it could have been a lot worse; they could have tried to cross the river in the dark and got washed down. They were half a kilometre along the other side and had stayed in some huts at a village overnight. They were fine.

The whole time we were up there, we were only a phone call away from some emergency. We got the weekends off, but if someone was robbed you'd go straight down to the office to resolve the problem. There were some silly things too. One of the expats had a local girlfriend and they used to get on benders including the local sauce and chewing the betel nut. During the day he seemed like a reasonable sort of bloke, but one Saturday I had to go round to his place because he'd apparently beaten her up and she was out in the street yelling and screaming. She wanted to go back into the home but the guard wouldn't let her.

There were a lot of these things where you're trying to help but then you've got to make a report and when you do you get grief. Someone calls and says, 'What are you doing sending reports back to Canberra about me? It's none of your business. Are you a spy? What's your job?'

The company had some administrative people who ran the vehicle fleets, accommodation repairs and the security of the compounds, but otherwise if I needed anything done I was pretty much on my own.

In our home we employed a local woman one or two days a week to help with Kenzie. She was pretty good and became a close friend. But there was no office assistant who could give me a break. On a couple of weekends we went away, once to Brisbane for a long weekend because our visas were expiring, and then to an island about 50 kilometres off Moresby, where we stayed in a bungalow. But Emily wasn't comfortable with it, and there were snakes just outside the front door, which didn't help.

We had a few day drives into the mountains. But in Moresby you wouldn't want to walk down the street, especially if you were a woman.

I'd go for a jog every second day, but I was really taking my life in my hands. You'd see guys sharpening their knives on the side of the street and looking at you. I wasn't armed at all. And I got robbed too. It was at Goroka in the Highlands. I was only there on a daytrip to see one of the officials in a resort-style set-up. When I returned to the town, which I'd been told was much safer than Moresby, I fell into that false sense of security. It was the end of the day, out at the airport before take-off, and I was thirsty.

There was a shop about 50 metres away and I thought I'd go over and get a Coke.

As I walked towards the shop, there was a young fella, probably about ten years old, standing outside, and he went to shake my hand. I sort of ignored him because I thought better of it. Just next to him about two metres away was an 18-year-old male leaning against the fence. I had my bag tucked tightly under my arm with its strap over my shoulder. All I had in it was my two-way radio, a camera and all my reports and paperwork. I got my Coke in the shop and when I went back outside he was still there. As I passed, the kid had his hand out again. I thought, Oh bugger, and I put my hand out. Instead of letting go, the kid pulled me off balance and at the exact same instant this other guy reached over and whack. He grabbed my bag by the strap, it snapped on one end and I held onto the other but it ripped through my hand and he was already running off as fast as he could. I chased him but I couldn't catch him.

As my contract was coming to an end, I was glad to get out of the place. Rather than help me get over my PTSD, it probably increased my problems. It was not good for Emily either, and we didn't want to have the baby in Moresby because the medical facilities were not the best. Come the end of the contract, they wanted us to stay on, but we said no, we're going. So in 2008 we came home and then I was out of a job.

About a month later Steve rang me up and said, 'Nev, we need a WA rep for our company for crisis management. You work from home, it's a reasonable wage, and every now and again you'll fly off to different parts of Australia or anywhere else to run crisis-management training.' It sounded pretty good. For example if a mine site had a major incident and someone was killed in an explosion, they needed to know how to handle all the moving parts of the situation. My job would be to train them how to respond, from the managers at head office to the people at ground level. I would brief them on how to get the assets they needed, how to coordinate the operation and how to deal with the police.

They liked that I'd had the police experience, Papua New Guinea and the SAS. And the money was pretty good too, so I said yes. But after a week at home doing very little, the anxiety of it was killing me. I rang him up and said, 'I just can't do it anymore. I just can't do it.'

He said, 'What do we need to do to keep you?'

I said, 'I don't feel I'm doing a good enough job.'

He said, 'You're one of our most tested and trusted employees. We just had you up in New Guinea for six months and you did a good job there, so we think you'll do a good job here.'

But my head was saying, I can't do it perfectly so I can't do it at all. I ripped the carpet out from under myself in just the same way I did when I told the regiment I wasn't going to do promotion courses anymore because my head wasn't in it. And in the months that followed, I did that many times in many jobs. I was out of work with not much income beyond a modest army pension and a bit of work at Swanbourne. The future looked grim.

26

AFTER THE SASR

It was the darkness before dawn. At last things started to turn around for me. First Emily gave birth to Jonathan, our lovely little boy. By then we had returned to Perth, and he entered the world at Joondalup Hospital on 11 February 2009. I was present for his arrival at about 8.30 a.m. and cut his umbilical cord as I had done for Kenzie at her birth. Initially he suffered from jaundice as well as reflux, which was very stressful for Emily. He soon recovered from the jaundice; the reflux took a lot longer but he came through great. He also had a peanut allergy for his first couple of years but outgrew that as well. He has completed our family for us; we are very lucky indeed to have both Jonathan and Kenzie.

I decided to call Peter, an SAS association advocate, to seek his advice about the PTSD. Pete said, 'Come and see me and we'll look at your case to see if we can give you some assistance.' He took one look and said, 'Why did you take a regular discharge? You are entitled to a medical discharge; you've already been diagnosed.'

I told him about the rumours that the government wouldn't pay some of your entitlements if you took that option and he said, 'No, that's bullshit. You're still able to access your entitlements if you've been injured or diseased or whatever.'

Pete was terrific. He said, 'I'm going to write a letter to Veterans' Affairs. We'll put your case to them and try to arrange for incapacity payments.' So that's what Pete did and we got a positive response. We even got a bit of back pay about nine months later.

I was almost debt free when I got out of the army. So we were now in a reasonable spot. Under the medical discharge arrangement I can work for about 20 hours a week, but the fact is that's all I can do physically anyway. We started a little business teaching advanced four-wheel driving and it went okay but after two or three days of driver training I'm really tired. I'll be going great guns until then, but suddenly I hit the wall. I'll be absolutely knackered. I just shut down and have to lie on the bed for two or three hours.

I never know what's going to set it off. It might be some little misunderstanding with Emily, or something has upset me, and I'll hit the wall and just have to lie down and rest. It can happen anytime. One minute I'm fine but the next

I'm out of it. I'd love to be able to do some meditation but you're supposed to stay awake and I'll be off in dreamland.

A couple of years ago I had an opportunity to go to Abu Dhabi and become a training supervisor in a civilian capacity with the Special Forces there. I was seeing a psychologist at the time and I asked him if he thought I could handle it. He said, 'Your capacity to do things is not what it was. You might think it's there but it's not.'

It came as a hell of a blow to hear that, and it took me a long time – because it was a very bitter pill – to swallow that loss of capacity. But if I push too hard, I know I'll hit that wall and I'll start to make those silly decisions again. It's no good going off to another country and getting paid a lot of money if you're going to quit after three or six months because of the anxiety and stress.

I think I'm now getting to know my limitations, and as long as I work within those limitations I can function well. I can now recognise when I'm not operating at the top of my game a lot sooner than I did before. I wouldn't have had that capacity when I was on team in 2004. I was just wondering why the hell things weren't working out as they should. I was shaking. I was locking up and not responding.

I don't have the flashbacks that people with PTSD sometimes talk about, but I have recollections of things during the day. It might be a smell or a sound – you remember them forever. And sometimes it's pretty weird. If I smell nail polish, for example, it makes me feel unwell.

It reminds me of dead bodies. I don't know why. If I hear a loud noise – say if Emily drops a plate in the kitchen – I can become very angry until I realise I have to settle down.

The dreams pervade your day. You can wake up and you might not remember the dream but you wonder why you're in a shitty mood, and you don't want to get out of bed and you wonder why you haven't got any energy. More than once I've woken up in a fury of punching and kicking on the bed, and I'm hot – shaking and sweating. Emily tells me that, when I sleep, I'll be kicking and punching. I can't hold her because I squeeze her tighter and tighter and she has to push me away. Often in the dreams I'm back in the SAS. I'm running the CT cell; I'm responsible for all these men again and I don't know if I'll be able to do the job. I'm on operations somewhere and someone's been killed and I'm eating body parts. It's awful, terrible. Why would I be dreaming such a thing?

It's corrosive. When people are doing and seeing things that they don't feel proud of – even though at the time it's part of the job and perfectly legitimate but as a person it doesn't feel right – then they'll have a sense of guilt and they'll struggle with it forever. And somehow they feel they're not adequate as a person.

I don't have many situations that I can relate to when I feel that I've done something bad. Even in Iraq when we were firing weapons, I wasn't standing within ten metres of people who were potentially being shot; they were hundreds of metres away. When I fired at that vehicle to stop it coming through the roadblock, I fired at the engine block. I probably would have been justified in shooting the driver but I didn't; it was a natural instinct to fire at the block and it worked. But if I had fired at the driver, that would have resulted in a whole new level of anxiety for me that I would have had to deal with for the rest of my days, because it's so personal. Looking through a windscreen at someone's face is a lot different to firing a machine gun at someone 300 metres away.

In clearing buildings in Afghanistan, I had to make instant decisions: is this guy a threat or do I just push him away and move on? Luckily, in most situations the threat was not adequate to justify pulling the trigger. But they are situations you never forget. They become part of you.

There's really no let-up when you're back at Swanbourne in hard training. In the 'CQB house', for example, where we do a lot of our CT training, there have been a few incidents of serious injury. One of the drills used to be quick-draw practice, like in the old Wild West – draw the weapon out, aim at a target and pull the trigger as quick as you could. There was a bad practice of two guys facing each other, and obviously they thought their weapons were unloaded or they weren't going to pull the trigger. But one of the guys did and he shot his colleague and killed him. That doesn't happen anymore.

When we were out on the boat off Bougainville, we had a very confined area where we kept all our equipment and our weapons. The guys would often go in there and unload the weapons or be checking and cleaning them when one of the blokes accidentally let a nine-millimetre round off. It hit the deck first and fragmented then hit my mate. He's got a scar on his backside. There are lots of guys with scars like that from when something's gone pear-shaped.

Someone once said about soldiers, 'Your job is not to question why.' But later on you think about it. At the time you're so busy trying to get things ready that you don't have time to think about what you're doing in Afghanistan or Iraq and why you're doing it. You get the command to go and officers will say, 'This is why you're doing this,' and they'll give you the government line. But you take that with a grain of salt, as they are fed that information.

Everyone has a personal opinion. But I can't see the contribution that I made while I was in Afghanistan as making any difference, and I can't see that a year or two after we leave that place it's going to be any better than it was. I do know that if my little boy in about 20 years' time joined the army and said he was going to Afghanistan, I'd be ropeable.

I think the SASR is a terrific environment for blokes who want to be good soldiers. It tries to get the best for the role, and the best part about being there is that everyone has the same level of professionalism and everyone is striving to get the job done to the best of their ability. You don't have slackers, except for the very odd one now and again. There might be slightly different levels of professionalism but generally everyone is focused on the task – especially on operations. And that's the best thing about working in a team where everyone's pulling together. They become like your brothers, a tight little team of blokes, and you're going through the same miseries together, but you're going through the same good times together as well.

So it's a top environment for a soldier; you couldn't ask for a better one. And the amount of hardship that you go through to get there in the first place means that you have respect for the people around you because you know they have been through the same ordeal.

I enjoyed most of my time there. There were very few times when I thought, That's crap; I shouldn't really be doing this. Ultimately it was the highlight of my time in the army and probably one of the highlights of my life as well. To be able to serve is really a great opportunity. It had a detrimental effect on my health, but any job can be like that whether you're working in the mining industry and you get injured driving a truck or whatever. But I'd like to emphasise a positive outlook and I think that generally my life in the regiment has been a positive experience.

Of course there are some who have never been able to adjust. Recently I met a colleague from my team on selection while I was crossing the Nullarbor on a camping trip with my family and another good mate with his family. We had stopped at a service station and I was about to pay for the fuel when I heard a voice call out, 'Nev Bonner.'

I was shocked to see my mate 'Darren' sitting in his ute at the petrol pump. He still looked the same: tall and lean with short army-style haircut. He had aged 20 years like me and it felt like we had been friends forever. I asked him where he was heading and he said Perth. He explained how he was now homeless and out of work.

I wanted to help and offered him the use of our vacant lot down south, where he could at least have somewhere to set up his camp trailer while in Western Australia. I didn't know what had happened to him since I saw him last but I surmised he had separated from his wife and family and was doing it tough. This is a common story, as I have heard of ex-regiment mates living in their cars or on the streets at night.

I have another mate, Ned, who lives in the UK and who is in the same situation. Ned was very close to Frosty and was a member of 1 Squadron when the Black Hawk accident occurred in 1996. Unfortunately he became addicted to gambling at the casino after the accident and sold many of his family possessions. He left Perth back in 1999 as his wife left him and took the children to live closer to her folks in Scotland. Ned followed but he had no friends for support in the UK. Public housing or the back seat of his car is his new home these days. He still emails me and lives on a shoestring. I often ask him to return but he can't be without access to his kids and is willing to live like a hobo for that.

I don't really know how the government intends to continue to fund the care and compensation for the ever-growing number of Defence personnel who contract diseases or are affected by mental-health disorders and other injuries from conflict. It may mean that in the future they will not be able to offer post-war service care at the same level they currently do.

Defence tells recruits to the army that, should you be injured in war service to your country, you will be looked after when you come back. They said this to me and my colleagues when I joined back in 1986. It gives you confidence to give it your best shot knowing that if you are injured or killed your family will be cared for. If this promise is no longer offered, the ability of the government to recruit for Defence would likely suffer as a result. It's important that our men and women in the forces are better advised about the likelihood that they may suffer the effects of depression and PTSD as a result of their service before they commit to spending their lives serving their country.

It is equally important that if the Australian politicians who all too eagerly commit our most precious resource, our sons and daughters, to such dangerous foreign places as Afghanistan and Iraq keep their promises and look after our service personnel when they return broken and needing help.

EMILY'S STORY IX

In 2012 Emily was accepted at Edith Cowan University for a preparation course to do counterterrorism and criminal psychology. 'I get goosebumps when I think of it,' she says, 'because for so long I felt I wasn't good enough. But I did it and I felt good.'

It also provided insights to the mental torture that both she and Stuart had suffered in the SAS experience. 'It's the families who are suffering PTSD as well,' she says. 'I sincerely believe that I have a form of PTSD. If I even see something to do with war on TV, I have to turn it off. Because when Stuart was away I watched everything live, all that bombing. I get sick watching anything to do with war . . . and any soldier that's passed away, died, I cry like it's my own husband because I know that could have been Stuart. It's painful.

'I even get jittery when I hear a sharp noise. I was in the shop last week and a lady came with a trolley and I was busy looking at something and she made like a bang and I jumped. It wasn't natural. At times like that you worry about your mental health.'

However, she has learned to seek help and the world of psychology is open to her. 'I have a very good psychologist,' she says. 'Stuart and I were having difficulty in communication and other issues, and I went to see this lady – oh my God, she's a blessing. She's very good. I think she sees a lot of the women in the regiment but she opened a big window for me to see things differently and not to blame myself. There is a lot of guilt. As a wife and woman, we are nurturers and have a tendency to instinctively try and help your loved one. Sometimes you feel "I wish I could just help", but you can't.

'I'd like to have more time with him, just the two of us. We go away a lot but it's with the kids. It's not just Stuart and me.'

But while the struggle continues, Emily has come to realise that she and Stuart are part of a much bigger problem. 'PTSD is a major factor in families of the ADF,' she says. 'There's so much pain, hardship and very difficult circumstances that families have to endure.'

And she is pleased to have the opportunity to bring it into the open. 'We should not make it a taboo subject, and we should be open about it and not feel ashamed to speak about PTSD,' she says. 'It is courageous and I applaud all those who have spoken about this crippling and devastating issue. You are more of a man to speak about it rather than sinking yourself in that big black hole. Loved ones will always support you.'

However, while the ADF acknowledges the problem, more action is needed. 'The ADF has to look after their own more rather than making it difficult with all that paperwork that our men and women have to fill in. Why should these brave men and women be subjected to that kind of treatment when they have put their lives on the front line to protect us? They have endured enough and so have the families.

'When those different behaviour characteristics start to show on your loved one, don't be afraid to talk to them and say it's okay to go and see someone, and there is no shame. For my family we are a strong partnership and we have had our difficult times and we still struggle, but we keep it going. We're a work in progress but we're doing good!'

•

I am now able to see a light at the end of the dark tunnel that is PTSD. It doesn't get easier to live with, but I have developed a better understanding of it and can now take steps to minimise its negative impacts. The military has been a great journey for me, and although there have been some downsides with illness it has been a full life for me so far.

Would I turn it down if I had my life over? Not join the army? Not join the regiment? I've had a life adventure, and even though it might have put me in a bad spot in certain ways post-service, I have enjoyed most of it. I probably would do it again but I might change one or two little things on the way.

LIST OF ABBREVIATIONS

2IC	second-in-command
ADF	Australian Defence Force
AO	area of operations
APC	armoured personnel carrier
CASEVAC	casualty evacuation
CO	commanding officer
CQB	close-quarter battle
CT	counterterrorist
DS	directing staff officer
DUI	driving under the influence
EA	emergency action
FAC	forward air controller
HIMARS	High Mobility Artillery Rocket System
HVTI	high-value target interdiction
IED	improvised explosive device

INTERFET	International Forces East Timor
JDAM	Joint Direct Attack Munition
LAV	light armoured vehicle
LRPV	Long Range Patrol Vehicle
LUP	lying-up place
MOE	method of entry
MPs	military police
MRE	meals ready to eat
Muj	Mujahideen
NCO	non-commissioned officer
NGO	non-governmental organisation
NVGs	night-vision goggles
OC	officer commanding (squadron commander)
PC	patrol commander
PJ	pararescue jumper
PT	physical training
PTI	physical training instructor
PTSD	post-traumatic stress disorder
QRF	Quick Reaction Force
RSM	regimental sergeant major
RTI	resistance to interrogation
SASR	Australia's Special Air Service Regiment
SBS	Special Boat Squadron
SLR	self-loading rifle
SOCCE	special operations command centre
SSM	squadron sergeant major
SUV	sport utility vehicle

LIST OF ABBREVIATIONS

UAV	unmanned aerial vehicle
UNTAET	United Nations Transitional Administration in East Timor
UXO	unexploded ordnance
WMD	weapon of mass destruction

Also by Robert Macklin

SAS Sniper takes us inside the closed world of the Australian Special Forces – it's tough to get in, but the fighting that follows is even tougher...

Rob Maylor has seen action in the world's most dangerous combat zones. From East Timor and Iraq to Afghanistan he has been places where no-one else wants to go. He was there when a Black Hawk helicopter crashed, drowning two of his mates. He was there at Australia's biggest battle in Afghanistan when a Taliban ambush left him shockingly wounded.

He has walked for hours, sometimes days, through hostile country until he has found the right position, sometimes more than a kilometre away from his target, then when the moment is right he aims, and with absolute precision, puts the bullet just where it is going to have the most effect...

This is a gritty, no-holds-barred behind-the-scenes look at life on the front line from an elite SAS sniper.

www.ingramcontent.com/pod-product-compliance
Ingram Content Group UK Ltd.
Pitfield, Milton Keynes, MK11 3LW, UK
UKHW041300180426
11947UKWH00009B/587